Frank E Hodgkin, J. J Galvin

Pen Pictures of Representative Men of Oregon

Frank E Hodgkin, J. J Galvin

Pen Pictures of Representative Men of Oregon

ISBN/EAN: 9783337033316

Printed in Europe, USA, Canada, Australia, Japan

Cover: Foto ©ninafisch / pixelio.de

More available books at **www.hansebooks.com**

PEN PICTURES

OF

REPRESENTATIVE MEN

OF

OREGON.

BY

FRANK E. HODGKIN.   J. J. GALVIN.

*COPYRIGHT APPLIED FOR.

-- PORTLAND, OREGON.
Farmer and Dairyman Publishing House.
1882.

INTRODUCTION.

Some one who evidently knew what he was talking about has said "Oh, that mine enemy would write a book." Well, we have written ours, and here it is for our enemies to make the most of. We expect and welcome criticism, realizing only too well that our little work is incomplete, and perhaps somewhat crude in detail. Our only excuse is the hurried manner in which it has been prepared and the difficulties encountered in securing the necessary data on which to base our sketches. We have in six short weeks written brief biographies of upward of two hundred and fifty of the representative men of our State, residing in all its distant nooks and corners. This has entailed no small amount of labor on our part. Such being the case, we would crave the friendly indulgence of our readers and ask of them, so far as consistent with their good nature, "to pass our imperfections by." While we would not have them imagine that we have written biographies of all our representative men, still, we do flatter ourselves that those we have secured stand prominent in their respective stations. We may at some future time complete the task that has thus far been but barely commenced. Meanwhile, we set this little waif afloat upon the almost boundless sea of literature, trusting that it may at least fill its allotted sphere; and, sometime, in the dim future, when those whose names are inscribed herein shall have passed away, serve to recall their virtues and bring to mind the then representative men of Oregon. If it will do this, and at the same time please our patrons, we are content. Thanking a generous public for the liberal support accorded us, we remain very respectfully their obedient servants, THE PUBLISHERS.

INDEX.

Abell, F.G.	104	Coldwell, E. L	188
Abraham, Sol	76	Colvig, G. W	21
Adams, E. G.	191	Collins, J. L	93
Adams, H. F.	101	Condon, S. W	xxv
Atkinson, J. F.	195	Congle, J. B	64
Baughman, J. H.	46	Condon, T.	88
Bailey, J. R.	100	Cook, W. T.	126
Babcock, F J	160	Crawford, G. F.	42
Bacon, C. P.	162	Crawford, T. H	155
Bachman, J.	165	Crawford, J. W	114
Barin, L. T	76	Curtis, W. R.	31
Berry, F. P.	150	D'Arcy, P. H.	69
Belt, G. W.	169	Davenport, T. W.	5
Bean, R. S.	xix	Deady, M. P.	142
Bennett, A. S.	xviii	Dement, R. M	92
Benjamin, W. F.	79	Denny, O. N.	179
Besser, L.	72	DeLashmutt, V. B.	87
Bilyeu, W. R.	13	Dolph, J. N.	ix
Blake, M. F.	189	Dorris, G. B.	7
Bleakney, J. G.	52	Dufur, W. H. H.	28
Blum, L.	112	Durham, G. H.	129
Blythe, S. F.	193	Eakin, S. B.	32
Boise, R. P	xvi	Earhart, R. P.	iii
Bonham, B. F.	166	Faulconer, T. N.	44
Boothby, W. F.	151	Fithian, J. B.	197
Bower, J. M.	135	Ford, T.	154
Boyd, H. C.	110	Fulton, C. W	100
Bronaugh, E. C.	79	Fullerton, J. C.	67
Brenner, J. H.	77	Gates, N. H	14
Brown, H. G.	45	Garrison, J. M	125
Bush, A.	57	George, M. C.	xi
Burnett, J. J.	188	Geary, E. R.	105
Burnett, G H	159	Gearin, J. M.	181
Burnett, J.	71	Gibbs, A. C.	68
Burch, B. F.	106	Gibbs, W. W.	131
Buchtel, J.	168	Gilbert, A. N.	46
Byars, W. H.	vi	Gill, J. K.	177
Carson, J. C.	37	Gregg, J. T.	74
Caples, J. F.	114	Haines, I. D.	16
Carpenter, H.	71	Hayes, R. B.	33
Cartwright, J. C.	111	Hall, H.	18
Casey, E.	198	Hare, W. D.	152
Cauthorn, T. E.	10	Hart, W. A.	162
Chadwick, S. F.	94	Harris, W. H.	25
Chamberlin, M. L.	109	Hanna, H. K.	xx
Chapman, W. S.	186	Hawley, J. H.	51
Chapman, W. W.	133	Hendershott, J.	111
Chapman, J. A.	115	Hendricks, T. G.	16
Child, J. A.	108	Himes, G. H.	61
Clinton, H. M.	189	Hill, R. W.	152
Clow, R.	20	Hill, W. L.	156

INDEX.

Hirsch, E	v	Moores, I. R	153
Hirsch, Sol	2	Moores, C. B	xxi
Hodgkin, F. E	xxii	Mulkey, M. F	81
Holmes, W. H	80	Myers, J	18
Holton, D	136	Newcomb, R	102
Holman, A	184	Newbury, W. S	131
Hoult, E	9	Nicklin, A. I	107
Humphrey, N. B	7	Nichols, B. F	53
Humphrey, G	96	Noltner, A	182
Hunt, J. A	30	Noyer, P. S	36
Hutchinson, J. C	116	Oatman, H. B	119
Ireland, D. C	108	Odeneal, T. B	xxv
Ison, L. B	39	Odell, W. H	185
James, W. S	63	Patton, T. M	103
Jessup, S. R	86	Paxton, O. F	124
Jessup, E	15	Patterson, F. A	45
Johns, C. A	117	Parker, A	26
Johnson, W. C	74	Pennington, S. M	6
Jones, M. L	44	Perkins, W. A	28
Josephi, S. E	66	Peebles, J. C	97
Keady, W. P	38	Pilkington, J. B	103
Kelly, P	39	Pittinger, J. M	98
Kelly, J	86	Plummer, O. P. S	49
Kelly, J. K	67	Powell, L. J	163
Kelsay, J	140	Prim, P. P	17
Kinney, A	82	Prentice, D. W	123
Kizer, F. M	36	Pratt, I. W	165
Knight, P. S	78	Reed, F. C	12
Ladd, W. S	140	Reid, W	174
Lee, J. D	10	Read, C. A	121
Lockhart, A	102	Rigdon, W. T	42
Long, J	48	Rice, J. N	51
Lord, W. P	xii	Ripinsky, S	136
Lundberg, W	99	Robbins, J. H	176
Marquam, P. A	40	Rock, J	191
Marston, H. L	50	Samuels, L	187
Mays, F. P	138	Sanders, I. N	118
Marshall, A. J	171	Suppington, J. W	48
Mallory, Rufus	172	Savage, O. S	161
McBride, G. W	24	Saylor, W. H	170
McBride, T. A	145	Scott, H. W	182
McCain, J	130	Scott, L. S	124
McConnell, W. J	1	Schwatka, Fred	65
McCornack, E. P	xxiv	Sewall, W. R	116
McCully, A. A	120	Sears, G. C	59
McElroy, E. B	viii	Shattuck, E. D	158
McKercher, D	119	Shaw, T. C	157
Merryman, J. D	126	Sharp, R. J	34
Merry, T. B	183	Showers, W	110
Miller, J. F	70	Shurtliff, F. N	171
Miller, W. P	80	Simpson, B	166
Mires, A	82	Siglin, J. M	11
Mitchell, J. H	146	Sifers, J. B	12
Moody, Z. F	1	Simon, Joseph	4
Moreland, J. C	97	Sinnott, P. B	130
Moreland, S. A	184	Skiff, L. S	123
Moomaw, D. L	101	Smith, J	47
Montgomery, J. B	55	Smith, T. F	137
Moss, S. P	27	Sperry, J. B	43
Morras, W	29	Stanley, A. C	51

INDEX.

Starkweather, W. A	8	Veatch, R. M	30
Stephens, J. B	121	Voorhees, J	9
Steel, G. A	139	Watson, E. B	xiv
Stearns, D. W	21	Watson, C. B	90
Stearns, L. B	60	Waite, E. M	118
Stewart, F. A	54	Ward, J. P	148
Story, G. L	173	Watkinds, W. H	128
Stott, R	xvii	Waldo, W	14
Stewart, C. H	113	Waters, A. W	20
Struble, W. R	197	Webb, H. P	33
Stites, T. J	190	Wheeler, A. F	xxiii
Stearns, L. B	60	Whitney, J. J	25
Struble, W	197	Whalley, J. W	160
Sutherland, T. A	185	White, E. D	149
Tanner, A. H	35	Whiteaker, J	178
Taylor, F. J	122	Witherell, A. W	113
Thompson, H. Y	177	Williams, G. H	127
Thornton, H	46	Williams, W. R	75
Thayer, W. W	173	Willis, W. R	75
Tolman, J. C	83	Wilson, B. W	132
Truitt, W	41	Wiley, J. R	194
Tustin, F. P	91	Wilbur, A. C	27
Tyson, R. H	19	Wright, D	22
Van Scoy, T	84	Yocum, G. W	149

ERRATA.

Page 31—W. "P." Curtis should read W. "R." Curtis.

Page 96—In S. F. Chadwick's sketch the name W. T. "Long" should read W. T. "Gray."

Page 189—"A." M. Clinton should read "H." M. Clinton.

STATE OFFICERS.

GOVERNOR Z. F. MOODY.

Zenas Ferry Moody, Governor of the State of Oregon, was born on the 27th day of May, 1832, in Granby, Mass. His father was Major Thomas H. Moody. His mother was Hannah M. Ferry, an aunt of Senator T. W. Ferry, of Michigan, formerly Vice-President of the United States. Gov. Moody comes of good old New England Revolutionary stock, his grandfather, Gideon Moody, having borne arms as a soldier during the Revolutionary war. He has proven himself worthy of his lineage, and the principles which he imbibed on New England soil have been the guide of his whole subsequent life. The sturdy virtues of that stock are too well known to require comment: they have become historical. The public men of New England have led the van in every reform, and have taken a most prominent part in molding all of that history of which the American people are most proud. New England ideas have been infused throughout the whole of our national life, and we have come to expect from men of that nationality those sturdy qualities, which have contributed so largely to our happiness and prosperity as a people. Mr. Moody's childhood was spent in Granby. In 1848 he removed to Chicopee, Mass., where he remained the ensuing three years. On the 13th day of March, 1851, he sailed from New York for Oregon via the Isthmus, with a company, among whom was Hon. Samuel R. Thurston, the first Delegate to Congress from the Territory of Oregon. He came direct to Oregon City, then the principal town of Oregon, landing there on the 21st day of April, 1851. From this time until 1853 he was engaged on the United States Surveys as one of the "Freeman party," so called after James E. Freeman, who stuck the first pin in the United States Surveys in Oregon, established the initial point of the Willamette Meridian, and extended this Meridian to the Canyon Mountains. In 1853, Mr. Moody removed to Brownsville, Oregon, where he engaged in the mercantile business. In the fall of 1853 he was married to Miss Mary Stephenson, his present wife. Four sons and one daughter now constitute the family group. In 1856 he was appointed Inspector of United States Surveys in California. After completing his duties as such Inspector he went to Illinois where he remained four years, during a portion of which time he was the Surveyor of Morgan county. He happened to be in Washington, D. C., when Fort Sumter was fired upon in 1861 and enrolled as one of a company formed to protect the city until the arrival of the regular troops. In the year 1862 he removed to The Dalles, engaging there in the mercantile business. In 1863, though still continuing his residence at The Dalles, he removed his business to Umatilla, the development of the Boise mines having contributed towards making this an important business point. Here he remained in business until the fall of 1865. In the spring of 1866 he built the steamer "Mary Moody" to operate on Pen d'Oreille Lake, and afterwards aided in organizing the

"Oregon and Montana Transportation Company." This company built two other steamboats, constructed portage roads, established Cabinet Landing and projected other enterprises with the object of securing the trade of the Kootenai mines, and diverting, if possible, the trade of Montana towards Portland, just as is now being done by the committee of merchants operating under the auspices of the Portland Board of Trade. The route selected by Mr. Moody in 1866 is the same as that over which the line of the N. P. R. R. Company now runs. This venture, however, was in advance of the times and resulted in heavy financial loss. In the fall of 1867 he engaged in the mercantile business in Boise city, where he remained for two years. In 1869 he disposed of his business interests there and returned to The Dalles, where he took charge of the extensive business of Wells, Fargo & Co. In the fall of 1873 he resigned this position, and in March, 1874, he was awarded the contract for carrying the United States Mail between Portland and The Dalles, and, in connection with this contract, established a line of steamers to operate between the points named. In 1875 he withdrew from the management and control of the transportation line, and in the following year resumed business at The Dalles, where he resided until called to the executive chair. Since his accession to the Governorship, his extensive business interests at The Dalles have been under the control and general management of his sons. Prior to the late civil war, Gov. Moody was a Whig. Since that time he has been an active and pronounced Republican, his first Presidential vote having been cast for Abraham Lincoln in 1860. While always active in the Republican ranks, he has not sought office, though he has for many years been prominent in the Republican councils, and has been frequently urged for high stations to be filled by the State Conventions of that party. In 1872 he was nominated by the Republicans in the Democratic county of Wasco for State Senator, and after an active canvass was elected by an undoubted majority. His election, however, was contested by his Democratic competitor, whose party friends, having a majority in the State Senate, awarded him the seat. In 1880 he was nominated by the Republicans of Wasco for Representative, and although this county is Democratic by an average majority of nearly 200, Mr. Moody was elected by a majority of 150. At the session of the Legislature immediately following this election he was chosen Speaker of the House of Representatives. So satisfactory was his discharge of the duties of this position that his name was from that time forth prominently mentioned in connection with the nomination for the Governorship.. The next Republican State Convention was held in Portland in April, 1882, and on the 21st day of that month, just thirty-one years from the day upon which he first landed in Oregon City, he was nominated as Governor of the State. On the 5th day of June following he was elected Governor over his Democratic competitor, Hon. Joseph S. Smith, by a majority of 1,452 votes, although his opponent was one of the strongest and most popular Democrats in the State. On the 13th day of September, 1882, just thirty-one and one-half years from the day upon which he sailed from New York for Oregon, he delivered his inaugural message as Governor of the State. Governor Moody is a man of business capacity, whose executive ability has been tested for many years in the management of an extensive wholesale business in Eastern Oregon. He brings to the executive office a well-trained mind, exact business methods, and a keenness of perception in financial matters that qualify him to make at once a successful and popular Executive. With a courteous manner that prompts him to accord a respectful hearing to all, he combines discrimination and firmness of purpose. Physically he is of a splendid type. He is of compact build, with a handsome, ruddy face that indicates sound health, a keen, sparkling eye, through which is displayed the cheerful and sociable nature, determined to extract all the good things from life consistent with sobriety, and an elastic step and a rapid movement that bespeak the busy man of affairs. One who lives well, appears well, and, in all, promises to do well, he brings to his office a popular manner, with a dignity and reserve such as the station demands. He is one who will make it his sole business to attend to the duties of his office, and will not use it as a stepping-stone to secure a greater prize. Judging from the nature of the man, from the habits which have characterized his business life, and from the disposition he has shown since entering upon the duties of the executive office, we are justified in predicting for him one of the most successful administrations known in the history of the State of Oregon.

HON. ROCKEY P. EARHART.

There is perhaps no more responsible position in the State government of Oregon than that of Secretary of State, embracing, as it does, the additional duties and responsibilities of Auditor and Comptroller in connection with his important duties as custodian of the Great Seal, and a more competent man than Mr. Earhart could not have been found to fill it. He appears peculiarly fitted by nature for the duties of public life, possessing that personal magnetism which affects to a more or less degree every one with whom he comes in contact. It seems to flow from him as naturally as light comes from the sun, and he is at all times brimming over with geniality and good humor. He is accustomed to look upon the bright side of life, and imparts the sunshine of good cheer to those about him. Whole-souled, genial and courteous, he gains staunch friends at every turn. Honest, upright and straightforward in all his dealings, he takes it for granted all men are the same until they show the cloven foot. He possesses the true instincts of a gentleman both in friendship and enmities, and in his official acts personal feelings never prompt results. He deals with all alike, and shows neither fear nor favor. Politics never come between himself and those with whom he has official dealings, and many of his staunchest friends and admirers are found in opposing political ranks. In his present position he has no friends to reward or enemies to punish, save such as earn favors at his hands which can be bestowed without in any measure compromising his official capacity. Punctuality and thoroughness are among the leading traits of his character, and it is to these qualities, added to his social worth, that he owes the popularity and respect which he has gained from the people of the State he so ably serves. Mr. Earhart was born in Franklin, Ohio, on the 23d day of June, 1837, and came to Oregon via the Isthmus in 1855. His educational advantages were received in select schools in his native State, and he made the most of the opportunities offered. Arriving here and meeting incidentally with some of the public officials of the day, his superior clerical abilities were very soon discovered and he received the appointment of clerk under Captain (now Commissary General) Robert McFeely, U. S. A., and Quartermaster (now General) P. H. Sheridan, then stationed at Forts Vancouver and The Dalles, under whose latter command he was until his promotion and departure from this coast in 1861. He was all through the Yakima Indian war of 1855-6, and rendered valuable service in the departments in which he was employed. He afterwards went into the general mercantile business in Yamhill and Polk counties, until he succeeded Col. Logan as United States Indian Agent at the Warm Springs Agency, where he remained until the appointment of Captain John Smith, the present incumbent, in 1865. He served for some time as chief clerk and Special Indian Agent under Superintendent Huntington and was Secretary of the Board of Commissioners appointed by the general government to treat with the Klamath and Modoc Indians. In 1868 he engaged in the mercantile business in Salem, in which he continued until 1872. Mr. Earhart was active in conjunction with other citizens in maintaining peace and quietude at the capital during the troublesome times when the civil war was raging and when an outbreak might have been made in our very midst but for the courage and cool-headedness of a few of our best citizens who were prepared for active service and could be ready for any emergency at almost a moment's notice. In 1870, when the stockholders of the Chemeketa Hotel, then just completed, were looking around for some popular and energetic man to manage it, they unanimously selected Mr. Earhart, who reluctantly accepted, and for year or more was its proprietor. He was chief clerk in the office of Superintendent of Indian Affairs in 1872-3. He also represented Marion county in the House in 1870, and was instrumental in securing the first appropriation for the erection of public buildings in this State. He afterwards moved to Portland and was for some time engaged in the business management of the "Daily Bulletin." In 1874 he was appointed chief clerk of the Surveyor General's office, which position he held until 1878, when he resigned to accept the office of Secretary of State, to which he had been elected. He entered upon the duties of that office in September of that year, and at once commenced a thorough and systematic overhauling of the books and records, and in a few months' time had the office in better shape than it had ever been prior thereto. So acceptably did he discharge his official duties during his first term in that office that he received the unanimous vote of the Republican State Convention for renomination and received a majority of over 2,500 at the general election in June, 1882. He identified himself with the Masonic order in 1863, and has held every office within the gift of the fraternity, being still active in its interests. He was elected Grand Secretary of the Grand Lodge in 1872 and served until 1878, when, in recognition of his past services in that body, he was promoted from the Secretary's desk to the high and honorable position of Grand Master, and was re-elected in 1879. He is at the present time Sovereign Grand Inspector and thirty-third of the Scottish Rite in the State of Oregon. He was instrumental in organizing the first Commandery of Knights Templar established on the North Pacific coast, and served for four years as its Eminent Commander, being presented on his retirement from that office with perhaps the handsomest Masonic jewel ever brought to Oregon. Mr. Earhart is also connected with the I. O. O. F. and the A. O. U. W. He was married July 2, 1863, to Miss N. A. Burden, daughter of Judge Burden, of Polk county, their family consisting of four daughters, who are general favorites in society circles. Mr. Earhart is a gentleman of ordinary height, rather heavy set, weighing about 170 pounds, with a full face, partially covered with beard, and brown hair. His features are pleasant and his manners are such as gain friends rapidly. He is an unusually engaging conversationalist, his descriptive powers being vivid and his mimicry complete. He tells and can keenly appreciate a good story, and ten minutes' general conversation with him will make you his friend. No man in Oregon is to-day more popular or has more friends than has Hon. R. P. Earhart. He is but just in the prime of life, and we have no hesitancy in predicting for him higher official honors than he has yet attained.

HON. EDWARD HIRSCH.

Some one has written "There is a Divinity that shapes our ends, rough hew them as we may," and the subject of this sketch is a living exemplification of it. When, away back in the "fifties," he landed a poor boy in the city of New York, among strangers in a strange land, and looked about him for honest employment in any capacity, how little he dreamed that, as years passed by, he would hold the purse-string for the then almost unknown Territory of Oregon, when but a few years later she should lay aside her swaddling clothes and emerge into the maidenhood of a young but prosperous commonwealth. Such has been his career, however, and no man in the State stands higher in the estimation of the people than does Hon. Edward Hirsch, our present State Treasurer. He was born at Wurtemberg, Germany, May 3, 1836, and came to America in 1855. Landing in New York City, he at once sought employment. Proving unsuccessful, however, he went over into the the neighboring State of Pennsylvania and secured a clerkship in a store in a little town in Mercer county, at the princely salary of $75 per annum. He remained there for several months and then went down into Georgia, where he remained nearly two years, the greater part of it being spent at Macon. He became thoroughly acquainted with Southern life in all its varied forms, and to this day bears pleasant recollections of his sojourn in the Sunny South. Becoming imbued, however, with the Western fever, he again went north, and in company with his brother, Hon. Sol. Hirsch, State Senator from Multnomah county, embarked on the steamer "Star of the West," booked for the Pacific slope, via Isthmus of Panama. They reached Portland about the middle of April, and a few months later opened a retail store at Dallas, in Polk county. They remained there about three years and then moved to Silverton, where they carried on a general merchandising business three years longer. They then dissolved partnership, and the subject of our sketch went to Salem and was employed for some time as salesman in the firm of J. B. and M. Hirsch. In 1866, having been elected President and business manager of the Eagle Woolen Mills, at Brownsville, he went there and remained in charge of the enterprise for about two years. In 1868 he returned to Salem, where he has resided continuously since. In 1869 he was interested in the mercantile firm of Hermann & Hirsch, of that city, and in 1870 the name was changed to L. & E. Hirsch. In 1878, when the Republican State Convention met in Salem, Mr. Hirsch's name was urged by a host of friends as candidate for State Treasurer. The contest was a spirited one, but Mr. Hirsch was successful, and a few months later was elected by a rousing majority. During the succeeding four years he devoted his entire attention to the responsible duties of his office, and so faithfully did he discharge the trust reposed in him, he was renominated for the same position by the Republican State Convention in 1882 and was again elected by a largely increased majority. His honesty, integrity, high social standing and unflinching adherence to the principles of the political party he espouses have endeared him to the hearts of the public. His honesty is proverbial and his popularity immense, having the respect of all and the enmity of but few. His liberality is acknowledged, although many of his acts of kindness are known to none but himself and the grateful recipient. He is an able financier, guarding with zealous care the interests of the people in all his official acts. Mr. Hirsch is highly respected as a citizen of Salem, and for two terms represented his ward in the Common Council of that city. He was also Chairman of the Republican County Central Committee in 1876. He belongs to both branches of the I. O. O. F., and is P. M. W. of Protection Lodge No. 2, A. O. U. W., of Salem. He was married May 10, 1868, to Miss Nettie Davis, their family consisting of seven children. Mr. Hirsch is destined to many long years of usefulness, and the people will not fail to take advantage of his abilities in the future as they have in the past.

HON. WILLIAM H. BYARS.

The experience of mankind has stamped with the signet of truth the popular saying that "success denotes merit," and when a young man attains a position of honor and prominence in a community, whether it be in the political or mercantile world, that fact should be taken as proof of merit of no ordinary kind, in the make up of the one winning such honor and distinction. Such an elevation as that of Hon. W. H. Byars to the responsible position of State Printer argues that his past life has been spent to good purpose, and that he has availed himself of his leisure time to store his mind with that fund of literary and political lore which stands him so well before the people of Oregon to-day. He was born in Desmoines county, Iowa, July 7, 1839, his father, Fleming Byars, being a Virginian by birth and his mother, whose maiden name was Anna Deardorff, a native of Ohio. The father died in 1847, leaving the mother with one son and three daughters. In 1851 she was married to John H. Mires and in 1853 they crossed the plains and settled in Umpqua (now Douglas) county, where they still reside. The subject of our sketch carried the United States mails from Oakland, Oregon, to Yreka, California, in 1856-7 and 1858, and, notwithstanding the fearful condition of the roads, the almost utter absence of bridges and an occasional race with the Indians, young Byars missed but two trips during that time, showing conclusively that he was possessed of indomitable pluck and energy and a hearty, robust constitution. During the winters of 1858-9 and 1859-60 young Byars attended the Columbia College at Eugene City, and taught school at Fair Oaks, in his own county, during the summer of 1859. In 1860 he ran for the office of County Surveyor but was defeated. He attended Umpqua Academy during the winter of 1860-1. He spent the summer of 1860 prospecting for gold on the headwaters of the Umpqua river. The summer of 1861 was spent in teaching school at Fair Oaks, and in the winter of 1861-2 attended school at the Willamette University, and during the years 1862-3-4 he was in the Eastern Oregon and Idaho Territory gold mines. On March 15, 1865, he enlisted in Company A of the First Oregon Cavalry, and was elected Orderly Sergeant, in which capacity he served until mustered out July 26, 1866, acting meanwhile as an escort and guard for the surveying party that located the Central Oregon Military wagon road, running from Eugene City to the eastern boundary of the State. Entering school once more he graduated from the Umpqua Academy in 1867, and in the winter of that year taught school at Calapooia school house. The year following he was elected School Superintendent of Douglas county. He was married to Mrs. Emma A. Reed (nee Slocum) on December 23, 1868, and their family now consists of three boys and two girls. In 1869 and 1870 he was one of the principals of the Umpqua Academy, and in 1870 was the nominee of the Republican party of Douglas county for the office of Sheriff but was defeated at the polls. He moved into Roseburg in 1872 and in 1873 purchased the "Plaindealer," then a Democratic newspaper published by W. A. McPherson, and at once converted it into a Republican organ, since which time he has continued its publication and has in a great measure assisted in making Douglas county one of the strongest Republican counties of the State. Mr. Byars is a practical surveyor and has acted as Deputy U. S. Surveyor for a number of years, and had several important contracts. Mr. Byars is a strong Republican and has been such ever since he cast his maiden vote for Abraham Lincoln in 1860. At the Republican State Convention held in Portland in April, 1882, Mr. Byars received the nomination of State Printer, and at the general election held in June following, he was elected by 2,438 majority over Hon. W. F. Cornell, the strongest man the Democracy could have nominated for that position. Mr. Byars is a quiet, unobstrusive gentleman, who rarely attracts attention. He is a good business man, however, attentive and prompt in the discharge of his official duties, and as honest a man as we ever met. He is a genial, whole-souled gentleman, and, socially speaking, stands high in the community. He is of low stature, heavy built, with a clear, penetrating eye, prominent features, heavy beard and hair and a strong constitution.

HON. E. B. M'ELROY.

Among the public institutions of our country none more deservedly attract the attention of all lovers of law and order than do our public schools. It is all-important, therefore, that each commonwealth should have some man of learning and ambition at the head to represent, as it were, in a single individual the individual interest of every child in the State. Especially is this the case in our own State, where we are in reality but just laying aside the swaddling clothes of self-government and endeavoring to lay broad and deep the foundations of a government for higher and more prosperous days to come. Not but what we are as far advanced in educational interests, perhaps, as we are in other interests of a public nature, but that what we are doing for the cause of education at the present time is but a poor sample of what we intend to do in the near future, when our valleys and hillsides are teeming with the fruits of the husbandman, and our wants and necessities in that direction become more general. In order, however, to prepare for this good time coming, it is requisite and necessary that we should make wise laws and most thoroughly systematize the workings of our common schools, and by these and other means better prepare them for their expansion and improvements in the future. Our legislators are sufficiently wise to make the laws, but no system of a uniform course of public instruction can be complete without a head center, and in this head center in a great measure depends the success or failure of the common school system under his control. Our State has, since the creation of the office of Superintendent of Public Instruction, been peculiarly fortunate in their selection of men of capability to fill the position creditably. Among those whose names have become almost a household word by reason of their incumbency of such office might be mentioned Hon. Syl. C. Simpson, Hon. L. L. Rowland, Hon. L. J. Powell, and last, but not least by any means, is that of Hon. E. B. McElroy, who, although he has been in office but a few short weeks, is already evincing a rare aptitude for his work and will, we feel fully confident, prove the equal if not the superior of his predecessors in that office. He brings with him the ripe experience of a successful teacher, the practical teachings of a like although minor position of a county school superintendent, the energy and ambition of a man who is just entering the prime of life, the love of the work inculcated into him by his long-continued connection with public instruction, the necessary qualifications of a successful business career, and a spirit of that progress to the overthrow of old-fogyism, if necessary, which will insure his educational work the advancement made by other public interests. As a man he is the very soul of integrity and is very highly esteemed by those who know him best. He is one of that class of men who, while you will fancy him the moment he addresses you, will none the less bear acquaintanceship and advance in your admiration and esteem the longer and more intimately you know him. Prof. McElroy is a native of Washington county, Pennsylvania, where he was born on the 17th day of September, 1842. His early life was spent on a farm, and he was educated in the public schools of Pennsylvania and at the Southwestern State Normal College of that State. He commenced teaching in the public schools as early as 1861. In September of that year, however, imbued with that noble patriotism so prevalent at that time among the bone and sinew of the North, he enlisted as a private soldier in the ranks of Company B, First Regiment West Virginia Volunteers, serving gallantly under Generals Shields, McDowell and McClellan. He was discharged in 1863, and at once re-enlisted in Company A, One Hundredth Regiment Pennsylvania Volunteers, serving in the Army of the Potomac until the close of the war in 1865. From then until 1873 he followed the several occupations of farmer, student and teacher at his old home and in West Virginia. In 1873 he caught the Western fever and immigrated to Oregon and again resumed his vocation as a teacher, and from 1874 to 1875 taught in the public schools of Corvallis, and in 1875 was elected to a Chair in the State Agricultural College, where he remained until elected to his present responsible position. While occupying a Chair in the Agricultural College he was three times elected Superintendent of Schools in Benton county, in the discharge of the duties of which office he gave universal satisfaction. He was married in 1869 to Miss Agnes C. McFadden, and their family at present consists of four children. He is an honored member of the A. O. U. W. and the I. O. O. F., and has been for a number of years a member of the Christian Church. Prof. McElroy lays no claims to good looks, although he is not homely by any means. He is very tall and slim and has prominent features, his face being smooth-shaved, with the exception of a short mustache, which, with his hair, is already liberally silvered with gray. His forehead is expansive. As a man and neighbor he is very highly spoken of by those who have known him longest. He, with his family, has recently moved to Salem, where he will hereafter make his home, and where he has already made a host of friends by his courteous and affable treatment of those with whom he has come in contact, and we bespeak for him a successful career as State Superintendent of Public Instruction. He is a true-blue Republican and takes a great interest in the success of that party.

HON. JOSEPH N. DOLPH,

United States Senator elect, was born at what was then called Dolphsburg, in Tompkins county, in the State of New York, on the 19th day of October, 1835. After arriving at the age of eighteen years, he taught school a portion of each year while acquiring an education and his profession. He studied law with Hon. Jeremiah McGuire, at Havana, New York, and was admitted to the bar at the general term of the Supreme Court of that State, held at Binghampton in November, 1861. He practiced his profession in Schuyler county, New York, during the winter of 1861-2, and in May, 1862, enlisted in Captain M. Crawford's company, known as the Oregon escort, raised under an act of Congress for the purpose of protecting the immigration of that year to this coast against hostile Indians, crossing the plains as orderly sergeant of the company, on the way losing all his clothing except the suit worn by him, together with every dollar of money with which he set out,—he arrived in Portland on the 31st day of October, 1862, with only the six months pay he had received from the government upon being mustered out of service at Walla Walla, W. T. Upon his arrival in Oregon Mr. Dolph at once began the practice of his profession. With the beginning of the year 1863 he formed a copartnership with Hon. J. H. Mitchell, which continued for more than ten years and terminated upon Mr. Mitchell's election to the United States Senate. He was appointed City Attorney for the city of Portland, in October, 1864, and held that position about one and one-half years, during which time he prepared and proposed important amendments to the city charter, which were afterwards adopted, and also revised for publication of the ordinances of the city. In January, 1865, Mr. Dolph was appointed by President Lincoln United States District Attorney for the District of Oregon, which position he held until September, 1866, when he resigned it to take his seat in the Oregon Legislature as State Senator from Multnomah county, in which capacity he served his county during the session of 1866, and took his seat at the beginning of the session of 1868, but his seat was contested upon the pretence that no allotment had been made at the previous sessions of the Legislature as required by the constitution, and Mr. Dolph was ousted by a strict party vote. He was, however, returned at the general election of 1872 by an increased majority of the votes of his constituents, and sat in the two succeeding sessions of the Oregon Legislature as a Senator for Multnomah county. Mr. Dolph has been an active participant in the politics of the State. He was Chairman of the Republican State Central Committee from 1866 to 1868. He has been an able and eloquent advocate of the principles of the Republican party. He was present at Salem at the meeting of the Electoral College in 1876, and after Governor Grover had given the certificate of election to Cronin, advised the course adopted by the Republican electors, and on the spot drafted the papers which were, by the Electoral Commission, adjudged sufficient to establish the election of Messrs. Odell, Cartwright and Watts. To his promptness, discretion and firmness the fortunate result of the matter is largely attributable. In 1876 Mr. Dolph was elected by the Most Worthy Grand Lodge of the Independent Order of Odd Fellows of the State of Oregon Most Worthy Grand Master, and he held that position with great satisfaction to the order for one year. At the last session of the Grand Lodge A. F. & A. Masons he was elected Most Worshipful Grand Master of the Grand Lodge of Oregon, which position he now holds. Mr. Dolph was, at the time of his election to the U. S. Senate, the confidential legal adviser in Oregon of Henry Villard, Esq., the able and brilliant financier who has done so much towards the development of the northwest coast during the last few years. He was the consulting attorney of the Oregon Railway and Navigation Company, the Oregon and California Railroad Co., the Oregon Improvement Co., the Oregon and Trans-Continental Co., and the adviser of the officers of the Northern Pacific Railroad Co. at Portland, and the attorney of other minor corporations. He was also the President of the Oregon Improvement Company, the Vice-President of the Oregon Railway and Navigation Company and of the Oregon and Trans-Continental Company. As a lawyer he is prompt, ready, reliable and successful. Few men possess the comprehensive knowledge and ability to successfully conduct such intricate, complicated and multifarious matters as have been intrusted to Mr. Dolph within the last few years, and it is understood that while he possesses in an unusual degree of friendship of his clients, they justly regard his election to the United States Senate as a circumstance unfortunate to their interests. In October, 1864, Mr. Dolph was married to Miss Augusta Mulkey, a beautiful and accomplished woman, who, rejoicing in the success of her husband, still graces his elegant home. They have six living children, the eldest a daughter just entering womanhood. Mr. Dolph has long held the foremost place at the Oregon bar, and has been for many years the hardest worked lawyer in the State ; without genius in the common acceptation of the word, he is a good example of what integrity, industry and determined application will do for a man under a government whose highest positions are accessible alike to all. In personal appearance Mr. Dolph is large in figure and of good presence, grave in demeanor and earnest in expression. As a lawyer, he is devoted to his profession, and has for many years enjoyed a large and lucrative practice, from which he has realized a competency. His family residence, recently erected at Portland, is the finest in the State and would be a credit to any city. It is understood that independent of his profession, and in addition to his salary as Senator, Mr. Dolph will have a property income which will enable him to dispense in a becoming manner the hospitalities due to the high station to which he has been called.

HON. M. C. GEORGE.

Our present Representative in Congress, while not born in this State has resided here since but two years of age, and ought by rights to be classed among our Oregon boys. He is possessed of all the necessary qualifications to entitle him to this distinction, viz: energy, integrity, ambition, perseverance and unsullied honor. He has had much to contend with and may well be called a self-made man, and the success that has attended his past life is due only to his own personal exertions. Good fortune has had little to do with it, and we detect in his make up those principles, partially inherited but more generally instilled in him by his own perseverance, which go to create the sinewed mind and talent of our fair young State. Slowly, but steadily, he has advanced in the estimation of the people of Oregon until to-day he occupies the proudest position that a grateful people can bestow upon him through their inalienable right of suffrage. He was born in Noble county, Ohio, May 13, 1849, his father being a native Virginian and his mother of Puritan stock. The family immigrated to Oregon in 1851, the trip across the plains occupying nearly six months. They settled on a farm near Lebanon, in Linn county, where he resided until he became of age, laboring during the summer months and attending the Santiam Academy during the winter. He also attended school at the Willamette University at Salem, and took a commercial course at the Business College at Portland. In 1870 he was the unanimous choice of the Republicans of Linn county, in convention assembled, as candidate for Representative, and received his full party vote at the polls. He was defeated, however, being unable to overcome the Democratic majority usually given in that county. He then removed to Albany, where he was engaged in business for a short time, and on the illness of his brother, Hon. H. N. George, who was then Principal of the Academy at Jefferson, he took his place and taught the balance of the academic year. His services proved so satisfactory he was offered charge of the Academy for the ensuing year, but declined the offer and returned to Albany and shortly afterwards accepted the position for one year of Principal of the Public Schools in that city. In 1872 he was again a candidate for the Legislature and once more suffered defeat, although running considerably ahead of his ticket. The canvass on the Democratic side, the first time he ran, was made by Hon. N. H. Craynon, and the last time by Hon. George R. Helm. In 1872 he was married to Miss Mary E. Eckler, and in the same year commenced reading law with Judge J. C. Powell, of Albany, and in 1875 was admitted to the bar, having completed his course of study with Colonel W. H. Effinger, of Portland. In 1876 he was nominated for State Senator from Multnomah District, receiving forty-six out of the forty-eight votes in the convention, and was elected by a handsome majority. It was in the midst of this session that his child died, necessitating his immediate return home. In the last session, which was Democratic, Mr. George received the votes of the Republican Senators for the honorable position of President of the Senate. In 1880 Mr. George was nominated Congressman at large for the State of Oregon, receiving 1,397 majority over ex-Governor Whiteaker, who was a candidate for re-election. In 1882 he was re-nominated by acclamation by the Republican State Convention, which was held at Portland April 20, 1882, and was re-elected by a majority of 3,365 votes over Hon. W. D. Fenton, the Democratic candidate, it being the first time in the history of the State where a member of Congress has been re-elected. Mr. George is an eloquent speaker and a gentleman of very pleasing address; genial, courteous, affable and good-natured. He is a man of indefatigable industry, and, as the Representative of the people at Washington City, is active and energetic. He stands high among the members of the House, and has received marks of great distinction by being placed upon several of the most important standing committees, chief among which and where he has been enabled to do Oregon a vast amount of good, is his appointment as a member of the Committee on Commerce. His friends are legion, and no man in Oregon stands higher in the estimation of the people than does Mr. George. He is tall and slim, yet of firm build, as his weight is full two hundred pounds, with a kindly expression of features, full auburn beard and dark brown hair. He has a pleasant word for everyone, and, being now but in the prime of life, his future none can foretell; but prophesy indicates that higher and more honorable positions are still within his grasp.

HON. WILLIAM P. LORD.

The subject of this biographical sketch has led an active life, both as a public man and as a private individual. Born in the State of Delaware, he early imbibed the down-east passion for mastering everything that promised emolument or honor. Beginning life with indomitable pluck and honorable ambition, he has succeeded in molding for the benefit of the community in which he resides a model citizen and a man whose word is as good as his bond. His unflinching integrity at once commands the confidence and respect of his fellow men. He is one of those honorable men who, when our country was in danger, risked life and limb in her defense. Such men should be rewarded with the highest office within their capacity to fill or the power of the people to bestow. Judge Lord's services, we are pleased to note, are meeting with just recognition, and he has become a favorite with the people of Marion county and the State at large. He was born at Dover, Delaware, in 1839, and during his early life received the benefits of a good education, having attended a select school taught by the Quakers, as well as receiving instructions in a private class taught by a well-known professor. He attended college at Fairfield, New York, from 1858 to 1860, graduating with the highest honors, and being chosen Valedictorian in the class of '60. In the fall of that year he began reading law with Hon. George P. Fisher, of Dover, Delaware, afterwards member of Congress from that State and Judge of the United States District Court of the District of Columbia. Having a natural taste for law, he applied himself very closely to his studies and made rapid progress, giving every indication of becoming just what he was before going on the bench a most successful attorney. In the spring of 1862, orders having been issued from the United States War Department to raise a batallion of cavalry in that State, Judge Lord was elected Captain of the first of the four companies comprising the batallion, Lieutenant Colonel N. B. Knight, of Salem, receiving the appointment of Major. The batallion was soon afterwards increased to seven companies, and Judge Lord was promoted to the office of Major and Colonel Knight to that of Lieutenant Colonel. The batallion was attached to the Army of the Potomac and participated in a number of the most important engagements of that time. In view of Judge Lord's well-known knowledge of the law, he was detached from his command a portion of the time and detailed to act as Judge Advocate on the staff of General Lew Wallace. At the close of the war he resigned his position in the army and resumed the study of law, attended the law school at Albany, New York, and graduated in the fall of 1866, and was admitted to the bar of the Supreme Court of New York the same year. That the Judge made an active and efficient military officer whose services were sought after by the Government is evinced by the fact that he was, at the completion of his studies, offered a Lieutenancy in the Second Regiment United States Artillery, which he accepted, and was ordered to San Francisco to join his company at regimental headquarters, and was assigned to duty at Fort Alcatraz. He was stationed there a short time and was then ordered to Fort Steilacoom, W. T., and from there was ordered to Alaska, where he remained four months and tendered his resignation. This being accepted, he came to Salem in the fall of 1868, and associated himself in the practice of law with his friend and former comrade-in-arms, Colonel N. B. Knight, where he has remained ever since. He served as City Attorney for several years, and represented the city in the celebrated Court House case and other equally important cases on trial in the United States District Court before His Honor Judge Deady. These cases were carried forward to a successful termination and were decided in favor of the city, which result was in a very great measure due to Judge Lord's personal efforts and his thorough knowledge of the case, which enabled him to present it in a clear and forcible manner and at once gave it an excellent standing in court. In 1878 he was nominated and elected State Senator from Marion county, which office he resigned in 1880 owing to his nomination as Supreme Judge by the Republican State Convention of that year. He was elected by a handsome majority, and having drawn the short term, during the succeeding two years presided as Chief Justice. So ably did he fill the place and so general was the satisfaction he gave to the bench and bar throughout the State, he was the unanimous choice of his party for re-nomination, and at the general election held in June last he was elected by 1,401 majority over Hon. E. D. Shattuck, probably the ablest representative jurist in the Democratic party of this State. Judge Lord is a hard worker and devotes much time and attention to his official duties. His decisions are written with a fearless fairness, and an opinion rendered by him in the name of the court bears upon its face the impress of the true intent of the law, and as such is extensively quoted abroad. Judge Lord is a gentleman of about medium height, slightly rotund, and built from the ground up; a well-shaped head, somewhat bald; smooth face, with the exception of a mustache; hair dark brown, with eyes of blue. He is jovial, genial, and enjoys a good, hearty laugh as well as any one we know. He is not demonstrative, but, if a friend at all, he will do to tie to. His friends are legion, and his enemies, if he has any, are few. He was married to Miss Juliette Montague, of Baltimore, Md., January 14, 1880, and they have one boy, of which it may be truly said "he is a chip off the old block." The Judge belongs to no secret order save the A. O. U. W.

HON. EDWARD BYERS WATSON.

Among the young men who have prominently come before the public, and who have attained high honor and distinction for sterling qualities and native talent, none have pursued a more upright course than Hon. E. B. Watson, Chief Justice of the Supreme Court of Oregon. Standing, as it were, upon the very threshhold of life, he can but feel an honorable degree of pride in the importance and responsibility of his present high position, and with an ambition to deserve the commendation of all honorable men, he has anchored himself to truth, honesty and justice. In him we perceive another example of the feasibility of young men being afforded an opportunity of making a record for themselves in public life. He has proved himself every way worthy of the great confidence reposed in him, and is daily adding laurels to those already won by him during his occupancy of the bench. His entire career has displayed a force of character and indomitable energy which, in the long run, never fails to land the possessor of these qualifications at the top. He is unassuming, and makes friends without an effort, and being full of good humor, relishes a joke when properly told, and is himself replete with anecdote. Judge Watson was born in Clayton county,

Iowa, October 7, 1844, and with his parents crossed the plains in 1853 and came to Oregon. They spent their first winter in Lane county, and in the spring of 1854 they moved to Douglas county and took up a ranch in the fertile valley of the Umpqua. The subject of our sketch helped his father on the farm during the summer months and attended the district school in winter. In 1861 he entered the Umpqua Academy and continued his studies there at intervals until 1863, when he went to Forest Grove and entered as a student in the Pacific University, which is second to none in the State for thoroughness and general excellence. Mr. Watson graduated in the class of '66, and at once returned to Douglas county and commenced reading law under Hon. J. F. Watson, who at that time was a young attorney in Roseburg. He was admitted to the bar in 1868, and in October of the same year went to Jacksonville and opened an office with Hon. B. F. Dowell, with whom he remained until June, 1871, when he formed a partnership with Hon. C. W. Kahler. In 1872 he was elected County Judge for Jackson county and served for four years. In June, 1878, he was elected County Clerk of Jackson county, and in 1880 he was placed in nomination by the Republican State Convention as one of its candidates for Supreme Judge. Although well and favorably known in his own county, the name was not familiar to the people generally. On the judgment, however, of the convention that had placed him in nomination and on the reputation accorded him by well-known citizens of Jackson county, and his extreme popularity in Southern Oregon, where he was best known, he was elected by a handsome majority over an opposing candidate, who was undoubtedly the strongest man the Democracy could have placed in the field against him. The first two years of his term he sat as an Associate Justice, but the rule of rotation made him at the commencement of the October term of 1882, Chief Justice, and be it said to his credit, he is filling his position and discharging its duties in a manner highly creditable to himself and every way satisfactory to the bench and bar beneath him. As a jurist he has displayed marked ability. His decisions are carefully prepared, thoroughly revised, and when presented bear upon their face the impress of a thorough and complete knowledge of the law, an earnest, conscientious research of authorities, and a ready command of language of sufficient simplicity to enable those outside even of the profession to understand the case and grasp with readiness the theories advanced and the position taken. He is an untiring worker and his vacations are frequently spent in laborious study and research. Aided and abetted by his able associates, Judges Lord and Waldo, the decisions of the present Supreme Court are considered substantial bulwarks of law and doctrine, and are extensively quoted in the higher courts of other States. Judge Watson has been twice married, his first wife being Miss Mary E. Owen, of Jackson county, to whom he was united July 11, 1872. She died February 9, 1875, and on May 28, 1879, Judge Watson married his present wife, nee Miss Ella C. Kubli, of Jacksonville, their family consisting of two children, a boy and a girl. The Judge is a member of the A. F. and A. M., Improved Order of Red Men and the A. O. U. W. Judge Watson is destined to many long years of usefulness, and the people will not fail to take advantage of his abilities in the future as they have in the past.

HON. REUBEN P. BOISE.

The subject of this sketch was born at Blanford, Massachusetts, in the year 1819. His father, Hon. Reuben Boise, was a farmer and a prominent man in the politics of his State, having been County Commissioner, County Clerk and member of the State Senate of Massachusetts. He also filled other offices of honor and trust with credit to himself and the State. In 1843 Judge Boise graduated at Williams College, in the classical course, and, being struck with the Western fever, he immigrated to Missouri, where he commenced his career as a school teacher and followed that occupation for two years, when he returned to his native State and began the study of law under his uncle, Hon. Patrick Boise, at Westfield, Massachusetts. In 1848 he was admitted to the bar and at once entered upon the practice of his profession at Chicopee Falls, where he remained for two years. Being again desirous of seeking his fortunes in a new country, he came by the way of the Isthmus to Oregon, and settled at Portland in the spring of 1851. He immediately commenced the practice of law, succeeding much better than he had anticipated. In about a year the Territorial Legislature elected him Prosecuting Attorney of the first and second districts. In 1854 he, in company with Hon. James K. Kelly and Hon. D. R. Bigelow, was elected Code Commissioner for Oregon. At that early date the Territory had no laws compiled in book form for its government, hence this was the first code ever prepared for Oregon. The Commissioners swept away much of the old common law that was cumbersome and intricate and founded our present mode of practice. He then purchased a farm near Dallas and moved thereon. In 1854 he was re-elected Prosecuting Attorney, and at the same election honored by Polk county with a seat in the Territorial Legislature. Two years afterwards he was again elected a member of that body, both terms taking a very prominent part in its deliberations. In 1857 he was one of the Representatives of Polk county in the Constitutional Convention, where he was Chairman of the Committee on Legislation, and prepared that portion of the Constitution relating to the Legislative Department, and otherwise materially assisted in furnishing Oregon with her fundamental laws. In this same year he was appointed by President Buchanan one of the Supreme Judges of the Territory. The next year, after the admission of the State into the Union, he was elected to that office, and from 1862 to 1864 was Chief Justice. Upon the expiration of his term in 1864 he was again re-elected for six years, during four of which he was Chief Justice. In 1870 he was again chosen by the people to fill that honorable position, but Hon. B. F. Bonham, his competitor, having commenced an action to contest his seat on the bench, and not desiring to stand the cost of a long and expensive litigation, he resigned and returned to the practice of his profession. In 1874 he was elected by the Legislature one of the Capitol Building Commissioners, which office he held until 1876, when he was again elected to his old position on the Supreme Bench. Two years later, the Legislature having divided the Supreme and Circuit Judges into distinct classes, he was appointed one of the Judges of the Supreme Court, and acquired considerable celebrity on account of his many dissenting opinions. In 1880 he was elected Judge of the Third Judicial

District, which office he now holds. There is, perhaps, no man in Oregon who has been called upon so often and so continuously to fill offices of honor and trust as Hon. Reuben P. Boise. He had not been in this State over three months before he was called upon to discharge the duties of Prosecuting Attorney, and from that time to the present, a period of over thirty years, he has, almost without intermission, been serving the people in positions that required great ability and integrity, and some of the time, before the laws of the Territory prohibited it, holding two offices at once. That great confidence is reposed in Judge Boise by the people is evinced in the fact that he has never been defeated at an election in his life. The Judge took a prominent part in the Independent move in politics, which showed great strength in the election of 1874. After what he thought the Independent party had been organized for was accomplished, he returned to the Republican ranks. He is an independent man in every sense of the word, and if men and measures have not been what he thought they should be, he has spoken out, regardless of party censure; and such men the commonwealth demand, mere time-servers never advance their country's welfare. Judge Boise is the happy possessor of one of the largest farms of Polk county, embracing over twenty-five hundred acres, the greater part of which he has owned since 1853; being raised on a farm in his boyhood, and having owned and operated one in Oregon for so many years, he takes great interest in the advancement of our agricultural interests. He has twice been elected Master of the State Grange of Oregon, which position he now holds, and in 1880 attended the meeting of the National Grange at Washington, D. C., as a delegate from this State. Being a classical scholar, he has always zealously worked in behalf of the cause of education, and is now a member of the Board of Trustees of the Pacific University at Forest Grove, the La Creole Academy at Dallas, and the Willamette University, of Salem, and takes great interest in their welfare. The Judge being descended from the old Puritans, has inherited their strict purity of morals and uprightness of character, not one word having ever been truthfully uttered against his honor. During his long career in public life, reaching over a quarter of a century, it has demanded many varied acquirements to meet all the positions Judge Boise has been called upon to fill, yet he has adorned all of them.

HON. RALEIGH STOTT.

Among those adding honor and lustre to the legal fraternity of this State, none stand higher in the estimation of both the bench and the bar than does Hon. Raleigh Stott, Circuit Judge of the Fourth Judicial District. Although comparatively a young man, he occupies a niche in the history of the legal lights of our own fair young State that makes him envied by many whose heads are whitened with the passage of years. He has won honor and distinction at the hands of a somewhat fastidious public, and in his official capacity has made new friends who, when an opportunity shall arrive, will gladly show their appreciation of his merit by voice or vote. Although not born in Oregon, his early life was spent here, and his adopted home has become endeared to him by many ties.

He has labored earnestly to master the intricate details of his profession, and, while none of us are supposed to be too old to learn, still we feel justified in saying that Judge Stott's knowledge of law is unsurpassed by any member of the bench in Oregon at the present time, and in comparison with the number of decisions he is called upon to render annually, and the limited time he has to prepare them, owing to the vast amount of work he is compelled to perform—taking into consideration all these facts— his decisions are very far above the average for accuracy and precision, and are as unfrequently reversed by the courts above. His opinions are rendered as the result of earnest research, careful study and an evident desire to dispense justice while obeying the strict letter of the law. Judge Stott was born in Indiana in 1845, and in 1851 came across the plains to Oregon and settled in Washington county, where his mother still resides, his father having died in 1880. The family was a large one, consisting of four girls and four boys. Judge Stott attended school at Forest Grove and graduated from the Pacific University in the class of '69, and at once commenced the study of law under Hon. John W. Whalley, of Portland, and was admitted to the bar in 1870. He commenced practice in Yamhill county, and shortly afterwards associated himself with James McCain, whom he terms "the Logan of Yamhill." There he remained until 1873, when he came to Portland and associated himself with the late Charles A. Ball, Esq. In 1874 he was elected a member of the Legislative Assembly from Multnomah county as a Republican on the "People's Ticket." He was appointed Chairman of the Judiciary Committee. In 1876 he was elected Prosecuting Attorney for the Fourth Judicial District. At the end of his official term in that capacity the firm of Ball & Stott was dissolved and Judge Stott then associated himself with Hon. John M. Gearin, under the firm name of Stott & Gearin. Their practice proved lucrative, and the firm was not dissolved until 1880, when Judge Stott was elected to the position he now so ably fills. Judge Stott was married in 1876 to Mrs. Susan C. Stout, widow of the late Lansing Stout, of Oregon, their family consisting of two children. He is a gentleman of tall, commanding appearance, with pleasant features, expressive of more than ordinary intelligence and forethought. He dresses plainly, although with neatness, and is one of those plain, every-day, sensible sort of men one delights to meet in the upper walks of life. There is nothing distant about him. He has always the same pleasant smile for the rich and poor alike, and is therefore honored and respected by all classes of society. His friendships are strong, and his enemies, if he has any, are among those who are least acquainted with him, for those who know him most intimately are his warmest and most enthusiastic friends.

HON. A. S. BENNETT,

At present Circuit Judge of the Fifth Judicial District, with his residence at The Dalles, was born in Dubuque county, Iowa, on the 10th day of June, 1854, and came to Oregon when he was but eleven years of age, crossing the plains in the footsteps of the thousands who had preceded him, and he has resided in this State or Washington Territory continuously since 1865. He received a common school education, but that he made the best use of his time when a student is shown by the prominence he has even at his present early age attained at the bar. He was elected County Superintendent of Schools for Wasco county in 1878. Naturally ambitious and realizing the scope that the practice of law afforded an active, energetic young man to attain fame and fortune, he early decided to adopt it as a profession. He read Blackstone, etc., under Hon. J. B. Condon, of The Dalles, and in January, 1880, having passed a very successful examination before the Supreme Court, he was admitted to the bar. He was elected a member of the House from Wasco county at the last general election, but resigned his office before the Legislature convened to accept the office of Circuit Judge of the Fifth Judicial District, tendered him by Governor Thayer upon the resignation, September 1, 1882, of Hon. L. L. McArthur. During the brief time he has been on the bench he has given universal satisfaction, showing an earnest and conscientious disposition to deal justly and at the same time hew closely to the strict line of the law. His opinions are indicative of careful study and a thorough knowledge of the common law. He is a pleasant, companionable gentleman and makes friends rapidly. Politically speaking he is a Democrat, and matrimonially considered he is a young bachelor, although not beyond redemption. He is six feet one inch high, weighs about 170 pounds, and is of robust, hearty health. As a friend he is valued, as a man he is esteemed, as an attorney he is respected, and as a Judge he is honored and revered.

HON. ROBERT SHARP BEAN.

"Every man has two educations— one which he receives from others, and one, more important, which he gives himself." Very early in life the subject of this sketch learned this important lesson, and the fruits of its strict observance are being enjoyed by him at present. Only twenty-eight years of age and an Oregon boy, it is certainly pleasant to record the wonderful success that has crowned his efforts. He owes his present success to no accident of birth or fortune, but he has earned it through the toilsome avenue of study and hard work. His early education was imparted to him in a district school during the winter months, when the plow of his father's farm stood idle in the granary. Who knows what dreams of future success flitted across the mind of the plow-boy when dreamily following the furrow behind the jaded team? Some whisper of the prosperity and honor in store for him must have been borne to his ears as an encouragement to him in the routine work of farm life. He was possessed of an active brain and undaunted courage, however, and in early life became imbued with a desire to follow the profession of law, and his school days were improved with that object in view. He was born in Yamhill county on the 28th day of November, 1854, and moved with his parents to Lane county at an early age, where he has resided ever since. He entered the Christian College at Monmouth in September, 1869, pursuing his studies during the winter and working on the farm during the summer months. He graduated with high honors in June, 1873. He worked at the carpenter's trade until November, 1874, when he commenced the study of law with the late Hon. John M.

Thompson, in Eugene City, and was admitted to the bar in December, 1876. He shortly afterwards formed a partnership with Mr. Thompson and was associated with him at the time of his death in February of the present year. Feeling deficient in certain branches of education, he entered the State University at Eugene City in September, 1877, and graduated in 1878, being a member of the first class that graduated from that now prominent institution of learning. He continued in the active practice of his profession until 1882, when he was honored with the nomination and election to the Judgeship of the Second Judicial District. He is one of the most popular young men in his district, his genial, good-humored and affable disposition making him friends everywhere. He is small of stature, weighing less than 140 pounds, trim built, neatly dressed, pleasant features, brown hair and beard, the latter full, a clear beaming eye, and is universally conceded to be good looking. Although young in years, he has brought to the bench of the district over which he presides an experience valued from the fact that it was culled from practical life, and, having ever been a deep student, he combines with such experience the result of zealous research in legal lore, and his decisions thus far have been viewed with great favor by the members of the bar. He is just in his rulings and prompt in his transaction of the business of the court. He was married in September, 1880, to Miss Ina E. Condon, second daughter of Prof. Thos. Condon, of the State University at Eugene City, and has one child. He is an honored member of the Masonic fraternity and a man among men wherever you find him.

HON. H. K. HANNA.

There is probably no member of the legal profession better or more favorably known throughout Southern Oregon than is the subject of this sketch, by reason of his long and intimate acquaintanceship with its leading men and active participation in all matters of public import that have tended to advance the interests of that section of the State. His enterprise and integrity have made for him friends among all classes of society, and his name is a synonym for honesty and industry. Judge Hanna was born in Steuben county, New York, May 22, 1832. After arriving at a sufficient age he attended the public schools of his native place until he was fourteen years old, when he entered a dry goods store as salesman. In 1848 he immigrated to Wayne county, Ohio, where he found employment in the Recorder's office. Succumbing to the Western fever, he came to California in 1850 and at once struck out for the gold fields of the interior. He remained in California for about eight years, and working his way northward, we find him a resident of Josephine county in 1858. He still followed his avocation as a miner with varied success, devoting his spare time to preparation for a thorough course in the study of law, which he afterwards availed himself of under the late lamented Hon. James D. Fay, and was in 1872 admitted to the bar. Prior to his admission, however, he was elected Prosecuting Attorney for the First Judicial District, and on assuming the duties of that office he removed to Jacksonville, where he still resides. He was re-elected in 1874 and again in 1876. When in 1878 the law was passed creating a separate Supreme Court, Governor Thayer appointed Judge Hanna Circuit

Judge of the First Judicial District in place of Hon. P. P. Prim, who was appointed Supreme Judge. In 1880 he was nominated and elected as his own successor, and he still occupies the same high and honorable position. Judge Hanna is a man of rare worth and intelligence. He is remarkably clear-headed and grasps with readiness any knotty problem of law, and is quick in forming an opinion and rendering a decision. None are more independent than himself, and neither fear nor favor control his acts in either public or private life. He believes in calling things by their right names and has the reputation of fearlessness in all he does and says. Socially speaking he is one of the pleasantest men on the bench and has a host of friends. He is full of enterprise, and although nearly fifty years of age, has the vim and energy of a man in the very prime of life. He is the personification of integrity and as a jurist is honored and respected. He is married and has three children, one of which is adopted. Judge Hanna is a Past Master Workman of the A. O. U. W. and Past Sachem in the I. O. R. M. He has won a warm corner in the hearts of the people of Southern Oregon, and we bespeak for him many years of usefulness.

HON. C. B. MOORES.

Some men attain the goal of personal or political prominence by reason of their wealth, some because of their knowledge of and recourse to political trickery, others because of their happy, genial disposition, social qualities and facility for making friends, while some, and they are few indeed, are honored with distinction through merit alone. The subject of this sketch has succeeded thus far in life simply because he merited success and at the same time is possessed of those qualifications which tend to make a man popular with the public, viz: industry, energy, ambition and affability, and no young man has brighter prospects for the future or gives better promise of fulfilling the expectations of sincere well-wishers and devoted friends than does Charles B. Moores, the private secretary of His Excellency Governor Moody. He is well qualified to discharge the duties and responsibilities of that office by virtue of his long residence in and extensive knowledge of this our commonwealth and his versatility as a correspondent. He is a plain, good-natured, pleasant young gentleman, with whom no ceremony—like his popular chief--is necessary beyond the common courtesy one gentleman owes to another, and he has already made a host of friends with those who for the first time, perhaps, have had any dealings with him. Mr. Moores was born in Benton, Missouri, August 6, 1849, and with his parents removed to Danville, Illinois, in 1851. In the spring of 1852 the family removed to Oregon, arriving in Salem in March, 1853, where he has since resided almost continuously. He was educated at the Willamette University and graduated in the class of 1870. The following week he accepted a situation in the land department of the Oregon and California Railroad Company at Portland as draughtsman, where he remained four years. He went East in 1874 and attended one course at H. C. Spencer's Business College, in Washington, D. C. He then went to Philadelphia, where he remained one year in attendance at the law department of the

University of Pennsylvania, taking one course of lectures. In September, 1876, he went to Ann Arbor, Michigan, where he continued his study of law and completed his course, graduating with high honors in March, 1877. In this connection we might add that while visiting Eastern cities Mr. Moores wrote some very interesting letters home, a number of which found their way into the columns of the "Oregonian" and "Statesman" and were read with deep interest, and were highly indicative of far more than ordinary talent in that line. Many of his friends have urged him to adopt journalism as a profession, appreciating his ability as a writer. He has, however, since his return to Salem in 1877, applied himself wholly to the practice of law, in which profession he has made rapid progress. In 1880 he was elected Chief Clerk of the House of Representatives, and in that position evinced surprising executive ability and was generally conceded to be as efficient an officer as that body ever employed. He was married November 1, 1881, to Miss Sallie E. Chamberlin, and is said to make a model husband. The responsibilities of married life, however, have not deprived him of his proverbial love for fun and frolic, and he is still the life of any social gathering in which he may be a participant. He is highly esteemed by all who know him, and we predict for him, with confidence, a life of honor, trust, prominence, and, we hope, of affluence, as he is certainly deserving of the greatest and best of Fortune's favors. Mr. Moores is a member of the I. O. O. F., and is at present P. G. of Chemeketa Lodge, No. 1.

FRANK E. HODGKIN,

An humble attache of the State Department, was born in Tecumseh, Michigan, March 8, 1846. Left an orphan at an early age, he was reared by his grandparents, Dr. and Mrs. William Bacon, now residents of Niles, Michigan, and who, by the way, if they live until February next, will celebrate the sixty-eighth anniversary of their marriage. With them "Frank" moved to Princeton, Illinois, in 1850, where his early life was spent and where he received the benefits of a common school education. He there learned the tinner's trade, which occupation he followed until coming to Oregon in June, 1870. In September of the same year he received the appointment of night clerk in the Portland postoffice under Hon. L. H. Wakefield, where he remained until the spring of 1872, when he went to Salem and for a few months acted as local editor of the "Statesman." In December of the same year he accepted a position on the editorial staff of the Portland Daily "Bulletin," where he remained until the summer of 1874. In January, 1875, he was appointed mailing and delivery clerk in the Salem post office under Colonel T. B. Rickey, and there remained until the spring of 1876. He then returned to Portland and was the first city editor of the Daily Evening "Telegram" of this city. He was afterwards associated with W. S. Chapman, Esq., in the editorial management of the Daily "Bee," which position he resigned in September, 1878, to accept the office of Assistant Secretary of State under Hon. R. P. Earhart, who that month assumed his official duties. Mr. Hodgkin, in September, 1881, was commissioned Assistant Adjutant General on the staff of Brigadier General E. Meyer, with the rank of Major, which position he but recently resigned. On Mr. Earhart's re-election as Secretary of State in 1882, he re-appointed Mr. Hodgkin as his Assistant, which position he still holds. He is also the Salem correspondent of the Daily "Oregonian" and San Francisco "Chronicle," and is now serving his third year as Secretary of the Salem Fire Department. He was married September 2, 1874, to Miss Frankie A. Dunbar, youngest daughter of Hon. Rice Dunbar, deceased, and their family consists of four children. He is a member of the I. O. O. F. and A. O. U. W., having "passed the chairs" in both organizations. His latest venture in the literary line is the publication of the present volume of "Pen Pictures," of which he is one of the authors.

HON. A F. WHEELER,

Who during the past four years has acted as Assistant State Treasurer, and has just entered upon his second term in that capacity, is a man just in the prime of life, and one who is by nature endowed with the very qualifications necessary to make him successful in the responsible position he occupies as the guardian and accountant of the public funds. He was born in Bristol, Indiana, December 9, 1844. His early life was a series of migrations from point to point until 1862, when he enlisted in Company I, Eighty-eighth Indiana Regiment, and in March, 1863, was discharged by reason of disabilities received while in service. In 1863, in company with his brother, A. Wheeler, Esq., now of Shedd's Station, he started for Oregon and reached Linn county in November of that year. In the Spring of 1864 he was appointed Deputy County Clerk of Linn county, where he remained until 1867, when he began reading law under Judge Powell. In 1868 he went to Salem and worked for a short time in the County Clerk's office, under George A. Edes, Esq. In 1868 he went to Corvallis and engaged in the photograph business, and in 1869 he taught school at Union Point, near Brownsville. He then went into the mercantile business with his brother at Brownsville, where he remained until 1871, when he disposed of his interest in the store and went to Harrisburg and kept books for W. H. Baber, and afterwards for E. Cartwright, Esq., of Albany. He had meanwhile learned the art of telegraphy, and in 1872 he was appointed by Hon. O. P. S. Plummer, then District Superintendent, as manager of the office of the Western Union Telegraph Company at Albany, where he remained for about one year, and in connection with P. H. Raymond, Esq., ran the postoffice and a book store in connection with the telegraph office. In October, 1873, he took charge of the Salem office, where he remained until September, 1878, when he accepted his present position under Hon. Edward Hirsch, State Treasurer. In 1876 Mr. Wheeler was elected County Treasurer of Marion county, in which capacity he served for two years, and in connection with his other business was, and is still, agent for several first-class insurance companies. Mr. Wheeler has been twice married, the first time to Miss Laura Nealy, of Polk county, who died September 11, 1880. In January, 1882, he was married to Miss Josie D. Stull, of South Bend, Indiana. He has one child, a daughter, by his first wife. Mr. Wheeler is a man of low stature and light frame, a quick, nervous disposition, and, for a man of his physique, a good constitution. He is a very competent accountant, a splendid penman, accurate and reliable in business matters, and possessed of a sufficient knowledge of law to qualify him to draw up important documents in legal shape; thoroughly honest, sober and industrious, and every way qualified for the important position he occupies. He is genial, and is calculated to make warm personal friends. He is a member of the I. O. O. F. and of the A. O. U. W. Mr. Wheeler is a fluent speaker, and when interested in a debate is capable of dealing telling blows in defense of his opinions, and he is noted for his bluntness and the poignancy of his remarks. In a word, Mr. Wheeler is a useful member of society, and with more such citizens we would have less of the sham and tinsel in this world of ours. We bespeak for him a more brilliant future than he has experienced in the past.

HON. EUGENE P. M'CORNACK,

Though a native of Illinois, might properly be called an Oregonian, as he has lived in this country since early childhood and has acquired his education here. His father purchased a farm in the vicinity of Eugene City, and in 1860 sent the subject of this sketch to wrestle with the spelling book in the district school of that village, where he remained for several years. In 1868 he entered the preparatory course in the Albany Collegiate Institute, where he remained two years, only partially completing the course. He then went to the Pacific University, completed the preparatory course, entered college in 1871, and graduated from that institution in the classical course in 1875; went to The Dalles, taught a year in the public school, began the study of law with Hon. L. L. McArthur, continued a year, when, finding his financial meal-tub empty, he went into the field as a Deputy United States Surveyor. Continued on the government surveys until the fall of 1878, when he was elected Clerk of the Board of Commissioners for the sale of school lands, etc., of the State of Oregon, and immediately entered upon the discharge of the duties of that office. This position he has filled during the four years of the last administration to the entire satisfaction of all. In the discharge of its duties he has been faithful and efficient. The Board, of which he is Clerk, constitutes the Land Department of the State, has the exclusive control and disposition of all lands belonging to the State, and the management and investment of the school, university and Agricultural College funds. The management of the office in all of its intricate details, requires great capacity, accuracy, systematic method and a most abundant stock of patience. Those not familiar with the amount and the character of the work done in this department, little comprehend the capacity required to successfully administer its duties. Mr. McCornack's administration of the office during the past four years has been, in every respect, most satisfactory. He has conducted it upon the most systematic business principles, and in now entering upon a second term of four years, he carries with him a valuable experience derived from familiarity with the duties of the office, and the confidence of all of those with whom he has been brought in contact.

HON. SEYMOUR W. CONDON,

Who has just entered upon his duties as State Librarian for the ensuing two years, is a young man of rare promise who is destined beyond a doubt to assume a prominent place in the ranks of the legal profession for which he is now preparing himself by a thorough and systematic course of study, for the purpose of pursuing which he became a candidate for his present office. He was born at Albany, Oregon, February 5, 1860. With his parents he moved successively to The Dalles, Forest Grove and Eugene City, in which places he attended school and made rapid advancement in his studies. He entered the State University at Eugene City in 1876. In April, 1880, he accepted a position as clerk in the office of Hon. R. P. Earhart, Secretary of State, where he remained until January, 1881, during which time, by his quiet, gentlemanly deportment, and his habits of industry and unflinching integrity he won the well-merited esteem of his employer, associates and acquaintances. Realizing the importance of the completion of his collegiate course before entering upon the active study of his chosen profession he resigned his position in January, 1881, and returning to Eugene City resumed his studies in the State University, spending his spare moments in the study of law under the late Hon. J. M. Thompson and Hon. Robert S. Bean, now Circuit Judge of the Second Judicial District. He graduated from the University in the class of '82, and shortly afterwards came to Salem and resumed his old position in the office of the Secretary of State. He received the caucus nomination of the Republican members of the Legislative Assembly of 1882, and was elected State Librarian by a flattering majority. He is the oldest son of Prof. Thomas Condon, of the State University, and, like his father, is a man of unsullied reputation.

HON. T. B. ODENEAL

Came to Oregon in 1853, crossing the plains in what was known as the "Boy train"—nine in number, ranging in age from eighteen, and the oldest not twenty-one. Hon. William Waldo, now State Senator from Marion, was senior, and captain of the company. Arrived in Salem on the 27th day of September, after a journey of five months and seven days, and commenced working for Hon. Asahel Bush, in the "Statesman" office, the next day. Was Chief Clerk of the House of Representatives of the Oregon Legislature at the session of 1855-6. Was elected and served as Clerk of Benton county from 1856 to 1860, and in that year was admitted to practice at the bar. He founded the Corvallis "Gazette" in 1863, and published the same until July, 1866. Served as County Judge of Benton county about two years by appointment from Governor Gibbs, and four years additional by election—term ending in 1870. Was appointed Assistant Assessor of Internal Revenue in 1870, for the division embracing all the counties of Oregon south of Clackamas and Washington; served until April, 1872, when the position was resigned to accept the office of Superintendent of Indian Affairs in Oregon, which was held until abolished by act of Congress September 1, 1873. Was appointed Clerk of the Supreme Court on the 1st day of August, 1880, which position he still holds.

SENATORS.

HON. W. J. M'CONNELL

Who, during the past two sessions, has so ably represented Yamhill county, and, during the session just closed, occupied the highly responsible position of President of the Senate, is a young man just in the prime of life and enjoys the reputation among the ladies of being the handsomest member of the body. He is a gentleman of ordinary height, weighing about 175 pounds, ruddy complexion, with full beard, a broad expanse of forehead and brown hair. He dresses neatly, but not loud, and is of pleasing address. As a presiding officer he has given universal satisfaction, his decisions as such having been rendered with a view of dealing justly with all parties concerned. He is prompt and energetic in transacting the business of the session, and, possessing a clear, ringing voice, he imparts a certain degree of vim into the proceedings and pushes business with rapidity. He is generous, genial, jovial and good-natured, appreciates a good story and is liked by all. He was born in Oakland county, Michigan, in 1839, and spent the first twenty years of his life on his father's farm, attending school in the meantime. Becoming imbued with the Western fever, he started for California in 1860, where he engaged in mining for about two years with indifferent success. He came to Oregon in 1862, en route to Salmon river mines. Was diverted from this enterprise, however, by discouraging reports, and settled in Yamhill county, where he engaged in teaching school at North Yamhill. In the spring of 1863 himself and John Porter, a miller, purchased six horses, together with a gardener's outfit, consisting of plow, garden seeds, etc., and started for the Boise mines in Idaho Territory. They shipped their animals to The Dalles, where, packing them, himself and his partner walked the entire distance, over the Blue mountains and along the Meacham trail. They located on a small tributary of the Payette river and commenced operations as gardeners. The enterprise proved successful, to the surprise of every one, and the young men laid by some money. The country at that time was infested with horse thieves and road agents, together with deserters from both armies; those from Price's rebel ranks largely predominating, and the civil authorities were powerless to protect citizens and travelers. After a long series of losses caused by the theft of horses and mules, Mr. McConnell was forced to protect himself by going in pursuit of the parties who had committed the depredations. This brought about a conflict between himself and a band of outlaws who originally came from Fort Union, in New Mexico, and led to the organization among the farmers of what was then known as a vigilance committee. Mr. McConnell's leadership of that organization attracted public attention and he was tendered the position of Depnty United States Marshal under Mr. Alvord, which he accepted, and was literally given entire charge of the office. The faithfulness and efficiency with which he discharged the duties of that office is a matter of history. It became necessary for Mr. McConnell to visit the Eastern States during the summer of 1866, and his departure was announced by a Boise City paper as having already taken place. Business matters, however, detained him a couple of days, during which time the editor of the "Idaho World" made an infamous assault upon his standing and character through the columns of that paper. Mr. McConnell had already started on his trip, but was overtaken by a friend and his attention called to the article. Not wishing to leave the Territory with even the shadow of a stain on his character, he at once returned to Idaho City to settle the matter. The result of that settlement is also an interesting scrap in the early history of that Territory. Mr. McConnell, having been detained several weeks in the final settlement of this matter, and the time having nearly arrived when he was to be married to one of Yamhill's fairest daughters, gave up his Eastern trip and returned to the Willamette valley. On the 15th day of September, 1866, he was married to Miss Louisa Brown, the wedding taking place at the residence of James M. Fryer, Esq., of North Yamhill, in the very house now occupied as a family residence by Mr. McConnell. He having resigned his position as Deputy Marshal, he went with his young wife to Humboldt county, California, where, for the next four years, he was engaged in the stock business. It not proving congenial to his taste, however, he returned to Oregon and engaged at once in the general merchandising business at North Yamhill, which he has conducted for ten years uninterruptedly. He has also conducted branch establishments in Eastern Oregon and Northern Idaho. At present his mercantile attention is confined solely to his business enterprises at Moscow, I. T., in connection with which he contracts with farmers for large quantities of flaxseed, his operations in that commodity being such as to control the market of the Pacific Coast. He still continues to live at his old home in North Yamhill, where he owns a fine farm and is interested in various other business enterprises. Politically speaking, Mr. McConnell is an uncompromising Republican. He was elected State Senator in 1880 and has ever proved active and efficient in the discharge of his public duties.

HON. SOL. HIRSCH.

There are few men who ever sat in the legislative halls of Oregon who can look back with more pride to a longer, more honored or useful career than can Senator Hirsch, of Multnomah county. Looking down the vista of years we see him at the foot of a hill, a poor boy, struggling with poverty and want; and, without at present recounting his adversities, we find him to-day at its summit, an honored citizen of this commonwealth, surrounded by all the comforts and many of the luxuries of life; and the recipient of the honor, esteem and confidence of his fellow men. These advantages and these blessings are not the result of a streak of good luck.

Far from it. They are the result rather of an unswerving ambition, an unsullied integrity, and an enterprising, active mind that will overcome all obstacles and knows no such word as fail. His position is always at the front and he is accorded the leadership in any movement in which he carries an interest. He is a man of remarkably strong constitution, clear and penetrating eyes, a prominent, well-shaped head, whiskers and hair of heavy growth and as black as jet. He is, in fact, the most intelligent-looking man in the Senate, and the fact is his looks do not belie him. He is cool, deliberate and collected in all his movements, with an iron will and naturally determined and stubborn when once he thinks he is in the right. He has a keen eye for the interests of his constituents, and, although not given to airing his eloquence, he generally manages to get the right word at the right moment in the right place. He was born in Wurtemburg, Germany, March 25, 1839. His youth was spent in the old country in attendance at the common schools of that day. He immigrated to this country in 1854 and at once secured a clerkship in a store in New Haven, Connecticut, where he remained a few months and then went to New York City to try his fortunes. He accepted a clerkship on Fulton street and remained there a short time, then going to Rochester, N. H., where he remained until 1858. Then joining his brother, Hon. Edward Hirsch, our present State Treasurer, together they came to Oregon, reaching Portland about the middle of April of that year. Together they opened a small retail establishment at Dallas, in Polk county, where they remained three years, and here it was that the subject of our sketch laid the foundation of his fortune. They then moved to Silverton, where "Sol." remained about three years, and, with a view of giving himself a broader sphere in which to exercise his acknowledged mercantile sagacity, he went to Portland and became interested in the wholesale dry goods house of L. Fleischner & Co., then located on the west side of Front street between Stark and Oak. Their business increased rapidly. Their quarters becoming cramped, the firm of Fleischner, Mayer & Co., as it stood in 1875, secured more extensive accommodations in their present location, and to-day occupy the proud position of the leading wholesale dry goods establishment on the coast, outside of San Francisco, their annual sales, in fact, exceeding by far many more pretentious establishments in California's metropolis. Mr. Hirsch's first appearance in the political arena was in 1864, while residing at Silverton. He took it into his head one day that his brother, Mayer Hirsch, then a leading merchant of Salem, would make a good delegate to attend the National Convention, to be held at Baltimore, Md. Acting on the impulse, he put in an appearance at the State Convention, which met at Albany, and—well, it is needless perhaps to add that Mr. Hirsch received his nomination, and, together with Josiah Failing, Fred Charman, Rev. T. H. Pearne, Hiram Smith and J. W. Souther, assisted in the second nomination of the lamented Abraham Lincoln. Senator Hirsch was a delegate to the Republican State Convention of 1872, that nominated Hon. Jos. G. Wilson for Congress, and he was that year elected a member of the House from Multnomah county, and as an acknowledgment of his well-known financial ability, was appointed a member of the Committee on Ways and Means. In 1874, the Republican party of Multnomah county nominated and elected him State Senator, he being the only candidate elected in opposition to the Independent ticket then in the field, his opponent being Judge Strong. In 1878 he was re-elected over Hon. J. B. Congle and in 1880 was honored by receiving the entire Republican vote of the Senate as President of that body, in which trying position he displayed marked executive ability, and by his fairness and impartiality won the esteem of both political sides of the Chamber. He was re-elected for the second time in 1882 as State Senator by nearly 1,200 majority over his opponent, Hon. John Catlin. This is by far the largest majority ever given in the State on the election of State Senator, and was highly complimentary to Mr. Hirsch. The Republican delegation from Multnomah county to the State Convention, which met in Portland, in April, 1882, unanimously recommended Mr. Hirsch as a member of the State Central Committee from that county, and he was afterwards unanimously elected as Chairman of that organization. His very successful management of the campaign of 1882 is a matter of history, the defeat of the Democratic party being as disastrous as was the success of the Republican party brilliant. Never was a campaign in this State better managed, its organization more complete, its work more effective, and its result more successful, and to Hon. Sol. Hirsch is, in a great measure, due the praise for the brilliancy of its success. In the session of 1882, Senator Hirsch was appointed Chairman of the Committee on Ways and Means, and, as ever, proved himself one of the most active workers on the floor. On the 1st day of February, 1870, Senator Hirsch was married to Miss Josephine Mayer, daughter of Jacob Mayer, Esq., of the firm of which Mr. Hirsch is an active member. She is an acknowledged leader in society and a mother in the fullest sense of the word to their four bright and intelligent children. Mr. Hirsch being just in the prime of life, it is safe to predict for him a bright and brilliant future.

HON. JOSEPH SIMON.

One of the first members to attract the attention of a stranger on entering the Senate Chamber is the Senator from Multnomah, whose name heads this sketch, not that he is either of commanding appearance or handsome, but because well just because he is not considered over burdened with either of these unnecessary virtues. He possesses, however, what is considered a superior, marked intelligence and keen perceptive faculties. He can detect a defect in any measure as readily as any member on the floor, and his opinion never fails to receive the careful consideration of his colleagues. He came to Oregon in 1857, when he was but six years of age, and with his parents settled in Portland, where he assisted his father in the mercantile business. He attended the public schools of that city and, being a hard and thorough student, was not long in securing such educational advantages as they offered at that day. Possessing a desire to study law he, in 1870, entered the office of Mitchell & Dolph as a student, and soon developed more than ordinary talent. He was a close student and, possessed of a retentive memory, he showed marked progress and was ready for examination for admission to the bar in 1872. He passed a successful examination and, having secured his "sheep-skin," was, within a very short time, admitted to partnership in the firm with whom he studied. He applied himself closely to his profession and no young attorney in the State stands higher in the estimation of the people than does Mr. Simon. In 1877 he was honored with the position of City Councilman from the Second ward, which position he held for three years, during which time he was for several months President of the Council and acting Mayor. He was Secretary of the Republican State Central Committee and had the management of the campaign of 1878, and was elected Chairman and directed affairs in 1880. In this arduous position he displayed excellent traits in generalship, and was greatly instrumental in securing the success of the Republican ticket. The same year be was elected State Senator from Multnomah county, and in the session of that year was Chairman of the Committees on Railroads and Assessments and a member of the Judiciary Committee. In the session just closed he was Chairman of the Committee on Commerce and a member of the Judiciary Committee. As a legislator he is a hard worker, and any measure in which his county is interested, or the interests of the State are involved, finds in him a zealous supporter. He is of low and heavy build, with a good-shaped head, clear piercing eye, high forehead and heavy chin whiskers. He talks with ease, but speaks slowly. "Joe" is unmarried, and the fault is his own. This, we believe, is the only objectionable feature he possesses in the minds of the fair sex.

HON. T. W. DAVENPORT

Was born in Columbia county, N. Y., July 30, 1826. He had the advantages of a fair education, which, with a view of studying medicine, he made the most of. He learned the drug business at an early age and devoted his spare time to the study of medicine and attended a course of lectures at Sterling Medical College, in Columbus, Ohio, in 1847. In 1851 he moved with his parents to Oregon and settled in Marion county, where he has resided ever since, devoting his attention to farming, and ranks among the most successful in that line of business. He was elected County Surveyor in 1864 and 1866, and a member of the House in 1868 and 1870, and was renominated in 1872, but declined to run. In 1874 he received the nomination for Congress on the Independent ticket and made a canvass of the State with Hon. Richard Williams, the Republican candidate. George A. LaDow, the Democratic nominee, being the successful candidate. He was elected State Senator in 1882. Mr. Davenport has been a prominent politician in Marion county for years and was one of the organizers of the Republican party of Oregon along in 1855. His father was an anti-slavery Whig and the son an original Abolitionist. In 1862 he was appointed Special Indian Agent on the Umatilla Reservation. He has been twice married, the first time, in 1852, to Miss Flora Geer, daughter of Hon. R. C. Geer, of Marion county. She died in 1870, from the small-pox contracted by Mr. Davenport while in attendance as a member of the House of Representatives in the fall of that year, his entire family being down sick with that disease. In 1872 he was married to Mrs. N. E. Wisner, of Linn county, their family consisting of six children. Mr. Davenport is an active member of the Legislative body and a hard worker. Having had considerable experience in that line, his advice and counsel is much sought after. He is a plain, every-day sort of a man, dresses with becoming taste, is of ordinary height and weight, with a well-shaped head, auburn hair and whiskers. He has been a deep reader and is well posted on all ordinary subjects. He is a ready speaker and indulges freely in the debates of the Senate. He is honest and conscientious in all his public acts, and by his neighbors is considered honorable and fair in all his dealings. He is an active member of the Good Templars' organization and has taken an active interest in the Grange.

HON. STEWART M. PENNINGTON,

Who is now serving his second term as State Senator from Umatilla county, is an uncompromising Democrat, and is considered one of the best men in that body. He is a quiet, unassuming gentleman, but keeps his weather eye open and is thoroughly posted on every question of importance that comes up for consideration. He was born in Monroe county, Kentucky, in 1824, and was the eighth of thirteen children. He received a common school education and with his parents moved to McDonough county, Illinois, in 1831, where he worked on his father's farm until April, 1847, when he started for Oregon in company with a train of emigrants. He disposed of his team at Fort Hall, and in company with John Danford, Joel McKee, John Monroe and Robert Greenvill, started on horseback for Oregon City. When near Fort Boise the Indians succeeded in stealing their animals, leaving them without means of transportation in a strange country. They succeeded, however, in trading some old clothes for Indian ponies with some friendly Indians, two hickory shirts being considered equivalent to a pony. With these animals they continued their journey, reaching Oregon City in September, 1847. He commenced work in Governor Abernethy's saw-mill at three dollars a day, payable half in cash and half in scrip, or orders on the store. He also farmed awhile on the Tualatin plains. In the spring of 1849 he went to California, where he spent about two years in mining and running a general provision store in Sacramento. He returned to Oregon in 1850 and took up his residence in Linn county, near the present town of Lebanon, where he was married to Miss Abigail E. Cooper. Here he spent about eleven years of his life between his donation claim of 640 acres, which he still owns, and his wagon shop in Albany, he being a practical wagon maker. While there, and while his party was largely in the ascendancy, he was repeatedly urged to accept some office, but persistently refused, preferring rather to pursue his regular line of business to entering the political arena. With his family he moved into Umatilla county in 1871, settling on Butter creek and entering the stock business, in which enterprise he is still engaged, although more recently residing at Pendleton. He was nominated and elected State Senator in 1878, and re-elected in 1880. He is a member of the standing Committees on Elections and Public Buildings and is an active worker. He has ever been an enthusiastic supporter of the free-school system and carefully guards the interests of his section of the country in matters of legislation. He is an honored member of the Masonic fraternity and a consistent supporter of the Baptist religion. He has raised a family of seven children and boasts proudly of being the grandfather of four little Webfeet. His attention to business is proverbial and his standing among Senators is first class, as they invariably regard him as honest, sensible and intelligent.

HON. N. B. HUMPHREY,

The Senator from Linn county, whose name and geniality of character is proverbial in our midst. He was born with a broad grin overspreading his features, and nothing in the ridiculous side of life escapes this happy man's notice. He was born in Louisa county, Iowa, January 30, 1840, and worked on his father's farm until he was sixteen years of age, when he commenced the study of law at Albia, in his native State, and was admitted in 1861, the year of his arriving at age. The war breaking out soon afterwards, he at once enlisted as a private soldier in Company D, 22d Iowa Infantry. He served nine months in the ranks and at Vicksburg, Miss., was elected First Lieutenant, where he served about one month and was promoted to the captaincy, in which capacity he served with efficiency until the close of the war, his company participating in several of the most important battles of the campaign. He was mustered out of service at Davenport, Iowa, August 4, 1865, and returned to Albia, where he resumed the practice of law. He was elected County Judge of his county in 1865 and resigned in March of 1866, when he started across the plains for Oregon, arriving in Albany, Linn county, in September of the same year, where he has resided ever since, engaged in the practice of his profession. In June, 1872, he was elected Prosecuting Attorney of the Third Judicial District, in the discharge of which duties he displayed his characteristic energy and persistence. He was elected State Senator from Linn county in 1880, at a time when the county was about 300 Democratic, his majority being about 290, with a known reputation as an uncompromising Republican. As a Senator and representative of the people Captain Humphrey is active, energetic and untiring. He is perfectly at home in debate and his remarks always command attention. His personal appearance is favorable, being of a little more than ordinary height, well-proportioned, broad shoulders, a pleasant face and an eye fairly twinkling with mirth at all times. His hair and mustache are slightly tinged with gray. He is undoubtedly the brightest wit of the Assembly and his jokes pass from mouth to mouth, exciting mirth whenever repeated, but none can tell his stories as he tells them himself. He is a companionable, social chap and we sincerely hope that his shadow may never grow less and his belief in the doctrines of the Presbyterian church increase.

HON. GEORGE B. DORRIS.

One of the most gratifying features of our republican form of government, and one of which has contributed largely to its perpetuity, is the fact that a wide field of honor, distinction and usefulness lies open to every young man of talent and ambition. No matter how poor his circumstances, with a proper amount of energy, determination and patience he can make of himself a useful citizen and a leader among men. The subject of this sketch is a fair example of this class of men. He was born in Nashville, Tennessee, on the 9th day of March, 1832, where he resided during the early part of his life, serving a regular apprenticeship at the tinner's trade and becoming a thorough master of the same. He moved to Clarkesville, Tennessee, in 1852, and applied himself to securing an education. By strict economy and close appliance to his trade, he managed to lay by sufficient means to enable him to pursue a course of instruction in the Masonic Academy of that city. He came to California, in November, 1855, and engaged in the stove and tin business at Crescent City, reading law meanwhile with Judge S. P. Wright, of that city. Came to Oregon in 1861 and settled at Jacksonville and continued the study of law under Hon. B. F. Dowell, and was admitted to the bar, in 1864, by the Supreme Court of this State. He settled in Eugene City the following year, and in May, 1866, was married to Miss Emma A. Hoffman, of Jacksonville. He has resided in Lane county since 1865, and is highly esteemed as one of its most influential citizens. He is a staunch Democrat and represented that county in the House of 1870 and was elected State Senator at the last general election. He is a prominent Mason and a member of the A. O. U. W. He has three children and enjoys home life rather than the excitement of a public career.

HON. W. A. STARKWEATHER,

Who is now serving his second term as State Senator from Clackamas county, was born in Preston, Connecticut, February 16, 1822. He was raised on the farm, but received the benefits of a very fair education, mostly derived from the common schools, aided by an occasional attendance at some select school. He prepared himself for teaching and followed this profession as a means of livelihood for a number of years. He left his native place in 1846 and went to Ohio and taught about two years in the schools of Redding and Lockland. He came to this coast in 1850, having crossed the plains. He remained but a few months in California and came to Oregon in the fall of 1850 and was with Governor Moody and others in the surveying party that located the meridian line in 1851. He took up a donation land claim near Scio in the following year, on which he remained until 1854, when he removed to Clackamas county, where he has since resided. He spent several years on a farm, and in 1861 went into the United States Land Office at Oregon City. He was elected a member of the House and attended the session of 1854-5, and has been so often a member of that body since that date that the data is forgotten. He was elected State Senator in 1878 for the term of four years. He was married to Miss Eliza Gordon in 1853 In 1857 he was elected as a member of the State Constitutional Convention Mr. Starkweather is an uncompromising Republican and stands high in his party. As a legislator he is an indefatigable worker and watches with zealous care the interests of his constituents and the entire State. Mr. Starkweather is a fine-looking old gentleman, with flowing white beard, prominent features, penetrating eyes and a well-shaped head. He occasionally indulges in debate, but is not given to airing his eloquence and is highly esteemed by all who know him.

HON. ENOCH HOULT.

Although naturally of a retiring disposition, no member of the Senate of 1882 was better posted on those subjects of paramount importance than was Hon. Enoch Hoult, of Linn county. As a citizen of our commonwealth he is universally esteemed; as a Democrat he possesses the entire confidence of his party, and as a legislator he is an active, energetic worker. He is a Virginian by birth, having first seen the late of day in Monongahela county in 1820. He turned his attention to farming and stock-raising, having but few educational advantages. His parents moved to Edgar county, Illinois, in 1832, and here Mr. Hoult found a life partner in the person of Miss Jennett Sommerville, to whom he was married in 1842, and whom he still survives, she having passed away in April, 1873. He came across the plains in 1853 and settled in Lane county, about ten miles north of Eugene City, continuing his vocation as a farmer. In 1863 he moved to Harrisburg, in Linn county, where he has resided ever since. He represented Lane county in the Constitutional Convention in 1857, and was elected State Senator from Linn county in 1870, serving his constituency faithfully. He followed the business of stock-raising with great success in Eastern Oregon. He has just served the first session of his second term. Politically speaking he is a Democrat, but not unnecessarily partisan in his views. He is a prominent member of the Masonic order and attained high honors in its various branches. He has a family of seven children, but one of which is of the male pursuasion; three of his daughters being married. He is a man of low stature, well-built, with pleasant features partially covered with a beard which, in sympathy with his hair, is slightly tinged with gray.

HON. JACOB VOORHEES,

The Senator from Marion, was born in Montgomery county, New York, on the 25th day of May, 1841. The greater part of his early life was spent on his father's farm, he receiving meanwhile the benefit of a very fair education by attendance at the common schools of his native place and a three years' course of instruction in the academies of Schenectady and Claywack. He engaged in school teaching for a year or more at Hogan's Mills, in that State, and in 1865 went to Minnesota, where, for about three years, he was engaged in the general merchandising business at Rochester and Minneapolis. He returned to New York in 1868, where he continued to reside until coming to Oregon in 1872. He settled on French Prairie, in Marion county, and engaged in farming. He took an active interest in agricultural pursuits and associated himself with the Grange organization, in which he has sustained prominent and important standing. His intelligence and integrity at once commanded the respect of his neighbors, and in 1882 he was put forward as a candidate for the State Senate. With his colleagues he made a canvass of the county, and although the combined force of the opposition was directed against him personally, he was elected, and has thus far taken an active part in the proceedings of the Senate. He is rather a fine-looking gentleman, of average height and weight, neat and trim in personal appearance, with heavy auburn beard and a kind, beaming eye. He is an easy man to approach and has the faculty of making friends. He is a' strong Republican and has been such ever since he was entitled to a vote. He is a prominent member of the Masonic order, having united with it in 1864. He was married in March, 1868, to Miss Anna M. Rice, of Rock Hill, Missouri, and they have a family of four children.

HON. THOMAS E. CAUTHORN.

Among the silent majority in the Senate, the subject of our sketch is an honored member, and represents Benton county. He is a pleasant, well-appearing gentleman, now in the prime of life. He has a full face, cleanly shaven, with the exception of chin whiskers. His voice is rarely heard in debate, but his vote is always cast, after a careful review of the situation, and his mind once made up it is not easy to change. He guards with zealous care the interests of the State, and proves an honest, conscientious public servant. He was born in Andraiw county, Missouri, in 1849, his younger days being spent in a store. With his parents he moved to Oregon in 1865, and settled at Corvallis. He went to Yakima valley in 1872, where he spent about three years in the stock business. Returning to Corvallis in 1875 he entered into partnership with his father in the general merchandise business, which he is still engaged in, and the firm to-day stands second to none in that city for enterprise and general business integrity. His parents are still living and stand high among the citizens of Benton county, and "Tom" is considered a chip off the old block, possessing the confidence and esteem of all who know him. He was married December 21, 1870, to Miss Sarah L. Jeffreys, of Corvallis, and with his accomplished wife occupy prominent positions in the social life of that city. He made his bebut in the political arena at the last general election, when he was elected Senator. Politically speaking, he is a Democrat, but is not considered a strict partisan, although he sustains a good political standing in his party. He is also an honored member of the Masonic fraternity.

HON. JOSEPH D. LEE.

Who is serving the last session of his four years' term as State Senator for Polk county, is, without doubt, one of the most popular men in that county, possessing the esteem and confidence of its citizens, both as a business man and a legislator. He is an Oregon boy, having been born and raised in the county he represents on the 27th day of July, 1848, his father, Nicholas Lee, having come to Oregon in 1847, and died at Dallas July 11, 1879, his mother surviving the husband's death just eighteen months. The subject of our sketch received a partial academic education in the La Creole Academy at Dallas. The greater portion of his boyhood, however, was spent on the farm or as a clerk in his father's store in Dallas. In 1872 he was admitted as a partner in the store, the name of the firm being N. & J. D. Lee, and in 1876 he purchased his father's interest in the establishment and assumed entire control, and to-day he occupies the position of leading merchant in that city, his attention to business and intricate knowledge of the trade having resulted in a most successful business career. He was appointed Postmaster at Dallas in 1870 and served as such for three years, and was a member of the first Board of Trustees in that place. In 1878 he was elected Representative from that county, the balance of the Republican ticket suffering defeat, and in 1880 he was elected State Senator by a handsome majority. He was married May 10, 1872, to Miss Eliza A. Witten, and they have a family of three children. He is a member of the M. E. Church and an honored member of the I. O. O. F. He stands about six feet one inch in his stocking feet, and is well-proportioned, weighing in the neighborhood of 200 pounds. His features are pleasant, his eye expressive, and his hair and whiskers auburn. He is an active member, indulges in debate but seldom, but always to the point. He guards with zealous care the interests of the State, and is inclined to be economical, but not parsimonious. He is a Republican in politics and was one of the original sixteen who, at the commencement of the session refused to enter or abide by the decision of the caucus.

HON. JOHN M. SIGLIN.

The hold-over Senator from Coos and Curry counties, is a gentleman who at once attracts attention on the floor of the Senate. He is of ordinary height and weight, with piercing black eyes and prominent features, black beard and hair and plainly dressed. When in street costume he generally wears a tall silk hat, which style this session is an exception rather than a rule. He often indulges in debate, and his opposition to a measure is generally vindictive and severe, while his support is considered a strong feature in its favor. He is a Democrat on general principles, but in obedience to what he claimed was the wish of a majority of his constituency, he was a strong supporter of Hon. John H. Mitchell, Republican nominee for United States Senator. He did not take this stand, however, until fully convinced in his own mind that there was no possibility of the election of a Democrat, when he naturally had his preference among the Republicans named. Mr. Siglin was born in Monroe county, Pennsylvania, in 1840, and at the age of twelve years moved with his parents to Illinois, where at Galena he received the benefits of an academic education. At the breaking out of the civil war he enlisted as a private in Company F, 13th Illinois Infantry, under the gallant Col. Wyman. For meritorious conduct at the battle of Wilson's Creek, in Missouri, he was promoted to a Second Lieutenancy and transferred to the 8th Illinois Cavalry, Company B, and was the youngest commissioned officer in that regiment. He participated in a number of engagements, including Fair Oaks and the seven-days' battle before Richmond, being compelled to resign in 1863 owing to failing health. Returning North, he commenced reading law and was admitted to the bar in 1867. He came to Oregon in

1872 and settled in Coos county, where he has resided ever since. He started the "Coos Bay News," the first newspaper published in that county, and was its editor for a period of eight years. He at once was accorded a prominent part in politics and has taken an active part in every campaign since his arrival there. In 1880 he was elected joint Senator from Coos and Curry, that being the first political office for which he was ever a candidate. By the way, Mr. Siglin is conceded to be one of the finest linguists in the State, he being able to speak several languages very fluently. He was married in 1863 to Miss Nellie Sherman, of Kane county, Illinois, she being the first cousin, once removed, of Gen. W. T. Sherman, U. S. A. In 1881 he was sent back to Washington City, D. C., on behalf of the citizens of his county, to press their claims for favorable action on the part of Congress in the way of appropriations for certain harbor improvements, and in his mission met with gratifying success.

HON. FRANK CROSBY REED,

The joint Senator from Clatsop, Columbia and Tillamook counties, was born in Woolwich, Maine, March 8, 1847, his early life being spent upon a farm, his only facilities for securing an education being such as were afforded by the common country schools of that early day and one term in the high school at Litchfield. He early imagined that he would adopt a seafaring life, but a trip from Boston to New Orleans and return satisfied him, and he abandoned the sea and commenced learning the carpenter's trade, and from 1867 to the spring of 1875 he applied himself to his trade, sandwiched with a job occasionally of fishing or log driving. In 1875 he was married to Miss Hattie E. Webb, at Woolwich, Maine, and soon afterwards started for Oregon, reaching Portland in April of that year. Spent the following summer among the canneries and took up their residence at Astoria in 1876. He secured an interest in the Fishermen's Co-operative Cannery, and in the fall of that year acted as their superintendent of construction. In 1877, when the fishing season set in, he was employed by the company as superintendent of the cannery, and held that position for three years. He had the misfortune to lose his wife in January, 1880. He was a candidate for joint Representative from Clatsop and Tillamook, but was defeated in the convention. After a short visit to the East in the spring of 1881, he built a new cannery under the firm name of C. Timmons & Co. Mr. Reed is a member of the A. F. and A. M., I. O. O. F., A. O. U. W. and K. of P., having attained places of distinction in each. He is a staunch Republican, an earnest worker in the legislative halls and alive to the interests of his constituents. He is a pleasant gentleman in social life and enjoys the confidence and esteem of all who know him.

HON. J. B. SIFERS.

This well-known member, who is now serving his second term as State Senator from Josephine county, was born in Morgan county, Iowa, January 7, 1832, and held the plow until he was about eighteen years of age, attending the common schools of the day, his educational advantages being extremely limited. In contact with the world, however, and making himself familiar with the current literature of the day, he has stored his mind with much useful knowledge and grasps with readiness the importance of leading or meritorious measures, and detects as readily the underlying defects of a job. He is a practical miller and mill-wright, having learned that trade before coming to this coast. He crossed the plains and arrived in Oregon City in 1854, where he worked for a few weeks at his trade and then went to Jacksonville and tried mining for awhile. He was appointed Deputy Sheriff in July, 1855, and in March, 1856, was appointed Clerk of the United States District Court by Hon. M. P. Deady, where he remained about two years and a half; he following various vocations until 1867, when he moved to Kerbyville and purchased the flouring mills, which he is still running. He served the people of his county four years as County Judge and was elected State Senator in 1880. He is of tall, commanding stature, and is one of the best-looking Senators on the floor. He is not given to debate, but votes intelligently and conscientiously. He was married in 1863 to Miss Mary Peninger, of Jacksonville, but is now a widower with two boys, his wife having died in 1874. He is an honored member of the Masonic fraternity, but has never sought distinction. Politically speaking he is a Democrat, but not a strict partisan, as was evinced by his voting for Hon. J. H. Mitchell for United States Senator in deference to what he considered was the choice of a majority of his constituents. His course was criticised somewhat, but having decided what course to pursue, Mr. Sifers paid no attention to their attacks and gained friends by his silence.

HON. WILLIAM R. BILYEU.

Among the Democratic members of the State Senate none are considered more stalwart than the subject of this sketch, who represents Linn county. He is the tallest Senator on the floor, of spare build, with chin whiskers and mustache, a broad forehead and glistening black eyes. He was born in Miller county, Missouri, in 1848, and received a common school education, his early life being spent on a farm. His parents moved to Oregon in 1862 and settled on a farm in Washington county, and from thence moving to Linn county in 1865. He there learned the carpenter's trade, at which he worked for several years. Becoming weary of the routine life of a mechanic he resolved to study law, and in 1873 entered the office of Mallory & Shaw, of Salem, as a student and was admitted to the bar in 1876. He then returned to Linn county and commenced the practice of his profession and soon stepped into a lucrative practice, he being a hard worker and applying himself closely to business and carefully guarding the interests of his clients. He is a member of the law firm of Powell & Bilyeu, of Albany. He was elected State Senator in 1878 and re-elected at the last general election. In legislative matters, as in law, he is an active worker and is an influential member. He is a ready debater and as such is conceded a leading rank by his Democratic colleagues. He is still unmarried and by the ladies is considered a hopeless case, although he is quite a society man; he is jovial and makes friends with all with whom he comes in contact.

HON. N. H. GATES

Represents the counties of Wasco and Lake in the Senate and is a man of great experience. He was born in Washington county, Ohio, in 1814, and was educated in the public schools of that State, being raised on a farm until along in his teens, when he learned the carpenter's trade. He was married in 1835 to Miss Mary Koontz, in Gallia county, Ohio, and shortly afterwards moved to Iowa, where he worked at his trade and practiced law, having been admitted to the bar in Ohio along in the year 1834. He resided in Iowa about eight years and then moved to this coast. Spent about two years in California, mining and trading, and came to Oregon in 1852 and settled in Portland. Went to the Cascades the following year and from thence to The Dalles, where he has resided ever since. He was elected to the Territorial Legislature in 1855 and was a member of the lower House for four consecutive years, being its presiding officer when Oregon was admitted as a State in 1859. Was elected County Judge of Wasco county in 1872 and served four years. He was appointed member of the State Board of Equalization in 1872 by his Excellency Governor Grover and held the office of Brigadier General under the same Executive. Was a member of the House in 1878 and in 1880 was elected joint Senator from Lake and Wasco. He took an active part in the Umatilla Indian war of 1877-78. His wife died in 1866, and he in 1868 married Mrs. Mary Schubnell at The Dalles. Politically speaking he is a Democrat, but not so strict a partisan as to prevent his voting for Hon. John H. Mitchell, Republican nominee for United States Senator, in obedience to what he considered was the wish of his constituents. He is an affable, courteous gentleman and makes friends readily.

HON. WILLIAM WALDO.

In producing our "Pen Pictures" we have undertaken no trifling task, and we realize our inability to do the subject justice when we endeavor to give a pen picture of Hon. William Waldo, State Senator from old Marion He must be seen, yes, more than that, he must be known, and known intimately to be appreciated. The writer has known him ten years, and still from time to time detects new virtues in his character to excite our admiration and esteem. Mr. Waldo is neither graceful nor handsome. In fact he prides himself on being peculiar in his personal appearance; but he is the very soul of integrity, and none know him but to esteem and respect him He is a perfect storehouse of information, having read extensively and being endowed with a retentive memory. His word is as good as his bond, and his standing among his fellow men is exceeded by none. He is tall, but not ill-proportioned, and plain featured. His beard is stumpy, his hair is bristling and his costume unpretentious. His eye, however, has a kindly expression and his voice is pleasant, and a dozen words with him will make you his friend. He rarely indulges in the debates of the Senate, but when he does his remarks are to the point and his criticisms are severe. He is strictly conscientious in all his public acts, and none dare assail his honor. He was born in Gasconade county, Missouri, in 1832, and with his parents moved to Oregon in 1843, settling in the Waldo Hills, one of the most fertile localities in Marion county. His father, Uncle Dan Waldo, was a man among men, and William is a chip off the old block. His educational advantages consisted of a two-years' course at the University in Columbia, Missouri, in 1855-6, and then three months' study at the Willamette Univesity at Salem. He commenced the study of law at Salem in 1860, under Hon. L. F. Grover, now U. S. Senator, and was admitted in 1863. His worldly circumstances are such that practice is unnecessary and he pursues his studies for the simple love of the profession. He has lived in the city for a number of years and has at odd times interested himself in business enterprises, among which was the erection a few years since of the flouring mills now owned by the City of Salem Company. Mr. Waldo is a Republican, but owes no allegiance to the claims of a caucus, and with his colleagues has stood out against the election of Hon. John H. Mitchell to the United States Senatorship in preference to any of the other candidates named. He is now serving his second term as State Senator, having been elected in 1880 and re-elected by a handsome majority in 1882. He served as a high private in the rear ranks during the Cayuse war of 1847-8, under Capt. Wm. Martin, now Sheriff of Umatilla county. He is a P. G. of Chemeketa Lodge, No. 1, I. O. O. F., of Salem, and acknowledges a "leaning" towards the M. E. Church. He is considered by the ladies a confirmed old bachelor; he denies the allegation, however, and insists upon it that he is still susceptible to the charms of the fair sex and will continue to receive proposals from matrons and maids for several years in the future.

HON ELIAS JESSUP,

Who represented Yamhill county in the Senate of the legislative session just closed, is a tall, well-proportioned gentleman, who will pull the scales at fully 225 pounds, and was consequently one of the heavy weights of that honorable body. He is literally a new-comer in this State, but has succeeded in establishing a most favorable reputation in his own county, and his legislative career has been marked by an evident desire on his part to be just to the State while partial to his own county. He was born in Hendricks county, Indiana, July 11, 1834, and was raised on a farm. He attended Erlham College for a short time, commenced the study of law and was admitted to the bar in 1859. He afterward practiced his profession at Danville until 1863, when he removed to Harding county, Iowa. Becoming favorably impressed with the medical profession, he there commenced the study of medicine and afterwards attended lectures at Rush Medical College in Chicago, Illinois. Returning to Iowa, he assumed the practice of medicine, remaining there for twelve years, serving two sessions meanwhile as member of the Iowa State Senate. He came to this State in 1880 and settled at Newberg, in Yamhill county, and is securing a lucrative practice as a physician. He was nominated and elected as State Senator from that county at the last general election; he was elected as a Republican, and was one of the sixteen Republican members of the Assembly who refused to go into caucus. He has proved an active and efficient public servant. He was married in 1856 to Miss Mary J. Morris, of Richmond, Indiana.

HON. ISRAEL D. HAINES,

Who represents Baker county on the floor of the Senate, has so often been a member of the Legislative Assembly that his name has become almost a household word in the history of our State. Mr. Haines is a gentleman of rather commanding appearance, tall and well-proportioned, neatly attired, pleasant features, with brown beard and hair, in which the silver threads are shining. He is a ready speaker, and takes an active part in the debates. He was born in Xenia, Ohio, in 1827; moved with his parents to Missouri in 1841, where he resided until coming to Oregon in 1849. He was then connected with the quartermaster's department of the Rifle Regiment, U. S. troops, commanded by Col. Loring. The regiment took possession of Fort Vancouver a few days after their arrival, under the U. S. treaty with Great Britain. Securing his discharge from the U. S. service shortly afterwards, he went overland to California in the following spring and spent the summer mining on Nelson's Creek. He returned to Oregon the following fall and remained in Portland until 1853, when he went to Jackson county. He remained there but a short time, when the Randolph gold excitement broke out. Mr. Haines went to Coos Bay and erected the first house there, using it as a hotel and general merchandise store. His goods arrived on the sailing vessel "Cynosure," commanded by Capt. Whippy; Mr. Haines acting as her pilot and guiding her across the bar, she being the first sailing vessel that, laden with merchandise, ever entered that harbor. He returned to Jacksonville in the fall of 1854 and carried on a general merchandising business until 1862. He that year represented Jackson county in the House of Representatives. He read law under Hon. P. P. Prim, and was admitted to the bar in 1864. He soon afterwards moved to Idaho Territory and practiced his profession there and in California. In 1867 he opened an office in Baker county, where he has resided ever since, interspersing his practice with successful ventures in farming and stock-raising. He was a member of the House from that county in 1876, and in 1878 was elected State Senator and was re-elected in 1882. He is a staunch Democrat and a strict partisan. He was married in 1871 to Miss Sarah M. Dorsett, their family consisting of five children. He is an active, influential citizen, and is highly esteemed by the people of the county he represents.

HON. THOMAS G. HENDRICKS,

The hold-over Senator from Lane county, is a member that does credit to his constituents and the party he represents. Politically speaking, he is a Democrat, and never swerves from his partisan principles. He is one of the best-looking members on the floor, dresses with taste, and is considered one of the most honorable citizens of Lane county, from whence he hails.

He was born in Henderson county, Illinois, in 1848, and, with his parents, reached Oregon the same year, settling in Lane county, where he has resided ever since. His parents died in 1878 at a ripe old age. The subject of our sketch lived on the farm until he was twenty-two years of age, when he commenced clerking for Bristow & Co., of Eugene City, of which firm he is now the successor, and carries on business on the same old corner where years ago he was but a clerk, and his sales at the present time amount to about $50,000 annually. He was married in 1863 to Miss M. A. Hazleton, who died a few years later. Mr. Hendricks has ever been an active supporter of the cause of education, and was highly instrumental in securing the location of the State University in that city, being the oldest member of the Board of Regents, and has been Chairman of the Executive Committee of that institution ever since its first organization. In 1868 he was married to Miss M. A. Stewart, and his family consists of three daughters. He has been mainly instrumental in the incorporation of the municipal government of Eugene City, and was one of the original charter members of the City Council, having served in that body several years, and is now Mayor of the city. He was appointed Assistant Adjutant-General with the rank of Major on the staff of Brig. Gen. Jno. F. Miller, and during his term of office took an active interest in the organization of the State militia. He is a prominent member of the I. O. O. F., with the rank of P. G., and served three years as County Superintendent of Public Instruction. In 1880, during his absence from the city and while in San Francisco on a business trip, he was nominated as State Senator from that county, and was elected by a handsome majority. He is active and conscientious in the discharge of his official duties, and is considered one of the most influential citizens of our fair young State.

HON. PAINE PAGE PRIM,

Senator from Jackson county, is a gentleman who has been prominently connected with the history of our State for a number of years past. He is a Democrat and is held in high esteem by his party. He was born in Wilson county, Tennessee, in 1822. He followed the plow on his father's farm until well along in years and graduated in the law department of the Cumberland University at Lebanon. He came to Oregon in 1851, his means of transportation being the primitive emigrant wagon of the day. He settled in Linn county and moving to Jackson county in 1852, commenced the practice of law. His knowledge of the profession, and his keen perception of technicalities, soon attracted the attention of litigants and he found himself possessed of a lucrative practice. The year 1857 marked two important epochs in his life, the most prominent being his marriage with Miss Teresa M. Stearns, which event was closely followed by his election as a member of the State Constitutional Convention. He continued the practice of law until the organization of the State Government in 1859, when he was appointed Supreme Judge and ex-officio Circuit Judge of the first Judicial District. This position he held until the act of 1878 was passed, making a separate Supreme Court, when he was appointed one of the Associate Judges. Being re-nominated in 1880, he was defeated, and, on doffing the ermine, again resumed practice and is now acknowledged as one of the leading attorneys of the first district. He was elected Senator from Jackson county at the last general election, and was the Democratic caucus nominee for United States Senator, receiving thirty-three votes for that honorable position. He is considered one of the ablest men of that body.

HON. JOHN MYERS.

Among those most prominent in the front ranks of the Democratic party is Hon. John Myers, Senator from Clackamas county. He is clear-headed, and watches carefully every measure brought forward. He is a fluent speaker, a strict parliamentarian, possessing a retentive memory and is a strong partisan. He is considered a good financier, and, in connection with the revenue laws of the State, has given the subject careful study. He is of heavy build, with clear-cut features, and his opinions on any subject never fail to receive the careful consideration of members of both political parties. He was born in Howard county, Missouri, in 1830, and was raised on a farm. He enlisted in the Mexican war in 1847, and was connected with the quartermaster's department for about a year. Returning home in 1848 he remained there until the spring of 1852, when he started for California, arriving in Stockton in October of the same year, where he engaged in mining and trading until January, 1857, when he was appointed Sheriff and was afterwards elected to the same office. Impressed with the idea that Oregon offered superior advantages to young men, he moved here, arriving in Oregon City in August, 1860. While on a previous visit he was married to Miss Sarah J. Hood, of Oregon City. He settled there and entered the mercantile business, in which he has been engaged ever since. He was elected Sheriff of Clackamas county in 1868, and represented that county in the State Senate of 1872, 1874, 1876, 1878, and has just been re-elected for another four years' term, his record in this respect indicating very forcibly the esteem and confidence reposed in him by the citizens of the county he so ably represents. He has a family of ten children, with one daughter married. He is a communicant of the Protestant Episcopal Church, and has always contributed liberally to its support. He has attained the honorable position of Past Master in the Masonic order and has always been a successful business man, and is to-day one of the most influential men of Oregon City, the citizens holding him in high esteem as one of their leading merchants.

HON. HENRY HALL,

Who represents Grant county in the Senate, is a plain, every-day sort of a man, such as commands the respect and esteem of those who have the welfare of the State at heart, and in whom they can with confidence repose the sacred trust of framing the laws for their governance. He is of low stature, dresses plainly, and is one of the quiet members of that honorable body. His vote, however, has been recorded on all important measures and has been cast after a careful consideration of the subject. He is of English birth, having first seen the light of day in Dorsetshire, England, in 1836.

He attended the common schools in the old country when not busy on the farm. He came to this country in 1858, and one year later arrived in Oregon, settling in Polk county, where he remained until the fall of 1861, when he went up into the Walla Walla valley with a band of cattle, and in the spring of 1862 settled in the John Day valley, in Grant county. He helped to open the first mining claim in that county and erected the first house, and there he has resided ever since, engaged in farming and stock-raising, a portion of the time being in partnership with Hon. T. J. Brents, now delegate in Congress from Washington Territory. His early life is replete with incidents of pioneer life, frequently interspersed with romantic incidents of Indian warfare. He is a staunch Republican and was elected County Commissioner in 1878, and at the last general election was chosen to represent his county for four years in the State Senate. He returned to England in 1871, and while there was married to Miss Ellen Killick, of Hungerford. He is an Odd Fellow and a consistent member of the Methodist Church, having been connected therewith for a period of thirty years. He is considered one of the solid men of Grant county, and has made friends with every member of the Senate by his paramount integrity.

HON. ROBERT H. TYSON,

Who represents Washington county on the floor of the Senate, is one of the most distinguished-looking members of that body. He is of ordinary height, well-proportioned, and is always neatly dressed. His face is smooth shaved, with the exception of a very heavy mustache. His eye is keen and his forehead expansive. Mr. Tyson was born in Macomb county, Michigan, January 7, 1840, his early life being divided between school and clerkship in a store. He moved with his parents to Springfield, Illinois, in 1856, and with his father went into the lumber trade, where he remained until 1862, when he came to Oregon "the plains across." He settled in Polk county, and, during the next six years, was engaged in teaching school and farming. He returned east in 1868 and remained there until 1870, when he returned to Oregon and resumed school teaching, and for about two years and a half was editor and publisher of the Oregon "Republican" at Dallas. He was also publisher of the Roseburg "Pantagraph" for about a year, closing it out in 1874. He moved to Washington county and taught school for about eighteen months, and then opened a general merchandise store at Middleton. His business being such that he could, without detriment, leave it in charge of others, he consented to become a candidate for the House in 1878 and was elected. In 1880 he was elected a member of the State Senate, and took a prominent part in the proceedings of that year. As a legislator, he is active, energetic and painstaking. He is a fluent speaker and participates frequently in the debates; he is a hard worker and guards carefully the interests of the county he represents and the State at large. He is a Mason, an Odd Fellow and a Granger, and prominent in each. He has been twice married, the first time in 1863 to Miss Emily Hagood, of Polk county, who died in 1865. He afterwards, in August, 1875, was married to Miss Hattie E. Olds, of Middleton, their family consisting of five children.

HON. ABNER W. WATERS,

One of the three Senators from Multnomah county, was born in Ashtabula county, Ohio, November 30, 1833. He received a partial academic education, having attended the academy at Mt. Pleasant, Iowa. He left Ohio in 1844 and settled in Warrick county, Indiana, where he resided until 1847, when he moved to Burlington, Iowa, residing there about three years. He came to Oregon in 1850 and settled at Harrisburg, in Linn county. He took up a donation claim and resided there for a period of eighteen years, during which time he was engaged in merchandising and trading in real estate. He recruited Company F, First Regiment Oregon Volunteer Infantry, and served as its Captain three years during the civil war. While in service he was at different times the commanding officer at Fort Hoskins, Fort Vancouver, Fort Walla Walla and Fort Lapwai. In 1868 he went up into Union county, and for several years engaged in stock-raising. In 1874 he purchased a controlling interest in the Salem "Statesman," which he managed until 1876, when he was appointed United States Marshal, which position he held for four years, proving an active and efficient officer. He was married in Linn county to Miss Mary A. McCully, who afterwards died, and in 1866 he was married to Miss Sarah McCartney, who also passed away during the summer of 1882. He is a prominent member of the Masonic order and a Knight Templar; he also belongs to the Knights of Pythias, A. O. U. W. and the Grand Army of the Republic. He was elected in 1880 to represent Multnomah county in the State Senate. He is a hard worker, either on the floor or in the committee room. His personal appearance is attractive and his voice is often heard in debate. He is an uncompromising Republican and is considered one of the shrewdest politicians in the State; he is genial as an acquaintance, faithful as a friend and honored as a citizen.

HON. ROBERT CLOW

Is one of those quiet, unassuming, intelligent gentlemen that seldom find their way into parliamentary assemblages, except as lookers on, but when once they do get there in a representative capacity, devote their undivided attention to their work in the same conscientious manner as though they were dealing in matters in which they only were personally interested. In the present body he represents Benton and Polk counties. In politics he is a staunch Democrat and has never swerved in his allegiance to that party. He was born in Berthshire, Scotland, in 1837, and emigrated with his parents to Canada in 1852, his early life having been spent on a farm. He left home shortly afterwards and lived for a few years in Iowa. He attended school a short time in Scotland and about three months in Iowa, which is all the educational advantages he had save those secured by judicious reading and a general knowledge obtained by intercourse with men of intelligence. He came to Oregon in 1862 and spent the first year in Wasco county, going to Idaho in 1863, where he spent a year in the mines. In the summer of 1864 he was appointed chief herder, and in fact had charge of the reservation, at Fort Boise, and accompanied the United States troops to Camp Warner, where he remained for about three years as wagon and forage master. He settled near Dallas in 1868, where he has resided ever since and followed the avocation of a farmer. He was elected a member of the House in 1872 and in 1880 was elected as joint Senator from Benton and Polk counties. He served for a number of years as officer and member of the Board of Trustees of the La Creole Academy and has ever evinced a warm interest in educational matters. He is an honored member of the Masonic fraternity, being a Past Grand Master of the jurisdiction of Oregon. He was married in Polk county, in the spring of 1868, to Miss Caroline S———, their family consisting of five girls and two boys. Mr. Clow is a good-looking man, of ordinary height, but heavy set, heavy beard, slightly tinged with gray. He is a ready speaker and commands the unqualified respect of all who are fortunate enough to merit his acquaintanceship.

HON. D. W. STEARNS,

Who represents Douglas county in the Senate, is one of those sedate, thoughtful and easy-going kind of men who attain prominence because of their honesty and worth in the community in which they reside. He is a heavy, thick-set man of small stature, with very heavy, black whiskers, a deep-set eye and prominent features. His voice is rarely heard in debate, but he never shirks a vote and it is generally conceded has conscientiously endeavored to subserve the best interests of the county he represents. He was born in Chesterfield, New Hampshire, in 1821, and lived in Chishire county until he was about 21 years of age. Up to that time he had received but the ordinary educational advantages, but afterwards attended three terms in the high school. Went to Massachusetts in 1843, where he was engaged in the mercantile business until 1849, when he started for California. He remained in the mines a few years, returning home in 1852, and came to Oregon in 1854, settling in Douglas county, where he has resided ever since. He was engaged in the mercantile and packing business until 1857, when he commenced farming. Was in the mines of Idaho Territory from 1860 to 1865. Returning to Douglas county he was nominated on the Republican ticket in 1872 as Representative, suffering defeat with the balance of the ticket. Was in 1874 elected Representative on the Independent ticket, and in 1880 elected as State Senator. He was formerly a Democrat, but voted for Abraham Lincoln, and has since been a Republican. Was married in Belchertown, Massachusetts, on January 3, 1846, to Miss Almira Fay, their family at present consisting of five sons.

HON. GEORGE W. COLVIG,

The energetic young Senator who for the last four sessions has so ably represented Douglas county, is comparatively a young man, but one whose experience in that body has made him an influential and valuable member. He was born in Knoxville, Missouri, in November, 1848, and came with his parents across the plains in 1850. Their first year of pioneer life was spent in Portland, and in 1851 they moved to Douglas county, where he has since resided. He helped run his father's farm until 1865, when he commenced paddling his own canoe. In 1872 he opened a drug store in Canyonville, and having meanwhile learned to manipulate lightning, has, in connection with his drug business, been the manager of the Western Union Telegraph Company's office at that place for years. He is a careful business manager and has succeeded in establishing a lucrative trade in that neighborhood. As a young man he never took any enthusiastic part in politics. Coming of age, he interested himself only as a good citizen should who has his country's welfare at heart. His popularity and integrity, however, made him the most available man to nominate for State Senator in 1876, and he was elected. So well did he discharge his duties as a legislator that he was re-elected in 1880. As a member of that honorable body he is active and energetic. His voice is often heard in debate and his vote is generally recorded on the right side of every important measure. He is a hard worker in the committee room and a popular member among his colleagues. He is a true-blue Republican and stands by his colors through thick and thin. He is an honored member of the I. O. O. F. and P. G. of his lodge. He was married in 1872 to Miss Mary C. Dyer, of Canyonville, and is the father of two girls and a boy. His standing at home is excelled by none.

HON. DUNHAM WRIGHT.

Whatever of praise may be due to the man who has, with the advantages of a collegiate education and abundant leisure for after study, risen to a position of honor and trust among his fellow men, we must accord a greater meed of praise to the young man who, without those advantages, has struggled with the waves of adversity and, by sheer force of ambition and native integrity, has elevated himself into a position of honor by the suffrages of his fellow citizens. The former is entitled to commendation for the ripened culture of the mind, while on the latter we must bestow the praise due to force of character and singleness of purpose. The Hon. Dunham Wright, who, like his cousin, the lamented Lincoln, started in life without any of these advantages, is indebted to no man or institution for the mental gifts which he possesses. They have all been culled from the practical field of every-day life. He is a plain-spoken man, thoroughly independent and honest in his dealings with his fellow man. He was born in Des Moines county, Iowa, and when but a child his father, who was a civil engineer, moved with his family into one of the frontier counties, where the subject of our sketch spent his younger days, deprived even of the advantages of a common school education. His education was received at a mother's knee, and in learning to write he was compelled to use a bullet hammered out to a point for a pencil and a smooth pine board for a slate. Nothing daunted, however, he took advantage of what was offered him, and, by perseverance, succeeded in conquering those elementary branches most essential in every-day contact with the world. He went to Colorado in 1862, and spent two years in the mines, and thence to Idaho Territory, where he sought for gold a short time and then commenced packing between the Boise mines and Umatilla landing. In 1865 he settled in the Grand Ronde

Valley, about 20 miles from Union, where he has resided ever since, and has been engaged in farming and stock raising with well merited success. His energy, integrity and business capacity excited the admiration of his neighbors, and in 1872 they elected him a member of the House of Representatives. His course in that body secured his re-election in 1874 and again in 1876. In 1880 he was elected State Senator, and is now serving the last half of his term. He is a well built man, of ordinary height, auburn hair and whiskers, broad and expansive forehead and a pleasant eye. He rarely indulges in debate, but his remarks demand attention when he does address the Senate. He is an earnest worker and takes pride in being present whenever the Senate is in session. He was married in 1867 to Miss Mishy Duncan, of the Cove, and they have one child. We confidently expect to see Mr. Wright returned to the Senate in 1884, as he stands very high among his Democratic constituents of that county.

Representatives.

HON. GEORGE W. M BRIDE.

The duties of Speaker of the House of Representatives require a ready sagacity, a correct and quick judgment, a bold independence and the capacity and disposition for hard work. The work which a Speaker must do while other men are asleep more severely tests all these qualities than does the public duty of directing the daily sessions of the House. In the Speaker's hand rests the burden of committee organization, and upon his judgment and fairness in this great duty hangs the controlling force of legislation; and in the duty of presiding, every hour calls for intelligence, decision and good common sense. Mr. McBride has made a good Speaker. We could not say more in a half dozen pages. His election was a high personal compliment honorable, because unsought; exceptional, because of his youth. Solicited by opposing factions, he stood unallied with either. His independence challenged the admiration of both, and their united vote gave him the place of responsibility and honor. He took his seat supported by the confidence and good opinion of both parties, and at the end of the session he retired from it with the warm personal friendship of every member of the House. All commended his judgment, all applauded his fairness. Mr. McBride is the first native Oregonian who has ever filled a high place in the official service of the State and the youngest man who ever sat in the Speaker's chair. He is the youngest son of the late Dr. James McBride, and was born in Yamhill county in March, 1854. The earlier years of his school life were passed at Lafayette, in Yamhill county, and St. Helens, in Columbia county, where he now lives. Later he spent one year in the Willamette University at Salem and two years in Christian College, Monmouth, under the tuition of President T. F. Campbell, quitting the latter institution a year before graduation on account of poor health, which a year of rest from severe study did not wholly restore. However, he entered the law office of Hon. J. C. Moreland, Portland, as a student, remaining three years, but ill health again prostrated him. For two years he was an invalid—an energetic and rebellious one, it is true, but a constant sufferer—and upon his recovery engaged in active business, abandoning for the while his purpose of practicing law, for which he was thoroughly disciplined and qualified. Mr. McBride has continued in business ever since, and is the principal merchant of Columbia county. Land owning and dealing is a passion with him, and his landed estates in Columbia county are extensive. For the past three or four years he has been an important factor in the politics of his county and of the State. Columbia, which formerly was a solid Democratic stronghold, has, since his participation in its affairs, become surely and solidly Republican, and last June rolled up something more than a handsome majority. Mr. McBride has, with the exception of two years spent in San Francisco, always lived in Oregon, and he always expects to. Oregon is his home and he shows the Scotch in his blood in his love for it. Personally he is a "good fellow to meet." He is cordial, but not boisterous, dignified but never stiff. He is always well mannered and well dressed, and though having a decided tendency toward student life, is fond of society and shines in it. Some may be interested perhaps in the fact that he knows the points of a horse and is a dead shot. Mr. McBride is not and never will be robust, but he has outlived his ill health and is a prodigious worker. He is of medium height, complexion neither deep only dark nor fair, has blue-grey eyes, weighs about 140 pounds, and wears a full, cropped brown beard. He only lacks the appearance of perfect vigor to be strikingly handsome. He is not married.

HON. WILLIAM H. HARRIS.

Among the silent majority of the House, the majority upon whom the State can look with pride, may be mentioned with unusual praise the gentleman whose name heads this sketch. He is a representative Oregonian, a man of few words, honest convictions and sterling integrity. Like all pioneers on this coast who have emerged into public life, Mr. Harris understands himself thoroughly and dares to pursue a course consistent with his ideas of right in the face of any and all prejudice, whether it be of a political or personal character. He was born in Adams county, Illinois, in the year 1832. He received the advantages of a good common school education and is possessed of a great amount of hard, practical sense, which has always enabled him to apply it to the best advantage. After residing in Illinois until he was twenty years of age, Mr. Harris immigrated to Oregon in the year 1852, since which time he has resided in the city of Portland. Mr. Harris has been twice elected a member of the Legislature of Washington Territory, and was also elected Clerk of Multnomah county in the year 1872. Having held office, as stated before, his election as a member of the House of Representatives of the present Legislative Assembly may be justly traced to his unsullied reputation and his large circle of warm personal friends. In person Mr. Harris is a compactly-built gentleman of medium size, having a full face and a twinkling, pleasant eye. Although he is a single man, he is not at all averse to the sweet links of matrimony, and when the proper young lady comes along we expect that he may become one of the "blessed." He is at present engaged in the ice manufacturing business, being the senior partner in the well-known firm of Harris & Salmon. In politics Mr. Harris is a staunch Republican.

HON. JOHN J. WHITNEY.

It is a pleasure to write of men in high places whose public-spirited generosity and acknowledged manliness recommend them to our favorable consideration, but it would be far more preferable if we enjoyed a larger acquaintance with the accomplished gentleman whose interesting history we are now transmitting in brief to posterity. The United States is prolific of that class of men who, with ordinary ambition, fair pluck and a proper degree of perseverance and industry, reach the top of the ladder. A man endowed with these simple attributes has no cause to complain if he meets with reverses when he first starts out in life. These little discomfitures always have a tendency to sharpen the intellect and urge their possessor on to renewed exertion, and when once he obeys the dictates of his better judgment, success is bound to crown his efforts. Many people reading of the achievements of others waste much valuable time wondering how they were secured, while if they would only jump into the current and ride with it, without troubling themselves too much about other people's business, they, too, might accomplish something. This order of things has always prevailed and will continue to the end of the world. Forty-two years ago, away back in Ohio, the subject of this sketch was born, and like all the boys of that day who came of good old stock, received his preparatory education in the common schools. Being blessed by nature with a well-balanced head, a good constitution and an aptitude for learning, he soon acquired a general knowledge of things. Full of energy and urged on by a disposition to win, he applied himself to the study of the law and entered the Albany law school, New York, and in the year 1864 graduated from that institution and was immediately admitted to the bar. He went to California in 1864, staying there but a few months, when he came through to Oregon, locating in the Willamette valley. Like many another young lawyer, finding himself in a strange and a young country, he turned his talents to good account by teaching school for one year, and then in the fall of 1867 went to Albany, where he commenced the practice of his profession. He was elected District Attorney in 1874 and again in 1878. He held the office of County Judge in 1870. Since his retirement from public office he has been practicing law in Albany. He is a useful member of the Committees on Judiciary and Elections, and in politics is a sterling Democrat.

HON. ALLEN PARKER.

It often happens that the inquiring student of biography, when delving among the musty tombs and records of the lives of distinguished men, is struck with the number of those who have commenced their life career on the farm. In such occupation the aspiring mind is brought face to face with the beauties of nature, the germs of after greatness very often unfold themselves and strike deep root in the fertile soil of ambition. In the present legislature more than one member can trace back the first promptings of his youthful mind to the happy days when he whistled after the plow and mimicked the shrill pipe of the blackbird in the balmy sunshine. Mr. Parker is a representative farmer and business man. He was born in Ross county, Ohio, in the year 1828. He remained there attending school until he was fifteen years of age, when his parents removed to Iowa. He lived in Iowa until 1852, on a farm, when he came to Oregon, locating in Linn county, where he has since resided, engaged in farming; he is also proprietor of a large saw-mill and also of a warehouse. He was elected Sheriff of Linn county in 1872, and he was elected Mayor of Albany in 1876; he was also elected Lock Commissioner of Willamette falls by the legislature in 1876. He removed to Benton county in 1878, and has lived there ever since, being engaged in the saw-mill business. In 1880 he was elected a member of the House of Representatives from that county, and was returned to the present session. Mr. Parker, therefore, has had his share of political glory, he has left an unta ished record, and has made a large number of staunch and admiring friends. In 1852 he was married to Miss Julia A. Umphrey.

HON. A. C. WILBUR.

There is, perhaps, no member of the House better acquainted with the routine of legislative business than Mr. Wilbur. In his youth he had the advantage of a liberal college education, has had previous experience as a member of the legislature, and is, therefore, one of its most serviceable members. He is a quiet gentleman and a superior counsellor, but is either too modest or lacking in confidence sufficient to play the orator or logician before the multitude. He is one of the Representatives from old Clackamas county, which constituency he also represented in 1880. Mr. Wilbur was born in New York in the year 1834, received the common school training of those days, and finished at Jefferson college, in Washington county, Pennsylvania. He emigrated to Oregon in 1870, and settled in Clackamas county, where he has since remained. Although Mr. Wilbur has always been a staunch Republican, he is by no means an extremist, and is always willing to examine any measure of legislation in all its lights, and do that which is best for the people of the entire State. Mr. Wilbur is an active member of committee on roads and highways.

HON. STEPHEN P. MOSS

Was born in Peoria, Ill., in 1840, and is now 42 years of age. He is the Democratic Representative from Lake county, and, although he is one of the quiet members of the House, every important measure receives his earnest attention, and, if meritorious, his warm support. He is an old Oregonian, and a very successful farmer and stock-raiser, well-known among the agriculturists of the entire State. He was educated in the schools of his native city, Peoria, until the age of twelve, at which time he came with his parents to Oregon and settled in Linn county, where he remained sixteen years, engaged in farming. In 1868 he sold out his farm, settled up his business affairs, and took a trip to California, where he remained four years, during which time he was engaged in stock-raising. After the expiration of that period, he returned to Oregon and secured a fine tract of land in Lake county, and engaged in raising stock. He has lived there ever since, and was elected in the year 1876 to the important office of County Commissioner. In politics, although Mr. Moss is not a bitter partisan, he is a strong adherent of the old Jeffersonian Democracy, and a respected member of the Democratic party. Mr. Moss was married in 1861 to Miss Sarah E. Robnett, who died in the year 1868; he was married in 1870 to Miss Margaret S. Casteel. He was a member of committees on internal improvements and assessments.

HON. W. A. PERKINS.

The farming element is well represented in the House of Representatives, and it is highly important that it is so. Many subjects affecting the most vital interests of our agricultural prosperity have been grappled with in every session of the legislature, and this great branch of industry should not be imperiled by sending unreliable or incompetent men to represent them. The fence law, destruction of noxious animals, the taxation of cultivated land and growing crops, the construction and maintenance of county roads, are questions that the farming population cannot ignore or neglect. They have shown that they appreciate the importance of these questions, and the necessity of properly attending to them by sending to the State Capitol men who are capable of grappling with the issues involved, and honest and worthy sons of the soil. Among the many good and true representatives of the agricultural element now in the House, although not at present farming, none are more entitled to a prominent place in this volume than Hon. W. A. Perkins, one of the representatives from Douglas. He was born in east Tennessee in the year 1835, went with his parents to Indiana in 1844, and during his youth received the common school advantages, and afterwards, by hard work and persistent effort, he succeeded in obtaining a first-class English education. While in Indiana he followed the profession of school teaching, and did some farming. In 1858 he went to Missouri, and, shortly afterwards, went to Kansas. He came to Oregon in 1875, and took up his residence in Oakland, Douglas county, where he has since continued to live. He taught school there for about two years, and afterwards became engaged in general merchandising, and was employed as telegraph operator at Drain station. At the present time he is the agent at Roseburg for the California and Oregon Railway Company. He was married to Miss R. J. McReynolds in 1853. Mr. Perkins has taken a strong interest in the great questions of woman suffrage and temperance, and used all his personal exertions and his influence in their earnest advocacy. Mr. Perkins was elected and served as Justice of the Peace a number of terms in the States of Iowa, Kansas and Oregon.

HON. WM. H. H. DUFUR.

Dean Swift, that grand old cynic, spoke many a splendid truth, but none more pertinent than his aphorism that "it is an incontroverted truth that no man ever made an ill figure who understood his own talents, nor a good one who mistook them." The subject of this biography will never make an ill figure. He is a representative of the young men of Oregon, and, at the age of twenty-eight, represents in our legislative halls one of the very finest constituencies in the State, in Wasco county, where he was elected almost without opposition. Mr. Dufur is the youngest son of Hon. A. J. Dufur, who has been repeatedly honored by his fellow Democrats, and by the entire people of the State, having been commissioner to the Great Centennial at Philadelphia in 1876, and a representative to the legislature from Multnomah county in 1862; he is also a brother of Hon. E. B. Dufur, who represented Wasco county in '74. Young William was born in Williamstown, Vermont, February 22, 1854, and came to Oregon with his parents at the age of six. He received his preparatory education in the common schools, afterwards entering Portland Academy, and finishing at the High School in 1873. He was a member of the county and State conventions this year, and in those bodies, although a retiring and thoughtful member, whenever he gave his opinion, it was listened to with marked attention and generally acted on. In the year 1876, on the 16th of July, he was married to a most estimable young lady, Miss May L. Alexander. Although Mr. Dufur comes from a strongly Democratic family, of the old school, yet he is an ardent Republican. He follows the free and manly business of farming and stock raising.

HON. WILLIAM MORRAS.

This gentleman is a valuable member of the present House. It is pleasing to note, in these days of wholesale extravagance, a disposition on the part of the people to return to the economical and home-like practices and habits of our forefathers; and we can only tell the sentiment of the people in this important particular through the representative men they send to the halls of legislation to make their laws. How long since — in fact, a very short time — is it, when a man who was known to be an open, avowed champion of retrenchment could succeed in an election if he wished to go to the Legislature? Mr. Morras is one of the men who has been exceedingly cautious in the matter of appropriating the people's money, and has taken the time and performed the amount of work necessary in an investigation of all such measures, and he has always taken a decided stand for appropriating the amount of money actually required and not a dollar more. If others were to pursue the same line of policy, and be as careful of the State's money as they are of their own, it would work great benefit to the people. Mr. Morras is a plain man, not in appearance, but in language; whenever he takes the floor to discuss the merits of a bill, what he says is short, plain and to the point, and he does not give up the subject till either he understands it or makes others understand him, according to the requirements of the case. He was born in Durham county, England, in the year 1828, and completed his education in the high school of that place. During his youth he remained at home on the farm, but afterwards became a surveyor, which business he followed for a number of years. The youth then emigrated to free America, and pitched his tent in the beautiful county of Fayette, in the wilds of Iowa, in the year 1850, where he enjoyed all the prerogatives of the independent farmer for three-and-twenty years. During that time his fellow citizens cast about them for a suitable person to represent them in the county Board of Supervisors, and fixing their eyes on the youthful William, forthwith elected him a member of that respectable body, in which he served two years. Hearing that Oregon was a fine agricultural country, and one which presented unusual advantages to the industrious and honest worker, he took a flying trip here in the year 1870 to see for himself. As soon as his practical eye rested on the soil of our young State, with its varied capabilities, he was captivated, and, flying back to Iowa, returned with his family in 1872, and planted himself in Coos county, where he has since grown and flourished. There he has served one term as a Commissioner of the County Court; he was elected as a representative in the House of 1880, and returned this session. He is a good parliamentarian, and his previous experience, added to this fact, has made him one of the foremost members of the House. He was married in 1851 to Miss Elizabeth Jaques.

HON. ROBERT M. VEATCH,

One of the Representatives from Lane county, is a Democratic member of whom his party and his constituency can feel justly proud. He is a quiet, unassuming gentleman, of medium size, with an intelligent and thoughtful face, and a wiry and well-proportioned figure. He does not take the floor for discussion very frequently, but when he does do so, it is after a careful study of the measure in all its bearings, and with a view to explain, as he understands them, to the House. He has been a school teacher for a number of years, and every measure which has been proposed affecting the educational interests has received his earnest attention, and if the measure has been deemed by him a beneficial one, he has used every endeavor to effect its passage. He was born in White county, Illinois, in 1843, and when four years old went with his parents to Iowa, where he attended the district schools until he was fifteen years of age. He then went to southern Missouri, where he remained four years working on a farm. At the breaking out of the rebellion he went to Iowa, but soon returned to Illinois, and in the spring of 1864, came to California, journeying across the plains. In 1865 he came to Oregon, locating in Lake county, from which place he went to Salem and attended the State University for one year. Taking a great interest in the cultivation of the soil, he attended the agricultural college at Corvallis for two years, from which institution he graduated. Mr. Veatch then engaged in the profession of school teaching, and was engaged at Cottage Grove five years and at Eugene City one year. He found that teaching was wearing upon his constitution, by reason of the confinement in doors, and, regretfully, he was forced to leave the school room; but, being a scientific as well as a practical farmer, he at once turned his attention to soil culture, and we hope to see him within a short time the "robust tiller of the soil." Mr. Veatch was the choice of the Democrats for the legislature from Lane county in 1872, and he was at that time beaten by only seven votes. He was married in 1871 to Miss Surphina Currin.

HON JOHN A. HUNT.

Representative Hunt, of Douglas, is one of those men whose life if written out would fill a volume with interesting reading matter. He was born in Union county, Indiana, in the year 1836. His father was a tradesman, and carried on an extensive business in the manufacture of wagons and carriages in the town of Liberty, and during his youth young John divided his time between the district school and his father's establishment, obtaining a fair amount of schooling and a practical knowledge of his trade. In 1847 he removed to Oregon and settled in Marion county, ten miles east of Salem. In that early day, when the country was comparatively uninhabited, and when the pioneer had to endure untold privations, young Hunt displayed an undaunted front and tenacity of purpose. Like thousands of others, he was attracted by the glitter of the California gold mines, and he went thither and spent some time in the northern portion of that State mining for the precious metal. His health becoming impaired, he was finally compelled to leave the mines, when he went to Washington Territory, and located a very desirable farm, but not being able to comply with the provisions of the pre-emption law, he gave up the farm and went to Portland, where he remained two years, and during which time he cast his first ballot for Abraham Lincoln. Some of his friends, who were possessed of more imaginary fear for the country than they were interested in the triumph of principle, inquired of Mr. Hunt why he voted for a Republican, which would certainly precipitate a war. He answered, "If that is the demand of the slave power—universal slavery or the dissolution of this union —here is one for Abraham Lincoln and universal freedom." And his answer was that of the true patriot. His early impression of government was, that in a republic subjects could not be half bond, half free; and that its permanency and perpetuation depended upon the wisdom and virtue of its subjects; consequently his vote and political ambition has been to leave our church, State and government in better condition than that in which he found them. The climate of Salem not appearing to suit Mr. Hunt's constitution, he removed to Southern Oregon, where, up to the time of his election, he has been operating a farm and grist mill. He was married in August, 1860, to Miss Ellen Amen.

HON. WM. P. CURTIS,

One of the Representatives from Baker county, is an exceedingly good-natured and pleasant little gentleman of sixty summers. He is hale and hearty, with a well-proportioned figure, an elastic step, and a peculiarly bright eye, and so far as general appearance is concerned, looks much younger than his years. His has been a varied experience, and in the course of his eventful life he has had his share of its joys and sorrows. Born in Owen county, old Kentucky, in the year 1822, in the days when the village master taught his little school in a log cabin, young William had an opportunity of daily interviewing the grim instructor of the youthful mind until the advanced age of ten years. He was then apprenticed to a hatter, and with that dignitary remained until he was master of the business. He worked for some time at his trade, and went into the general merchandise business in Monterey, in the same county. Hearing of the great gold discoveries in California, he settled up his business affairs and set out for the land of promise. The trip across the plains was a long and tedious one, and, after a five months' journey, Mr. Curtis had the pleasure of entering the historic place called "Hangtown" or Placerville, in El Dorado county. From there he went to Placer county and remained two years, and in 1854 went north to Yreka. He remained but one year in his new abode and then returned to Placer county, where he engaged in mining and stock-raising, in the meantime being elected to the office of Justice of the Peace. In those days the Justice was the oracle in the mining camp, and a man was never selected to fill that office unless he was possessed of character, sense and nerve; he was the arbiter of all differences and the advisor in all important matters. Mr. Curtis came to Oregon in 1864, locating in Canyon City, where he remained but one year; we next find him in a small mining camp called Clarkesville, in Baker county, where at last have his wanderings ceased and his spirit, as it were, found rest, and we find him representing that county in the Legislature of 1878, as well as in the present body. In 1872 he was elected Justice of the Peace there, and has been since re-elected twice. As an instance of his popularity, let it be said that the session of the Legislature of 1878 had no sooner closed, than he was once more made a Justice, which office he held until elected a member of the House in 1882. He is a frank, plain, open-hearted little man, and has hosts of personal friends. He was married in California in 1858 to Mrs. Margaret House, who died in 1863, and he has since been a widower.

HON. STEWART B. EAKIN, JR.,

Is the only Republican who represents Lane county on the floor of the House. As he comes from a strongly Democratic county, he certainly owes his election to a host of good and true friends. Mr. Eakin is a very pleasant-looking gentleman, of affable manners and accommodating habits; in fact, one of those men whom no one would hesitate to approach for any necessary information regarding a subject of which he himself was ignorant. He is, in every particular, a self-made man, and, like others of the same type, he looms up grandly to the front, not by virtue of accident or good luck, but entirely owing to the fact that he is an assiduous worker, a man of push, and not easily daunted by defeat. He was born in Elgin, Kane county, Illinois, on the 28th of August, 1846, and with his parents moved to Bloom, Cook county, Ill., when eight years of age. He remained there until 1866, when he came "the plains across" with mule teams, the trip requiring four months and two days, to Eugene City, Lane county, Oregon, the place of his present residence. Mr. Eakin has been in public life a great deal, and has left that indelible mark upon the record of being one of the men who "have been tried and found to be true." He was elected to the office of Sheriff of Lane county in the year 1874, and, as a reward for his faithful services, he was re-elected twice, in the years 1876 and 1878, holding that responsible position for the term of six years. During that period Mr. Eakin had numbers of our very hardest and most unscrupulous criminals to deal with, and was very frequently placed in a position where it required all his great nerve and cool headed judgment and physical strength to extricate himself without receiving any great personal injury. During the present exciting senatorial election, Hon. Stewart B. Eakin has maintained an unequivocal position, having been one of the very staunchest and most valuable supporters of Hon. John H. Mitchell. He was married in 1871 to Miss E. J. Hadley, and that their life may be as blissful in the future as it has been in the past, is the heart-felt wish of him who writes these few lines.

HON. RICHARD B. HAYES.

In the tempestuous legislation which has characterized the present session, none have pursued a more consistent and calm, straightforward course than Mr. Hayes. He has ever kept the true interests of the State in view, and directed his every effort to accomplish the greatest good for the greatest number. In this he has been eminently successful, and he deserves the highest credit for the ability he has displayed and the honesty of purpose permeating his efforts. He represents Lane county, and is eminently qualified to advocate the views of the class of people who form the majority of the citizens of that section. He is engaged in stock-raising and farming and brings to the House that free, breezy disposition so characteristic of "the men of the hills." He is one of those true lovers of humanity who believes in the integrity of man, and who, while exercising a certain amount of cool judgment in estimating the efforts of those who come in contact with him, does not regard his every day companions with the suspicion that some men are too prone to harbor against those with whom they have dealings. He was born in Warren county, Tennessee, in 1831, and went with his parents to Missouri in 1839. During his boyhood he received the benefits of a common school education. Like thousands of others, actuated by a desire to dig for gold, he went to California, the "plains across" in 1850. He came to Oregon in 1852 and located on a farm in Lane county, where he has since remained. Mr. Hayes was honored by his fellow Democrats in 1874 by being elected a Representative to the Legislature, and he was re-elected in 1876. He was married in Lane county in 1858 to Miss Lucy Brown- that was also the maiden name of the wife of our esteemed ex-president—so Mr. Hayes and his good wife, both before and after marriage, were the exact namesakes of the general and his wife. Mr. Hayes did good service during the Rogue river war as a scout, having served under Colonel Chapman and under Colonel Martin in 1855 and 1856.

HON. HIRAM P. WEBB.

Mr. Webb is one of those positive men who, like Davy Crockett, is first sure he is right, and then "goes ahead." He seldom makes a mistake, relying, as he does, on the dictates of his good judgment. He is a man who views every question in its various bearings, and acts coolly, almost apathetically, apparently, in everything he undertakes. He occasionally expresses himself on questions before the House, but he is, by no means, a lover of long-winded speeches, and was the staunch advocate of the five-minute rule, believing that brevity is the soul of wit, and that a man who can condense his thoughts into a succinct and concise statement will produce the most lasting effect upon his hearers. He is a medium-sized, full-bearded gentleman, with a clear eye, and a kind expression. He represents Douglas county and deserves the highest credit from his constituents for the able manner in which he advocates their interests. Mr. Webb has seen a great deal of public life, and understands particularly well the affairs of county government, having held the position of County Treasurer in Nebraska for eight years, and ever since he has taken his seat in the House, he has watched with eagle eye every bill that took money from the county treasury, and he has on many occasions given most satisfactory and important information on the condition of county affairs, particularly the cash-box. Hiram was born in Sangamon county, Illinois, March 14, 1842, and after receiving his preparatory education in the common schools of his native State, he entered North Sangamon Academy at the age of eighteen, remaining there three years, after which he went to the State University at Bloomington Indiana, from which he graduated in 1865. After completing his college course he went home and taught school the following winter, and the following year he studied law, and completed the regular law course of the State University in 1867. In 1868 he went to Beatrice, Nebraska, where he resided for ten years, practicing his profession for a time, then being appointed clerk of the district court and afterwards for four consecutive terms was elected county treasurer. In 1878 he immigrated to Canyonville, Douglas county, where he has since resided, having been engaged in teaching school and the practice of law. He was elected as a member of the present House by a large majority, where his previous experience has served him in good stead, and made him one of the most efficient workers. He was married October 21, 1873, to Miss Jennette Maxfield.

HON. ROBERT J. SHARP.

This gentleman is eminently a self-made man. His entire career has displayed a force of character and indomitable energy, which in the long run never fails to land the possessor of these qualities on top. He represents Clackamas county, and although not a frequent speech-maker, is a hard worker and is ably representing the interests of his section, while devoting his native energy and talent to the interests of the whole State. Mr. Sharp belongs to the positive school of legislators, and whatever he advocates may be depended upon as the honest convictions of the man—a rough and ready quality undoubtedly acquired through a varied experience with the world and the necessity of earning everything he possesses. He was born in Burlington, Iowa, March 10, 1844, and went with his parents to Henry county in 1848, in which year his father died. He attended school for a few years and afterwards learned the carpenter's trade. At the breaking out of the war young Robert, who was then only seventeen years of age, and whose forefathers had all fought for their country, imbued with that spirit of daring and patriotism which is so characteristic of the American lad, enlisted in Company G, 11th Iowa Infantry, under Capt. Samuel McFarland.

He fought during the entire war, and was under Generals Halleck and Grant at the battles of Shiloh, Siege of Corinth and the Vicksburg campaign in 1863, and in 1864 he served under Sherman in the Atlanta campaign, and accompanied that gallant General on his march to the sea; he also fought in the campaign of the Carolinas. He was mustered out of service at Louisville, Kentucky, and returned to Iowa, where he attended school for one year; then he removed to Kansas in 1866, where he remained eight years. While in Kansas the Indian war broke out, and young Sharp immediately fell into line and fought it out with Custer. He came to Oregon in 1874 and settled in Clackamas county, where he still resides, engaged in farming. Mr. Sharp was a member of the last Legislature and while a member of the House made a good record. He was married in 1869 to Miss Phœbe Freeman.

HON. ALBERT H. TANNER.

" Pitch thy behavior low, thy projects high.
So shalt thou humble and magnanimous be.
Sink not in spirit, who aimeth at the sky
Shoots higher much than he that means a tree."
—[Geo. Herbert.

These are golden words and should be impressed upon the tablets of every young American's memory in imperishable letters. The subject of this brief notice knew the wisdom contained in them at an early age, and, it seems, wasted very little of his time. He was born on the bank of the Columbia river, near Portland, in 1855. During his early years he attended the public schools of Yamhill county, and having completed his preparatory studies, entered the Monmouth Christian college at the age of sixteen years, from which institution he graduated in 1874, sharing the highest graduating honors. His inclination was for the law; so he entered on his legal studies in the office of the eminent attorneys Dolph, Bronaugh, Dolph & Simon, and pursued them so assiduously that he was admitted to the bar in 1879 at the age of twenty-four. Mr. Tanner is at present a practicing attorney in the city of Portland, Multnomah county, which constituency he represents in the House. He possesses a magnificent speaking voice, his elocution is deliberate and impressive, and when experience shall have inspired him with greater confidence in his own powers, he will use it to some effect in the political world; although at the present time Mr. Tanner is only twenty-seven years of age, he is recognized as one of the ablest members in the House, and when he takes the floor to discuss the merits of a measure, every word that he utters is listened to with marked attention; he is the youngest member, and as a just recognition of his legal ability, has been appointed to fill the responsible position of Chairman of the Judiciary Committee. On the 25th of October, 1880, he was married to Miss Sarah M. Kelly, daughter of Hon. John Kelly, ex-Collector of Customs. Mr. Tanner's success in life is essentially that of his own making, being possessed of those great and high attributes which inspire confidence and which command respect. In the near future he will occupy one of the very foremost positions as a party leader and will bring to that cause which he espouses great strength and wise counsels. In politics, Mr. Tanner is a pure Republican, and since his election has labored incessantly to promote harmony and good will, and is favorably regarded by his brother Representatives.

HON FRANCIS M. KIZER

The Democracy has reason to be proud of its representatives now in the Legislature. As a minority it makes a respectable showing of respectable men who were elected in many instances from counties boasting a Republican majority; it speaks well for the personal worth and popularity of such men when elevated to high positions of honor and trust by the people, not because of party affiliations, not because of wealth or position, but because of their own sterling worth. Stability of character and practical push are what are needed as the prime elements in the character of the successful man; without these the graces of nature, the adornments of art, and that luster and polish which education gives are so much dead weight in the race of life. The gentleman whose name is mentioned above is one of the old, practical, substantial type of the country farmer and stock-raiser. He was born in Cedar county, Iowa, forty-four years ago, and adheres to the principles of true Democracy, which were instilled into his veins in early boyhood, beneath the blue skies of his native home. He was educated in the common schools of his western home, and came to far-off Oregon in the year 1853, locating in Linn county, where he has since resided. He has been identified with the farming interests, and this is his first experience in politics. He has met with considerable success as a farmer and stock-raiser, and by industry and sobriety he has become the fortunate possessor of many a rich acre of waving grain. Like all true farmers, he has always taken a lively interest in the success of the grange, and is a prominent member of subordinate grange Charity, 103, of which he is master, and has for years been and is at present a member of the State grange. He was married to Miss Mary Wigle in 1859. He is an active member of Committees on Counties and Claims.

HON. PETER S. NOYER:

In the early days of the Republic sterling worth was a much more common element in the political character than it is now. This is a sad confession to make, but "pity 'tis 'tis true, and more's the pity." Hard-headed, practical common sense has been the chief characteristic of some of the greatest statesmen that America ever knew. Andrew Jackson, Abraham Lincoln and General Grant were of this class; men who had very little to say, but very much to do, and what they did do they did thoroughly and well. Coming down into the humbler paths of life we find individuals of the same type who would have acted in precisely the same manner had they accepted the responsible positions of the statesmen we have named. In this category we feel justified in placing the name of Hon. Peter S. Noyer, the whole-souled representative from Clackamas county. The subject of this notice was born in Richland county, Ohio, October 19, 1837, and in 1840 moved with his parents to Illinois. In 1845 the family went to Texas, where young Peter received the advantages of a common school education. In 1853, attracted by the great gold discoveries, he went to California, by the way of New Orleans, Nicaragua and San Francisco to the gold mines. He remained there till May, 1855, when he immigrated to Oregon and located in Clackamas county. In 1857 he was married to a most estimable young lady, named Miss Delilah C. May, who came with her parents from Illinois in 1847. In 1862 Mr. Noyer traveled through the wilds of Eastern Oregon and Western Idaho, which territory was at that time infested with marauding bands of hostile Indians, but he fortunately escaped with a sound scalp and no regrets. In 1874, as a recognition for his services to the grand old Democratic party, he was elected a member of the Legislature, and in 1882 he was returned. He has been a life-long Democrat of the Jackson school, and his probity and character are above suspicion.

HON. JOHN C. CARSON.

When the Republican county convention of Multnomah county were last spring casting about for honest representative men with whom to trust the interests of the people in the House of Representatives, one of the names mentioned was that of Hon. John C. Carson, of Portland, and his nomination followed almost immediately. His nomination was nominally equivalent to his election, and his constituents have not been disappointed in their estimate of the man. He has labored night and day for the best interests of the State at large and for the proper advancement of the interests of his own county, having never allowed a single opportunity to pass whereby a point could be made for those whom he represents. He was born on a farm in Center county, Pennsylvania, February 20, 1825, and with his parents removed to Richland county, Ohio, in 1832. He received very fair educational facilities, having attended the common schools in early life and entered Ashland academy, in Ohio, along in 1842, where he remained three years under the tutorship of Prof. Andrews, afterwards a Brigadier General in the Union army and the President of Kenyon college, where ex-President Hayes graduated. Mr. Carson supported himself during his academic course by working at the carpenter's trade. He afterwards commenced the study of medicine under Dr. Kenneyman, of Ashland, Ohio, and with him came to California in 1850 to start an hospital in San Francisco. The project was abandoned, however, owing to ill health, and a year later young Carson pushed on to Oregon, reaching Portland in September, 1851, where he has resided ever since. He followed the business of a builder and contractor until 1857, when he erected the first sash and door factory built in that city, it being located on the water front at the foot of Jefferson street. His business increased so rapidly that he was compelled to seek more extensive quarters, which he found at Weidler's mills, in the northern part of the city, where he has now the most extensive establishment of the kind on the northwest coast and is doing an immense business, his sales reaching about $150,000 annually, and constantly increasing proportionate with the growth of the city; his business office being located at the corner of Third and E streets. He was a member and President of the Common Council in 1855-6, and has represented the third ward in that body several terms since. He was a member of the board of experts appointed to effect a settlement between the United States Government and the Hudson Bay Company in 1865-6. He was elected a member of the House from Multnomah county in 1870 and again in 1882. He has been twice married, his first wife being Miss Elizabeth Talbot, to whom he was united in 1854, and who died in 1859. In 1860 he was married to Mrs. Eliza A. Northop, of Portland. They have a family of five children, one being married. Mr. Carson is a consistent member of the Congregational Church and contributes liberally to its support. He is also one of the oldest members of Samaritan Lodge, No. 2, I. O. O. F., of Portland. He is rather tall, of commanding physique, full face, beaming with health and good nature, pleasant features, brown eyes, smooth chin and light side-whiskers and gray, bushy hair. He is a pleasant man to converse with and is not cold or distant with new-made friends, and you are favorably impressed with him upon even short acquaintanceship. He made a host of new friends among his colleagues in the House, and we have no hesitancy in predicting that his legislative career has not yet ended.

HON. WILLIAM P. KEADY.

Among the many creditable Representatives elected to the Legislature just closed, by the Republicans, there is none more worthy of commendation than Hon. W. P. Keady, Representative from Benton county. He was born in Washington county, Pennsylvania, April 1, 1850, and when but three years of age removed with his parents to Illinois in 1853, and settled in Iroquois county, within the malarial confines of the Grand Prairie. Here he learned the printer's trade in his father's office, who at the time was editor and publisher of the "Iroquois Times." He came to California in 1869, where he worked at his trade and found his way to Oregon in 1872, and settled at Salem, where he resided for several years and was a power in politics from the very outset. He followed his trade, however, and was engaged in various enterprises in connection therewith, including the publication of the "Daily Statesman," four years' incumbency of the foremanship in the State printing office, establishment and publication for several months of the "Oregon Educational Monthly." In 1879 he went to Corvallis and entered into partnership with Hon. W. B. Carter, then State Printer, in a job printing office. Mr. Carter died in 1880 and Mr. Keady was appointed State Printer, by Gov. Thayer, to fill the vacancy then existing. Mr. Keady has a very thorough knowledge of the "art preservative," and has been in a very great manner instrumental in pointing out and correcting the abuses of the law governing the State work, and has acted as expert on several occasions by special appointment on behalf of the State. In 1881 he was appointed paymaster and right-of-way agent for the Oregon Pacific Railroad Company, in which capacity he gave very general satisfaction. In 1882 he received the nomination as Representative from Benton county, and was elected by a handsome majority. He has never been an aspirant for public office, but in the discharge of his official duties he has been honest and conscientious, and the pledges he took before the people he has kept faithfully at all hazards. He has proved a hard worker, was always in his seat and had his eyes open to every proposition. Although not particularly fond of speech-making, he has at various times during the session exhibited a command of language and a comprehension of the subject matter in hand which could only have been acquired by years of study and reflection. He is a man of slight build, pleasant face, with chin whiskers and mustache and brown hair. He was married in 1874 to Mrs. Julia G. Crump, of Salem, and their family consists of three children.

HON. PENUMBRA KELLY

Was born in Kentucky in the year 1845. His father immigrated to Oregon in 1848, and remained that winter with his family in Oregon City. In 1849 the family, which was a goodly-sized one, Penumbra being one of fifteen children, removed to East Portland, and since then the subject of this sketch has there resided, growing up from boyhood to manhood and earning a reputation for soundness of character and strength of purpose which has frequently made him the recipient of public trust and public office when he would fain have enjoyed the quietude of private life on his pleasant and valuable farm two miles from East Portland. Mr. Kelly was married in 1875 to Miss Mary E. Marquam, daughter of Judge Marquam, and has three interesting children. In 1874 he was elected a member of the House of Representatives from Multnomah, and in 1876 he was elected County Commissioner. He was again elected to the Legislature in 1878, and since that time he has been twice re-elected. Mr. Kelly's experience as a legislator, together with the fact that he is a thorough parliamentarian, a deep thinker and sound adviser, has made him one of the most valuable members of the present session, and many times has his counsel extricated the house from troublesome complications.

HON. LUTHER B. ISON

Is one of the Representatives from Baker county in the House. He is a medium-sized, well-proportioned and fine-looking gentleman, with a clear eye and a full face. At times you would think this man had genius, but you are immediately confronted with the stern reality that he has not. On entering the House, he goes straight to his desk, takes out his book containing legislation which is up for consideration, and buries himself in the work of investigating the merits and provisions of the various measures. When he proceeds to address the House, the listener is struck with the forcible manner in which he speaks and the great earnestness of his language. His style of oratory is one peculiar to himself and withal pleasing. Although Mr. Ison is not eloquent, he is, by far, the most acceptable speaker in the present House. He begins to talk in a moderated tone of voice, which gradually changes to one of decision, sometimes appealing, again persuasive, and again endeavoring to convince. His sentences are short, and seldom does he utter a clear-cut, round Edmund Burke construction.

He is an able man and a diplomate, and would make a popular candidate for any office that required addressing the people in large bodies assembled. He was born in Garrad county, Kentucky, in the year 1843. In 1849 his parents emigrated to Grundy county, Missouri, where young Ison attended the public schools until he was prepared to enter Grand river college, where he remained some time, and afterwards finished at Fayette college in Howard county. In 1866 he came to Oregon and located in Baker county, where he mined and taught school from 1866 to 1870. He was then elected county clerk, and subsequently re-elected twice to the same office. During the time which he served as county clerk, he studied law, and was admitted as a professional lawyer in October, 1876. In June, 1876, he was elected district attorney of the fifth judicial district, and was re-elected in 1878. At the expiration of his term of office, he became associated with A. J. Lawrence in the law business, and has since been engaged in the practice of his profession. He is a staunch Democrat, and his long life of usefulness as a member of that party, together with the many offices that have been thrust upon him, are sufficient indications of the esteem in which he is held. Mr. Ison was married to Miss Josie Cates, of Union, August 12, 1870.

HON. P. A. MARQUAM.

The man who has enjoyed all the advantages of a collegiate education, and the riches which are bestowed upon him by his family, is deserving of praise only for the obstacles he has to meet and encounter. Hence, when a man enters life without any of these bestowed advantages and works his way upward from the poverty of youth to a respectable position in the community and an honorable office before the people, and owes his advancement to his own blameless life, his strength of character, and an iron will that failure only serves to render stronger, we must place upon his brow the chaplet that belongs to the victor in a hard-fought fight — not the prize drawn by lucky chance in the lottery of life. Representative Marquam is one of those men who were born without the immediate advantages of wealth, but by his pertinacity of purpose and natural ability he has risen not only to honorable position and the attainment of a large fortune, but we might say he stands pre-eminent as a citizen and as a jurist. He was born in "old Maryland, My Maryland," in February, 1823, where his ancestors settled in the Revolutionary days. He is a grandson of Henry Poole, who was one of the largest planters and most distinguished men of his time. When quite small young Marquam's father moved with his family to Indiana, where they lived on a farm. As his father was quite poor, the boy assisted him by helping with the farm work, and at the same time whenever an opportunity offered he would take up his books, and it was there, following the plow and lying under the shade of the wide-spreading tree branches that he laid the foundation of an education which fitted him for the important place he was to fill in after life. After obtaining a sound English education, he studied Latin, together with the higher mathematics, and then having a strong inclination for the legal profession, he secured the necessary books and studied at home under the direction of Godlove S.

Orth, who is at the present time a Representative in Congress from Indiana. He completed his studies at the Bloomington law school, and was admitted to the bar at Lafayette, Indiana, in the year 1847. He then practiced there a short time and in 1849 crossed the plains to California in search of the "golden fleece." As soon as he arrived at his destination he went to work in the mines and remained there during the winter of 1849 and the spring of 1850, occasionally relieving the monotony of the pick and shovel by going on expeditions to repel the bands of marauding Indians, who in those days were the mortal enemy of the hard-working miner. In these engagements he received several serious wounds, which laid him up for several weeks, and after recovering his fellow-citizens with one acclaim elected him Judge of Yolo county, which position he held one year, and then resigned to come to Oregon. He arrived in Portland in the latter part of the same year and at once commenced the practice of his profession. He was successful from the very beginning, and within a year had a large and lucrative practice. In the year 1862 he was elected County Judge of Multnomah, and, as an endorsement of his services, was re-elected at the next election. After retiring from office Judge Marquam refused to take an active interest in politics, and he confined himself almost exclusively to transactions in real estate. He saw that Portland was some day destined to be a metropolitan city, and with the eye of a wise business man he looked around him and secured some of the most valuable property in Portland and the suburbs, a very large part of which he still owns. Amongst his large purchases was that of 298 acres, known as Marquam's hill, which is one of the very prettiest sites in the city of Portland. Some of this large tract he has disposed of, and the remainder he has retained for his own use, and on which his residence now stands. At the State election Mr. Marquam was nominated without his consent, and notwithstanding that fact he received the highest vote on the ticket. He was married to Miss Emma Kern, May 8, 1853, and their union was blessed with eleven children, four of whom are boys and seven girls, and all of them are now living and enjoying the best of health. In politics Mr. Marquam has always been a staunch Republican, and the many public offices he has been called upon to fill indicates the esteem in which he is held. His record, which is open, speaks for the man; from nothing, by his own exertions he has become the eminent citizen that he now is, and we regretfully close writing of the career of a gentleman whom we would gladly write a whole volume about.

HON. WARREN TRUITT.

This gentleman is one of the Representatives from Polk county. In appearance he is a thoughtful-looking man, with clearly-cut features, kindly, yet searching, eye, and a mouth the contour of which unmistakably indicates great strength of character and a determined will. The Judge, as he is familiarly called, is of pleasing address, plain and outspoken in all his dealings with the world, and possessed of a vast store of useful knowledge gained by close application and a judicious taste. He is a ready debater, but speaks very seldom, and then only on matters of great importance, and from his conduct in the House I should judge that he has an abhorrence of the habit of bobbing up and down in order to speak on every proposition. He was born in Green county, Illinois, in the year 1845, and educated in McKendree college, Sinclair county, from which he graduated in the class of 1868. He then entered the law office of Judge Snyder, Belleville, St. Clair county, Illinois, and was admitted to the bar in 1870. In the spring of 1871 he came to Oregon, taking up his residence in Polk county, where he has since continued to live. He was teacher in the Bethel academy three years, and was then elected County Judge in 1874, which office he held four years. At the expiration of his term of office he entered upon the practice of his profession at Dallas, and he now has a fine business. He was elected a member of the present Legislative Assembly by a large majority, and during the session has been a close and valuable worker and a member of the Judiciary Committee. He was married in the year 1874 to Miss Mary Basey.

HON. W. T. RIGDON

Is one of the Representatives from Marion county on the floor of the House. He was born in Powesheik county, Iowa, in the year 1849. In the year 1850 his parents immigrated to Oregon and sought a home in Marion county, where he has ever since resided. In 1852 the father of the family died, when young Taylor was but three years old. Left without a father at that infantile age, his story is that of many another boy who, deprived of the blessing of a father's presence and the consequent advantages that accrue therefrom to boyhood, has had to battle with the world alone and single-handed, and to his honor be it said that by application to his book around the family fireplace and working during the day for the maintenance of his mother and a large family, he, by his own efforts, obtained a good education and grew up to a useful and respected manhood. At the age of twenty-four he became a teacher in the Jefferson Institute, where he remained two years, and afterwards taught three years in the district schools. Mr. Rigdon was married to Miss Mattie J. Smith in the year 1878, and their union has been blessed with two little daughters. Although this is the first time that Mr. Rigdon has been before the people as an officeholder, he has always taken a leading part in the politics of Jefferson, is an ardent advocate of the cause of temperance and an active member of the M. E. Church. He is a Republican, and has done good service in the present session, having taken a particular interest in the passage of temperance measures.

HON. GEORGE F. CRAWFORD.

A good Democrat is the noblest work of the teachings of Jefferson, and Mr. Crawford, who represents Linn county in the House, is one of that stock. He was born a Democrat, bred a Democrat, and will very probably die in the faith. He is one of those political apostles who, while pursuing a thoroughly consistent course himself, can perceive good in the Nazareth of other parties, and is ever ready to award credit wherever he thinks it is due. He is one of that honest, conservative minority that we have so frequently spoken of in the course of these biographies, and a fanatic only upon questions of right and justice. He is of a grave disposition, and a studious demeanor, a man whose opinion is carefully weighed before it is pronounced, and, when delivered, carrying conviction to the fair and impartial mind. He possesses a vast amount of reserve power—he is a thinker. He is one of the most valuable men in the assembly, mainly on account of his individuality, a quality possessed by him in an eminent degree. Mr. Crawford was born in Grayson county, Virginia, in the year 1818. He attended the common schools of the county and afterwards learned the trade of tanner, in the meantime studying medicine. He immigrated to Illinois in the year 1844 and located in Warren county. Here he commenced the practice of his profession as a full-fledged M. D., and in the following year he moved to Henderson county, where he continued to practice for one year, attaining quite a reputation and meeting with a fair amount of success. In the year 1852 he came to Oregon, taking up his residence in Albany, Linn county, where he has since remained. He was elected a member of the House of Representatives from that place in the year 1874. Ever since the organization of the Albany Farmers' Warehouse Company he has been associated with it, and is at the present time one of its board of directors and its president. Mr. Crawford is the oldest member in the House, being sixty-four years of age, and is of a fine, hale and hearty appearance. He is what one would pronounce at first sight a picture of the regular old country gentleman, appreciating a favor and anxious to perform a kindness. In the year 1845 Mr. Crawford was wedded to Miss Mary Ellen Gilmour, a daughter of Dr. Gilmour, one of the physicians under whom he studied.

HON. JAMES B. SPERRY

Is one of the Democratic Representatives on the floor of the House, and hails from Umatilla county. He is six feet in height, weighs about 200 pounds, is well-proportioned and one of the quiet but hard workers of the minority. He has lived in our State thirty-two years, and can look back over the useful years of his life with the happy satisfaction of knowing that his character has ever remained unblemished, and his every action pure beyond question. Although, as we have said, Mr. Sperry is one of the quiet members, he has used every exertion in behalf of his constituency, and on one occasion, when a bill was up for passage which had for its object the division of Umatilla county in a way that would work injury to his people, he made one of the plainest, most vigorous and effective speeches of the session. Mr. Sperry was born in Ohio in 1835 and went with his parents to Iowa in 1840, where he remained until 1851, receiving there his school training, and afterwards worked on his father's farm. In 1851 he crossed the plains to Oregon and located in Linn county. He remained in that county until 1877, when he moved to Umatilla county, Eastern Oregon, where he has since resided. In 1870 he was honored by his fellow-citizens with the office of Assessor, which he held two years. He was married in the year

1856 to Miss Rebecca Rice, with whom he lived happily until 1875, when that lady died. He was again married in 1877 to Miss S. V. Spencer, of Umatilla. Mr. Sperry served in the Indian war of 1855 and 1856 under Capt. King, in Southern Oregon.

HON. MADISON L. JONES.

Among the young men of the assembly, none have brighter prospects for the future, or give better promise of fulfilling the expectations of sincere well-wishers and devoted friends, than the young gentleman whose name heads this brief sketch. Modest, unassuming and gentlemanly in his every action, Mr. Jones has gained the unqualified respect of every member of the House. He is a ready debater, and all subjects discussed by him have been treated in a forcible and logical manner. His style is concise, and when he has presented his case with the ability native to his character, he refrains from further urging and consequent weakening of the effect of his argument. In this he invariably displays a talent peculiar to but few men in public life, namely, the talent of knowing when to cease—the knowledge that at certain times "silence is golden." Mr. Jones was born in Indiana in the year 1849, and came to Oregon with his parents in 1853, remaining here ever since. He received his early training in the district school, and afterwards entered Willamette University, where he graduated in the class of 1871. After completing his educational course, he studied law with Shaw & Mallory, and afterwards with Shaw & Burnett. He was admitted to the bar in the year 1879. He was married in 1880 to Miss Emma Novenden. In politics, Mr. Jones is a strong Republican, and is esteemed as a promising young man of the future.

HON. THOMAS N. FAULCONER.

This gentleman is of a plain, quiet, unassuming nature, and has done very good work as a member of the House of Representatives. He has lived in Oregon for thirty-one years, and is considered, by those who know him best, as a hard-working and industrious man and a worthy citizen. He was born in Missouri in 1830, where he resided with his parents on a farm until the age of twenty. In the year 1857 he crossed the plains and settled in old Yamhill, which constituency he represents in the House. He has farmed there for the last twenty years, with exception of a few years spent in Wasco in the stock business. He was also in the mercantile business in Sheridan precinct for ten years, and was elected Justice of the Peace there, which position he also held for a period of ten years. He was married in 1861 to Miss Lucy H. Morgan, with whom he has lived happily ever since, and raised a comfortable family. During the Yakima war, when that murderous tribe of savages attempted to overrun and massacre the white settlers of Washington and Oregon, Mr. Faulconer was one of the fearless men that stepped to the front and tendered his services for the protection of their lives and property, and he made a good record, and one of which his family may feel justly proud. In politics he is a staunch Republican.

HON. F. A. PATTERSON.

The gentleman whose name graces this page is a native of Illinois, having been born in Sinclair county in 1835, and combines within himself much of the rough vigor and gentlemanly polish for which the natives of that State are so justly celebrated. His forty-seven years have not at all diminished his energy or dulled the brightness of his spirits. Mr. Patterson came across the plains to California in 1852, and after many hair-breadth escapes by flood and field, and lonely nights in the mountain glen and days of hard toil in John Town, a lively mining camp in El Dorado county, he went to Prairie City, Sacramento, where he mined a short time, then returned to old El Dorado, and finally came to beautiful Oregon in 1857, locating in Benton county on a farm, where he remained one year. Mr. Patterson was married to Miss Caroline Tatom in the year 1859, and is at the present time the happy father of ten splendid children, the first nine of whom are boys and the youngest a fair daughter. Shortly after his marriage he moved to Washington county. He lived there but one year, and then returned to Polk, where he has since lived. He was elected a Representative to the Legislative Assembly of 1880, and earned such a reputation for reliability and capacity that his fellow citizens returned him to the present session. In appearance Mr. Patterson is a medium-sized gentleman, with a full beard and and a sparkling eye. He is a good parliamentarian, a ready talker and well informed in the routine of legislative work. In his county Mr. Patterson is very well and favorably known, and is recognized as a staunch and prominent member of the Republican party.

HON. HENRY G. BROWN

Was born in old New Hampshire January 15, 1833, and was brought up on a farm until the age of seventeen. In May, 1852, he came to Oregon and engaged in the packing business from Scottsburg to Southern Oregon, and Yreka, Cal., and so continued until the end of the Indian war of 1855 and 1856. Mr. Brown was with the Knott Bros., at Loose creek, on the 9th day of October the terrible day that the general Indian outbreak occurred, and saw seven men between there and Rogue river lying by the roadside presenting the ghastly spectacle of an Indian killing. Mr. Brown himself was reported killed at the same time, but to the joy and surprise of his many friends he returned safely, and was married on the 15th of September, 1856, to Miss Priscella Stearns. Immediately after his marriage he purchased a farm fifteen miles from Scottsburg, where he has since resided. Mr. Brown has been honored before by the Republican party with the nomination of Senator and Representative, but he, together with the entire ticket, was then defeated. In appearance Mr. Brown is a very pleasant-looking gentleman, with eyes fairly beaming with good nature. He has made a fine record as an able member of the House, and has taken advantage of every opportunity to secure the passage of proper and necessary legislation. He is a Republican of the old school, and voted for J. H. Mitchell as long as there was a prospect of his election.

HON. HENRY THORNTON

Is a Republican Representative from Josephine county. From his infancy he has been identified with the farming interest, and is, therefore, peculiarly well qualified to represent the people of his county. Since the beginning of the session, Mr. Thornton has been an industrious member, and has introduced some of the very best measures for the benefit of his constituency. He was born in Tippecanoe county, Indiana, in the year 1832. When three years of age his father immigrated to Iowa, and became one of the farmers of that State. Young Henry remained on the farm, occasionally attending school until the year 1853, when he came to Oregon, arriving here the same year, after a tedious and dangerous journey across the plains. He settled in Umpqua county, securing there a fine farm, and in the year 1858 he was elected treasurer of the county. In the year 1865 he was married to Miss Josephine Haines, and the following year he moved to Jackson county. He lived there until 1875 and then went to Josephine, where he has since resided. In the year 1877 he was elected Commissioner of that county, and Representative in 1882. Mr. Thornton has always maintained his reputation as a consistent Republican, and a vigorous party worker. He is well acquainted with the routine business of legislation, is well posted on all subjects and has rendered valuable services to the people of his county.

HON. J. H BAUGHMAN,

Of Marion county, was born and raised to manhood in Illinois. His educational advantages were limited in the extreme. He emigrated to Oregon in 1850 and has ever since resided in Marion county. Naturally possessed of an investigating turn of mind, he gathered knowledge rapidly, ever keeping prominently in view the axiom that there never can be any real excellence without labor in any deportment of life. Very few read the newspapers with greater avidity than he, and still fewer have a higher appreciation of their worth to those who in early youth have been denied the rich boon that weekly or daily newspapers confer. Honest, upright and generous to a fault, he soon became a marked man in his neighborhood. The temperance cause now coming into prominence always found in him a fast friend and a firm supporter, the Sabbath school an able teacher, and society generally one of God's best gifts, an honest man. In the person of Mr. Baughman, the people of Marion county have had a good Representative, and one who has done as much as any other to secure the passage of proper and effective legislation. Upon the floor of the House, he has done good service, and can have the satisfaction of knowing that the open record of votes has always found him on the side of the people.

HON. ANDREW N. GILBERT

One of the Representatives from Marion county, is a gentleman who is well qualified by birth, attainments, capacity and connections to be a leader of the people. Born in Grand View, Illinois, in the year 1840, he attended the common schools of his native place and finished his education at Waveland

Collegiate Institute, Indiana, and was still a student at the breaking out of the civil war. Young Gilbert, together with a number of other brave young fellows, formed a company to fight for the unity and preservation of their country, and applied for admission in Lew Wallace's famous regiment, the Eleventh Indiana Volunteers; but the young company came too late, for the formation of the regiment had already been completed, and they consequently were rejected. Mr. Gilbert disappointed, but not discouraged, and fired by the feeling of patriotism so characteristic of the young American, returned to Illinois and enlisted in the Twelfth Illinois Volunteers, serving in that regiment three years. At the expiration of that time he re-enlisted at Pulaski, Tenn., and was in active service until the close of the war, when he was mustered out at Springfield, Illinois. During his life on the field his regiment was in the Army of the West, under General Sherman, and he participated in the battles of Fort Donaldson, Pittsburgh Landing, the advance on Corinth, and marched with Sherman to the Sea. Wonderful to relate during all this fighting our young friend received not a wound, although the deadly missiles dealt out death all around him. In 1866 Mr. Gilbert came to Oregon, by way of the Missouri river and across the Mullan route. Arriving here he took up his residence in Salem and engaged in the boot and shoe business, which he conducted successfully for many years. In 1870 Mr. Gilbert was married to Miss Estelle McCully, daughter of David McCully, Esq., of Salem, and is now the father of two fine boys. In politics Mr. Gilbert has always been a pure Republican, and has been honored by his party repeatedly. In 1872 he was elected City Treasurer, and at the expiration of his term of office he was re-elected. In 1874 he was elected a Representative to the Legislature, and he was re-elected in the years 1876 and 1882. Every time Mr. Gilbert has been elected he has received the largest majority on the ticket. Such in brief is a short sketch of the gentleman who at the age of forty-two has served his country faithfully on the battlefield and been honored by his fellow citizens in public life. He is at present engaged in the grocery business in Salem, and has a reputation for honesty and business sagacity that will commend him to the friendship of all. He is Chairman of Committee on Ways and Means.

HON. JASPER SMITH

Is one of the Representatives from Tillamook county, and a pioneer of Oregon. He is a plain, sensible man, with sound ideas on all matters of general interest, and with a particular desire to serve and advance the interests of the farming element. He was born in Laporte county, Indiana, in the year 1842, where his parents resided until he was five years of age. In the year 1847 the family came across the plains to Oregon and remained in the city of Portland about one month. While living there the father of the family, after having encountered all the hardships and privations of the trip, was taken sick and died in the land where he had expected to make a new home for his family. Mrs. Smith then removed with her family of young children to Yamhill county and took up a piece of unsurveyed land,

and for three or four months lived upon boiled wheat. Although the widow felt the loss of her husband deeply, she was enabled to live and get along well with the assistance of young Jasper and his industrious brothers, and after the lapse of a few years she was again married to Mr. J. C. Geer, a gentleman well known to old Oregonians, and died in 1854. About three years ago Mr. Smith went to Tillamook county, where he has since remained on his farm. He was married in 1866 to Miss Sarah Abigail Harper, and now is the happy father of eight children, seven of whom are boys. In politics Mr. Smith is a Republican.

HON. JOHN W. SAPPINGTON.

The world, as Emerson says, "is no longer clay, but rather iron in the hands of its workers, and men have get to hammer out a place for themselves by steady and rugged blows." This is true, indeed, of the present age, as men can no longer go at one leap into eminent positions, but must work on steadily in such a way as to prove by the stuff that is in them their capabilities and fitness. This might be said of him whose brief experience we are considering. He is a stout, fine-looking and full-bearded man, who has seen some of the ups and downs that follow in the wake of adventure. He was born in Montgomery county, Kentucky, in the year 1837. His parents removed to Missouri in 1838, and he attended the village school. He left Missouri in 1845 and came to Oregon, locating in Yamhill county. When the Yakima Indians commenced their depredations upon the white settlers in that county, young John was one of the first to tender his services and joined the Oregon volunteers, under command of Colonel Cornelius; he did good service until the suppression of that troublesome tribe was accomplished, when he returned to his home. In 1859 he moved to Wasco county and remained there until 1861, when he removed to Yamhill and remained till 1865, at which time he changed his residence to Washington county, where he now resides and is engaged in the healthful and independent business of farming and stock-raising. Mr. Sappington was elected Justice of the Peace in Washington county in 1878, and was elected to the House of Representatives this year by a large majority. He was married in 1857 to Miss Lucinda Laughlin.

HON. JOHN LONG.

This gentleman is one of the Representatives from Lane county. He is of very pleasing address, and, in his social relations, is the embodiment of courtesy. In personal appearance, Mr. Long is more fortunate than some of his colleagues. He is six feet in height, and weighs 180 pounds, with an elastic frame, and a pleasant, though penetrating, blue eye. In his legislative work he has seemed rather to devote his closest attention to a conscientious study of the merits and defects of the measures proposed in the House, and the result of his earnest scrutiny is apparent in his votes. It is safe to say that the voting record of Mr. Long is as consistent as any ever made in the halls of legislation in this State. He does not express himself much in debate, but the quiet influence he exerts among the conservatives

of his party is greater than many members give him credit for. He was
born in Butler county, Ohio, the grand old "Buckeye" State which has
given the nation more men than any other State in the Union, an assertion
which no caviller can gainsay. In his youth he lived on a farm with his
parents, attending the schools of the vicinity. He went to Missouri with
his parents in 1859, here the family remained for a number of years, young
John being enabled to obtain a very good ordinary education, which he afterwards brought to a very high degree of culture by his own exertions. In 1870 he
went to Dakota, where he remained two years teaching school. He came to
Oregon in 1872 and located in Linn county, where he taught school until 1876,
when he removed to Lane county, where he has since resided, teaching
school and being engaged in the lumber business. Mr. Long was married
in 1872 to Miss Annie Johnson. Although the position which Mr. Long
took in the last Senatorial election brought upon him the censure of some
few thoughtless and loud-talking men, yet it is a well-known fact, which
the record will prove, that Mr. Long's action throughout that bitter fight
was strictly consistent and highly creditable to him. He is an ardent Democrat and represented one of the most respectable constituencies in the
State in Lane county. For one long week Mr. Long voted for a Democrat
for U. S. Senator, and understanding full well that it was impossible for a
Democrat to be elected, he changed his vote and supported that Republican
candidate who was the choice of two-thirds of the Republican party and
whom he believed to be the best man for the people—Hon. J. H. Mitchell.
In taking this action Mr. Long was congratulated by every right-thinking
man, and the criticisms of his enemies only add luster to his good name.

HON. O. P. S. PLUMMER.

One of the most popular men in the Assembly is Dr. Plummer. His courteous manner, gentlemanly instincts and generous charity for the mistakes
and shortcomings of others has rendered him an object of sincere respect
to all with whom he comes in contact. His speeches on special subjects are
models; they are fluent, concise, and convey the impression to the listener
that the speaker is not only thoroughly conversant with his subject, but
that he brings to a consideration of the question under discussion a vast
amount of careful study and conscientious thought. Dr. Plummer possesses in a large degree the peculiar faculty of opposing the argument of
"the gentleman on the other side" with a genial and happy irony that
never fails to please even the member whom he is for the moment opposing.
It seldom occurs that he employs biting sarcasm or withering satire, but
the fact that he has occasionally dealt trenchant blows indicate that he is
thoroughly competent to use them effectively. He is one of the two who
were honored with a re-election from Multnomah county, having served the
people faithfully in the eleventh session of the Legislature. As a consequence he combines experience in legislative matters with his theoretical
knowledge of the business of the office he occupies. As a debater and parliamentarian Dr. Plummer has few equals, and his clear perception of the
merits of the question at issue has on several occasions rescued the House

from parliamentary difficulties. He was born in Greenville, Mercer county, Pennsylvania, in the year 1836, and is a fine and pleasant-looking gentleman with a clear eye and full, grayish beard, in the possession of the very best of health, physical and mental. After completing his preliminary studies he received a thorough medical education and graduated from the celebrated Jefferson Medical College in Philadelphia at the age of twenty-one. He resided at Rock Island, Illinois, several years, and during the first two years of the rebellion rendered the Union valuable service in the hospital and telegraph service in the southwest. In 1863 he with his family crossed the plains and arrived in Portland in the spring of 1864, where he has since resided. Immediately after his arrival Dr. Plummer was tendered the position of first manager of the telegraph office after connection with San Francisco was established. He continued in the telegraph service about ten years, during six and a half of which he filled the important position of Superintendent of the Third or Oregon district. As a surgeon Dr. Plummer established an enviable reputation, having performed many very difficult and trying operations, with remarkable skill and good judgment. With a dislike for the every-day cares of professional life and having a taste for business pursuits, he some years ago launched into the drug business, and became the head of the well-known firm of Plummer & Byerley, of Portland. The Doctor is well known throughout the State, and he secured a reputation for probity and business sagacity that commands him the respect of the business community, and in private life his character is without a blemish. He is a thorough Republican, firm in his conclusions and unflinching in purpose.

HON. HENRY L. MARSTON

Is one of the Representatives of Yamhill county. He is a representative business man in appearance, in action and in standing. Although this is his first experience in our legislative halls, he has a good knowledge of deliberative proceedings, is a pleasing and polished talker and is blessed with the possession of good judgment. He was born in the Pine-tree State, in the year 1843, and lived there with his parents until he was eight years of age, when the family removed to California and took up their residence in the quiet little village of Centerville, Alameda county. There he attended the schools for a period of five years, when he went to San Leandro and became a telegraph operator, which position he held two years, and then went to Oakland, the beautiful little sister city of San Francisco. He lived in Oakland some time, and then seeing a good business opening he started for Portland as the agent of the Perkins & House non-explosive lamp. In the introduction of this article he met with great success, and was enabled to embark in an extensive grocery business on corner of Third and Yamhill streets. After remaining in his new quarters one year, he went to Gaston, Washington county, Oregon, thence to North Yamhill, and finally to Carlton, in the same county, where he now lives, engaged in the general merchandise business, and honored by his fellow-citizens as their Representative in the House. Mr. Marston has traveled around considerably, and wherever he has lived has been known as a gentleman of reliability and character. He was married to Miss Annie Bond in the year 1868.

HON. JAMES N. RICE.

This gentleman is one of the Representatives from Linn county. He was born in Campbell county, Tennessee, on the 17th of March, in the year 1832. When quite young his parents moved to Missouri, where they lived on a farm until the year 1850. Young James attended school a certain number of months in each year, and the remaining portion of his time was spent in assisting his father with the farm work, so we find him in the year 1850, when he came to Oregon, a good specimen of the intelligent, sturdy, self-confident farmer lad of the West. On arriving in Oregon he took up a farm in Linn county, and has resided there since, happy in the cultivation of his acres and the presence of his browsing stock. In the year 1857 Mr. Rice, then twenty five years of age, was married to Miss Nancy Bobnett, and they have now nine children living and in the best of health. He volunteered his services in the years 1855 and 1856 in the Rogue river Indian war, and served throughout that campaign with much distinction, receiving a very painful and severe wound at the battle of Little Meadows, by being shot through both thighs. The people of Linn county made a good selection when they sent Mr. Rice to the House of Representatives, and he has watched their interests faithfully, and served his people well.

HON. J. H. HAWLEY

Is one of the Representatives from Polk county. He is a fine-looking and warm-hearted gentleman, with a face expressive at once of gentleness and stability of character. He is about six feet tall and his face is covered with a full brownish beard intersprinkled with the silvery threads. He was born in Canada in the year 1834, and when yet an infant his parents removed to Michigan, thence to Iowa, from which place they went to Missouri. They came to Oregon in 1844 and located in Yamhill county, where for us John followed the plow for thirteen years. In 1857 he removed to Polk county, where he has since resided. During the last ten years he has been engaged in the general merchandise business at Bethel. He was elected Justice of the Peace in 1862, and served in that office six years. In 1857 he was married to Miss Eliza Mulkey, who is a cousin of Mrs. J. N. Dolph and of Prosecuting Attorney Mulkey, of Multnomah. Mr. Hawley is a retiring and unassuming man, and although he says very little, entertains pronounced views on every question of importance, and if he does make a remark it is generally "the right word in the right place." He is a Republican, of good party standing.

HON. ARAD COMSTOCK STANLEY.

There are some men so happily constituted that with nerves of steel they can watch the play of passion as it flashes through the actions of men and never feel its magnetic influence in their own natures, or, if they do possess the power, having the inclination to suppress every evidence of the feelings which the outside influences are producing upon them. The expression "a looker-on in Vienna" expresses the character of men who are thus constituted, and as far as the display of unnecessary excitement is concerned, are cold, impassible spectators only. This has been the disposition of Mr. Stanley when the House chamber rang with the battle cries of passionate combatants in the arena of debate. He has never allowed his prejudices to get the better of his judgment, and has been thus enabled to view all sides of a hotly-contested question, and in cool deliberation draw just deductions from the conflicting arguments advanced. And yet he is by no means a drone in the hive. He does not stand idly by while others toil and spin. He is ever on the alert for an opportunity to further the interests of the State and his constituency, and with earnestness of purpose and sound judgment he attends to his duties which, notwithstanding the fact that he does not take an active part in debate, are by no means light. He has introduced several excellent measures, and worked hard for their passage. He was born in Missouri in 1835. He received the rudiments of knowledge in the village school and afterwards attended Trenton Academy in Grundy county. After completing the academic course, he studied medicine and became a physician. He entered upon the practice of his profession in Grundy county and remained there four years. He removed to Nebraska in 1862, where he practiced his profession two years, when, in 1864, he journeyed to the "Golden State" and took up his residence in the beautiful Sacramento Valley, and he purchased a farm there, on which he passed the time of seven years as a tiller of the soil. In 1875 Mr. Stanley came to Oregon and located in Jackson county, where he has since resided. He represented that good old Democratic county in 1880 and was re-elected a member of the present session. Although he has a large and valuable farm of 320 acres, Mr. Stanley still practices his profession, and he is recognized as one of the most reliable physicians in Jackson county. He was married in Missouri in 1856 to Miss Sarah Burus, who lived only four years after her marriage, and in 1863 he was married to Miss Susan Martin. Mr. Stanley is a member of the Committee on Corporations, and an active member of several special committees.

HON. J. G. BLEAKNEY

Is one of the Republican Representatives from Marion, and is fifty years of age. He is one of the men who has battled for his country, and who, in the perilous discharge of his duty to the principles he held paramount to his life, has willingly sacrificed his heart's blood, and such a man is entitled, not only to the respect and esteem, but to the deepest gratitude as well, of every true patriot in the land. The man who, for a principle, risks life and limb, can hold his head high among the proudest of his fellow men. Hon. J. G. Bleakney has attained this proud distinction, he battled bravely for the preservation of this union, and now that the war is over, he can have the satisfaction of knowing that he lives in the esteem of his countrymen.

He was born in Indiana county, Penn., in the year 1832. Received a limited education, and passed his younger years on a farm. He afterwards learned the trade of blacksmith and wagonmaker, and in 1856 removed to Illinois, where he settled in Henry county, and farmed until the breaking out of the civil war. At that trying period, when the union called on her faithful sons to preserve her inviolable, young John, on April 17, 1861, enlisted in company D, Twelfth Infantry Illinois Volunteers, in which company he served till August, 1861, when he was mustered out at Cairo, Illinois, and on the same day re-enlisted in the 19th regiment Illinois Volunteers. His regiment was assigned to a place in the army of the Cumberland, and he passed through the various battles from Cairo to Atlanta, under General Thomas. He was again mustered out on August 24, 1864, having passed through thirteen of the hardest fought battles of the war. He immediately returned to his home in Illinois, and took up once more the rusty plowshare. He was married to Miss Mattie Bellows January 1, 1865. In 1867 he removed to Jasper county, Iowa, where he farmed until 1870, when he, with his family, came to Oregon and settled in Marion county, where he has since lived. He has been a staunch Republican ever since the birth of that party, having voted for J. C. Fremont in 1856, and has been honored himself with several offi3es by the people in the different States in which he has resided. Although there was a break in the ranks of the Republican party at last election, Mr. Bleakney was elected by a handsome majority. He is a member of Committees on Claims and several special committees. He has always been an ardent temperance man, and active member of the Good Templars for sixteen years. He is also a respected member of order of Odd Fellows.

HON. BENJAMIN F. NICHOLS.

It would be base ingratitude were I not to make brief mention of this excellent gentleman. A tall, commanding-looking man, with long and silky hair and whiskers, as black as jet, a clear blue eye, prominent nose, fine shoulders, magnificent physique and easy carriage--he walks along the streets of Salem as erect as an arrow, this good-natured, generous, mirthful man of fifty-seven summers. He was born in Clay county, Missouri, in 1825. He received the education awarded by the common schools of Clay county. When yet a boy, he worked on a farm in Northwestern Missouri, and after his day's work was finished he would get his book, seat himself by the fireplace and study hard until the clock announced the hour of bed time. In this way young Benjamin obtained a store of practical knowledge that fitted him for the responsible positions he has been called upon to fill in after life, and the duties of which he has discharged in a way that reflected credit upon himself and made for him a large circle of steadfast friends. He came to Oregon in 1844, and wintered at Dr. Whitman's station, near Walla Walla, the next year moving to Oregon City, where he remained three or four months, and in 1845 went to Dallas, where he resided until 1877, most of which time he spent in farming. He was the first sheriff of that place under the provisional government, and afterwards, when the territorial government was organized, he was re-elected sheriff, which office he held four years. After Oregon was admitted as a State, he was elected county clerk of Polk county, which office he held one term, meantime studying law and becoming an attorney. In 1877 he moved to Wasco county, from which place he was sent as a Representative to the present Legislature. During the present exciting senatorial election, it was sought to attempt to secure his vote for a certain candidate by the promise of a large amount of money, but the great heart of the man throbbed with indignation, and he forthwith made public the base proceeding, and, after an examination and investigation before a special committee appointed by the House, his course was commended as that of a high-minded and honorable gentleman. Mr. Nichols was married in 1850 to Miss Sarah Ann Gilliam. He is at present a practicing attorney in Prineville.

HON. FRANK A. STEWART.

Whatever of praise may be due to the man who has, with the advantages of a collegiate education and abundant leisure for after study, risen to a position of honor and trust in the government of the country, we must record still greater meed of praise to the youth, who, without those advantages, has struggled with the waves of adversity, and, by sheer force of ambition and native integrity, has attained an education and elevated himself into a position of honor by the suffrages of his fellow citizens. The former is entitled to commendation for the ripened culture of the mind, while on the latter we must bestow the praise due to force of character and singleness of purpose. The Hon. Frank A. Stewart started in life without any of these advantages. He is indebted to no man for the mental gifts which he possesses, and the degree of erudition to which he has attained. He is a plain-spoken man, thoroughly independent and honest in his dealings with his fellow man. Frank was born in Cass county, Illinois, in 1843, and emigrated to Oregon with his parents in 1854, and in that same year was left an orphan by the death of his mother. He resided from 1855 to 1858 with W. C Brown at Dallas, Polk county. He was educated at Belpassi, Marion county, and after going through the course of instruction in the schools, became a professional teacher, which calling he followed for several years. He went to Curry county in 1866, and has resided there ever since. He was for ten years a merchant at Ellensburg, during which time he established a reputation for probity and good character unblemished. During his varied career in Oregon, Mr. Stewart has also been engaged in salmon fishing, mining, lumbering, etc. He has also been a contributor to many of our leading journals, and his articles and poems have been very widely copied. At present he is residing on a stock farm at his home in Curry county, and is engaged in the occupation of stock-raising and mining.

Distinguished Men.

JAMES BOYCE MONTGOMERY

Of Portland, Oregon, was born at Montgomery's Ferry, on the Susquehanna, twenty-five miles above Harrisburg, the capital of Pennsylvania, on the 6th of December, 1832. His educational training was conducted under the supervision of his uncle, Henry C. Moorhead, a lawyer of eminence and learning, until James was sixteen years of age. He was then sent to Philadelphia to learn the "art preservative of all arts," and remained in the office of the "Evening Bulletin" three years on the case and as proof reader. In the year 1853 he was tendered the position of associate editor of the Sandusky (Ohio) "Daily Register" by Gov. Henry D. Cooke. Young Montgomery was then but twenty years of age, and he discharged his duties in such a manner that in the following year he was afforded a much better opportunity for the display of his ability as a journalist, he then becoming one of the editors and proprietors of the Pittsburgh "Morning Post." He retained his connection with this paper for three years, and in 1857 disposed of his interest to Gen. James P. Barr, who is still the sole proprietor. Just about this time Col. John W. Forney started the Philadelphia "Press," and he secured the services of Mr. Montgomery as the Harrisburg correspondent of that paper, a position which he accepted for one year. In 1858 Mr. Montgomery threw aside his pen and sought a new and widely different field for his energies. It was about this time that railroad construction became a profession with many men whose strength of will, self-confidence and equanimity of purpose enabled them to overcome what appeared to others to be insurmountable obstacles. Mr. Montgomery, having determined to try this line of business, with that cool deliberation characteristic of the man of iron will, went straight ahead, and in the same year secured, together with two other gentlemen, a contract to build a bridge across the Susquehannah river at Linden, Penn., for the Philadelphia and Erie Railroad Company. The contract was completed most successfully, and he afterwards helped to finish other portions of the same road, becoming one of its directors in 1866 and remaining as such until the latter portion of 1869. Mr. Montgomery was awarded the contract to build the Bedford and Hopewell railroad in 1859, and in 1861, in connection with Captain Wm. Lowther, of Newport, Pennsylvania, he undertook to build the Nesquehoning Valley railroad, but the breaking out of the great rebellion necessitated a suspension of work for the time, and he afterwards helped to complete the road in 1868-9. In 1866 he built the wire bridge, 1,000 feet long, across the Susquehanna river, at Williamsport, Pennsylvania. Mr. Montgomery came to the Pacific coast in 1870 and to Portland in 1871. Immediately on his arrival he offered to build the first twenty-five miles of the Pacific division of the Northern Pacific railroad, and being the lowest of sixteen bidders, the contract was awarded to him. He subsequently built fifty miles additional of the same road, and also the drawbridge across the Willamette at Harrisburg, Oregon, for the Oregon and California railroad. Mr. Montgomery was also one of the owners of the charter of the Baltimore and Potomac railroad, and in connection with Thomas A. Scott, George W. Cass, Joseph D. Potts and J. Donald Cameron, succeeded in making arrangements for the completion of this most important highway between Baltimore and Washington City, and in 1866 and 1867 he was interested with Shoemaker, Miller & Co. in the completion of 400 miles of the Kansas-Pacific railroad extending into Denver. As an instance of Mr. Montgomery's energetic character and as an illustration of his enterprise, it will not be out of place to mention the following incident: In 1879 he went to Great Britain for the purpose of organizing the Oregonian Railway Company (Limited), which built and acquired 163 miles of railroad in Willamette valley, and of which he himself constructed seventy-eight miles, and in which he is the largest stockholder. On his trip across the ocean Mr. Montgomery formed the acquaintance on board the steamer Bothnia of Captain Gilmore. Captain Gilmore informed Mr. Montgomery that he was on his way to Cardiff to bring out the ship Edwin Reed, which was laden with railroad material destined for Portland, Oregon. Mr. Montgomery told Captain Gilmore that he himself was on the way to England for the purpose of organizing a company to construct a railroad in the Willamette valley. When Mr. Montgomery arrived in Great Britain he succeeded in organizing the company, and then proceeded to Stockton-on-the-Tees and contracted for the manufacture of rails, and then went to London and chartered ships, which sailed six weeks after the departure of the Edwin Reed, Captain Gilmore. Mr. Montgomery left by steamer for New York, bought in Philadelphia and Pittsburgh the necessary cars and locomotives for the road, which were shipped overland, and then started for Oregon. On arriving he immediately put surveyors in the field and proceeded to the construction of the road. When Captain Gilmore arrived some time after he sought an interview with Mr. Montgomery, and to his surprise learned that not only had Mr. Montgomery's material arrived, but that fifty miles of the track had already been laid. Although this feat of rapid railroad construction may seem somewhat remarkable to the reader, it is only fair to say of Captain Gilmore that his ship's cargo had shifted and he was compelled to put into Rio for the purpose of rearranging it. In the year 1872, when the general government undertook the removal of obstructions in the upper Columbia—noticeably the troublesome John Day Rock, in John Day rapid, which was 170 feet long and 80 feet wide, and on which many a good steamer had been wrecked it was Mr. Montgomery who received the contract to perform the difficult work. The operation was a dangerous one much more so than that of the celebrated Blossom Rock in San Francisco harbor, which received such world-wide comment, and the work was accomplished without the loss of a single life and so successfully that Mr. Montgomery received many other contracts for the removal of smaller obstructions in the rapids of the Snake and Columbia rivers. Of the enterprises in which Mr. M. has been lately engaged, the building of Montgomery warehouse at Albina, which is the largest private dock in Portland, is probably the most important. In the year 1861 Mr. Montgomery was married to Miss Rachel Anthony, daughter of Hon. Joseph B. Anthony, of Lycoming county, Pennsylvania. This lady died in 1863, leaving one son; he was again married in 1866 to Miss Mary Phelps, only daughter of Gov. John S. Phelps, of Missouri. In politics, although Mr. Montgomery is a staunch Republican, he has never held public office. He was elected a delegate from Lycoming to represent the Republicans of that county in the Pennsylvania Republican State Convention in the years 1866, 1867 and 1868. In 1866 he was on the Committee on Resolutions, and together with Thadeus Stevens, Wayne MacVeagh and others, reported a resolution recommending the nomination of Ulysses S. Grant for President. This was the first State Convention that presented the name of that illustrious soldier for the position of Chief Magistrate of the Republic. Now, patient reader, in closing this brief biography of a gentleman of whom we would be pleased to write a volume, we would simply say that we have not, even in what we have written, been able to do him half justice. He is sedulously reticent as to his personal history, his many successes and his brilliant associations, hence the few facts which we have been able to gather regarding him are to us a small portion of the open record, and while it would afford us great pleasure, and we entertain the hope that we may some time be able, to do Mr. Montgomery justice in a more complete biography, we must for the present remain satisfied in presenting this very incomplete sketch.

HON. ASAHEL BUSH.

The name that heads this sketch is one well known throughout Oregon. He who bears it is now well nigh three score years of age, but he apperrs much younger and is possessed of a greater degree of vim and energy than is ordinarily displayed by men of younger years. His career has, indeed, been an interesting one, and to enumerate even the more prominent events of his life, and to do justice to his energy and enterprise in one brief sketch would be impossible, as it would occupy more space than we can spare in our little volume. Mr. Bush was born in Hampden county, Mass., in 1824, and received an academic course of instruction in the institution of learning in his native village. About 1840 he went to Saratoga Springs, New York, and commenced learning the printer's trade, serving a regular three years' apprenticeship in the "Sentinel" office of that city. He held a case on the State work in Albany in 1845, and in his day was considered an expert and remarkably correct compositor. He returned to his native town in 1846 and commenced reading law, studying leisurely until June, 1850, when he was admitted to the bar at Springfield. During the time he was studying law, he for nearly two years edited a weekly paper in the village, and was, for some time, town clerk, a position of much honor and distinction in that early day, when the citizens of a town or borough in mass-meeting assembled made the laws that governed them. He took the western fever in 1850 and started for Oregon, reaching Portland in September of the same year, and in the spring of 1851 issued the first copy of the Oregon "Statesman" at Oregon City. It was not until 1853 that the paper was moved to Salem, and Mr. Bush continued as its editor until 1860. As a journalist, Mr. Bush has few equals and no superiors on the northwest coast. His editorials were extensively copied, and wielded a powerful influence, and are often quoted even at this late day. He was a pungent writer, indulging freely in cutting sarcasm and criticism, and the paper was largely sought after and of great political influence while under his editorial management. He was Chief Clerk of the House of Representatives in the session of 1850-1, which was held in Oregon City, and was Territorial Printer from 1851 to 1859, at which time Oregon was admitted to the Union, and State Printer from that time until 1863. In this office Mr. Bush, by careful management, succeeded in saving some money, with which, after disposing of the "Statesman," he became a silent partner in the merchandising establishment of L. Heath & Co., at Salem. In 1868 he associated himself with Hon. W. S. Ladd, of Portland, and established the banking house of Ladd & Bush, with which he is still connected, and of which he is the resident manager. He is also President of the Salem Flouring Mills Company and the Oregon City Flouring Mills Company, both of which are important business enterprises in our midst. As a financier, Mr. Bush is considered very successful, and understands thoroughly the art of making money. He is gifted with an active mind and unusual power of forethought. He is quick to detect an advantage, and, while willing to indulge in risks to a certain degree, is nevertheless endowed with sufficient cautionary faculties to insure him against serious loss in any business transaction. He is apt to want his own, and has his enemies as a natural consequence, but he fears no man, and is considered strictly honest and honorable in his transactions. When properly approached, Mr. Bush is liberal hearted and gives freely of his abundance. He is somewhat peculiar, however, and is strong in his likes and dislikes. He never forgets a friend and rarely forgives one who has knowingly and purposely done him an injury. He has done much towards improving Salem, and when not directly opposed to his business interests, he never refuses to contribute to its advancement. He is by some considered cold and austere, but what little he possesses of these traits were born and bred in him, as he is not given to affectation. His life has not been all sunshine by any means, and during late years he has been more or less wrapped up in his own family. He has a warm heart, however, for those who reach it, and those who know him are enthusiastic in his praise. His enemies, and he who has no enemies does not amount to much, can never harm him. He is impregnable to their abuse and cares less for it than do his friends, who oft times realize the abuse is unjust and unmerited. He is rather tall, of light build, a quick, nervous disposition, a glittering eye, which, at times, fairly twinkles with merriment, for he appreciates a joke most thoroughly, bristling brown hair, deeply tinged with gray, and full chin whiskers and short mustache. His life is more or less seclusive, although his intimate friends will ever find a cordial reception at his home, and as a host Mr. Bush has few superiors. His wife having died in 1863, the care of his home falls upon his daughter. Before closing this sketch we would do him an injustice were we to omit mention of his successful incumbency of the office of Superintendent of the Oregon Penitentiary during the past four years, under appointment of Gov. Thayer. His supervision of the institution has been marked with a spirit of economy rarely evinced in the management of public institutions. His first two years' services were donated to the State, and at his own request the salary for the ensuing two years was reduced from $1,800 to $800 per annum. In all matters of public or private life Mr. Bush has won the confidence and esteem of all who know him, and by his integrity in business matters he will continue to hold the same as long as he may remain among us.

GEORGE C. SEARS.

The present efficient Sheriff of Multnomah county, is a man who stands high among his constituents and is the fortunate possessor of a host of warm personal friends, who in their admiration of his numerous sterling qualities would make almost any sacrifice to enhance his success. He was born within the rock-bound borders of the Granite State, Vermont, near Richford, in the year 1842. His father, Hon. Alden Sears, was a prominent man in the political and trade circles of Northern Vermont. He emigrated with his family to California in 1850. George struck out for himself at an early age, clerking in various stores in Columbia, California, until he was about seventeen years of age, when he accumulated his savings and with them paid his college expenses during a four-years' course at Oakland. At the breaking out of the civil war in 1861 Mr. Sears enlisted and served until the close of the war and was mustered out of service with the rank of a First Lieutenant. He afterwards engaged in the mercantile business in Contra Costa county, California, under the firm name of Penneman & Sears, where they transacted a heavy business for several years. He disposed of his interest in that business and moved to Santa Cruz, where he erected a saw-mill and conducted the same for a few years, when he sold out and engaged in the cattle business, which he carried on extensively. Owing to a heavy and long-continued drouth he disposed of his stock and came to Oregon and located in Portland, purchasing a half interest in C. M. Martin's grocery establishment, in which business he continued about two years. He then bought the Dexter Livery Stable and continued in that business until he was elected Assessor in 1878. In this position he gained many warm friends and made some bitter enemies, owing to his unswerving fairness in assessing property, which duty he performed without fear or favor, with an honesty of purpose that gained him hosts of enthusiastic admirers. As a recognition of his services he was unanimously renominated and was reelected by the largest majority any candidate ever received prior to that date in Multnomah county, leading his ticket by several hundred votes. In 1882 he was elected Sheriff of that county by nearly one thousand majority, the largest by far that any candidate for Sheriff had ever received in that county. He is discharging the duties of that office with his characteristic energy and ability, and in his prompt execution of the law is meeting with the approbation of all good citizens. Mr. Sears is a member of nearly all the secret benevolent organizations, and has held high offices in all of them. He was the Freat Sachem of the Improved Order of Red Men of the State of Oregon; Secretary of Harmony Lodge of Masons, and is at this time Post Commander of George Wright Post No. 1, Grand Army of the Republic; D. D. Grand Chancelor Knights of Pythias; Treasurer of Mount Hood A. O. O. Forresters; Treasurer of the Portland Fire Department; President of Tiger Engine Company No. 5, and a member of the Board of Portland Fire Delegates. At the time of the last Indian war in Eastern Oregon, when the call was made for volunteers, Mr. Sears enlisted a company of one hundred men and was elected captain. Governor Chadwick accepted his company and ordered them to the field, but owing to the Government being unable to furnish arms for the men they could not be used, but they certainly deserve the same credit that they would had they gone, as they showed themselves ready and willing to do all in their power to assist the people in their great distress. As a politician he is, from his having so many personal friends, a very strong man in his party, is a good political manager, an honorable politician, and we can truly say that George C. Sears, as a politician or a social friend, is a man whom any person might well be proud to claim. He is a fine-looking gentleman, of a little more than ordinary height, well proportioned, with pleasant features. He wears a full beard and mustache of light brown, and his large eyes of brown beam kindly on all with whom he comes in contact. He is a hail fellow well met, and is the very personification of geniality and good humor. He is noted for his liberality, and his purse-strings are always loosened when an appeal reaches him from a worthy source. He was married in 1864 to Miss Jennie M. Aldrich, of Oakland, California, their family consisting of three girls and one boy. With Mr. Sears' well established personal popularity, and the esteem in which he is held by constituents who are not even acquainted with him, but who have full confidence in his official integrity and efficiency, it is difficult to form even a prophesy as to the probable brilliancy of his future career.

HON. LOYAL B. STEARNS,

Now County Judge of Multnomah county, is another one of our young men whom by rights should be classed among the earlier Oregonians, having arrived here in 1853, the year of his birth, which important event in his life took place at Keene, N. H., in May of that year. Arriving in Oregon, his parents settled near Scottsburg, where they still reside. The subject of our sketch attended the public schools of that section of the country until 1868-9, when he attended the Umpqua Academy, and in 1871-2 he was a student at the Bishop Scott Grammar School in Portland. During the years 1872-3 he studied medicine under Dr. W. H. Watkins of Portland, and attended one course of lectures at the Willamette University of Salem. He abandoned the study of medicine, however, and in 1873 commenced reading law under ex-Governor A. C. Gibbs, and was admitted to the bar of the Supreme Court in December, 1876, and afterwards went into partnership with Governor Gibbs, remaining with him about a year. He then opened an office and practiced alone for about a year, and in January, 1879, he was appointed Police Judge of the city of Portland, and having been re-elected he held that responsible position for some three years and a half. In the discharge of his official duties in that capacity he never failed to give satisfaction to all lovers of law and order, while at the same time it cannot be said that he failed to temper justice with mercy. He was prompt and efficient on the bench, and added dignity and precision to the sessions of a court wherein some of our most hardened criminals are arraigned and examined prior to their appearance in the courts above. His re-election was a flattering endorsement of his official acts as Police Judge, and while serving in that capacity he won the admiration and esteem of not only the members of the bar, but of the public generally, who felt a great degree of confidence and security in the integrity and faithfulness of the judicial officer who first presided over the trials of the desperadoes, then so numerous in that city. Upon his resignation at the close of his term he was elected City Attorney, which position he filled until June, 1882, when he was elected County Judge of Multnomah county, which important position he still occupies and is filling in a matter highly satisfactory to the tax-payers of that county, observing the established rules of economy without practicing those little schemes of parsimony so prevelent on this coast in county affairs. In 1878 Judge Stearns was elected a member of the House from Multnomah county, and as such served his constituency faithfully, watching carefully the interests of Multnomah county and the State at large. He served on several of the most important committees and proved an important factor in that organization. He is a well-built and well-preserved, rather short and heavy built, with features of a pleasant cast, a winning smile, expansive forehead, heavy mustache and brown hair. He is at present unmarried, but with him it is a case of "Barkis is willin'," and he is considered a ladies' man.

GEORGE H. HIMES,

Oldest son of Tyrus and Emeline Himes, whose progenitors were Puritans, coming from England to America in about 1670, and oldest of eight children, was born in Troy, Bradford county, Pa., May 18, 1844, and removed with his parents to Lafayette, Stark county, Illinois, in May, 1847. Began school in same town at age of five, continued three to six months a year until March 21, 1853, when with parents he began the journey across the plains. Walked most of the way. Reached destination, Olympia, Washington Territory, October 21, 1853, by the way of Nachess pass, leaving the old emigrant road at or near the present town of Pendleton a perilous journey, full of narrow escapes from floods, starvation and Indians. Attended three months country school taught by a "boarding-around" school master, each year from 1854 to 1858. In October 1855, with his parents was compelled to flee from home on account of Indians, and remain in forts until late in the fall of 1856. Stood guard many times, and though youthful, felt himself to be a valiant home guard. He spent the remainder of the time at various farm occupations, such as chopping, rail splitting, ditching, plowing, harvesting, etc. especial choice of work chopping until June 10, 1861. Then he began learning the printing trade in Olympia, W. T., in the office of the Washington "Standard," John Miller Murphy editor and proprietor. Remained in that office until March 10, 1864, when he practically left home for the first time, and started March 11 for Portland, Oregon, arriving March 12. Inasmuch as he felt that all moneys earned during his minority belonged rightfully to his parents, especially as they had hard struggles, owing to misfortunes on the plains, and afterwards loss of property by Indians, upon arriving in Portland he had $2 in his pocket. On March 13th he began work as compositor on the Daily Morning "Oregonian," continuing there until September 20, 1864, when the proprietor of the "Oregonian," then State Printer, telegraphed him to go to the capital. Here he remained employed on State work until the Legislature adjourned. He then resumed labor on the Daily "Oregonian," and continued until June 3, 1865. On June 26, same year, being tired of monotonous round of duties belonging to the life of a compositor on a morning newspaper, he apprenticed himself to W. D. Carter, a job printer, for one year, at the expiration of which time he emerged a full-fledged journeyman job printer, and continued in Carter's employ until October 5, 1868. He then formed a partnership with his employer to carry on the job printing business. He remained in partnership until April, 1870, since which time he has conducted the business alone. He published a small four-page paper in 1869 for about four months called the "News Budget." It not proving a financial success it was abandoned. In June, 1873, he bought the "Commercial Reporter," published it for seven months and sold it, not having the necessary time to devote to it, owing to the demands of his jobbing business upon him in that respect. He was one of the proprietors of the Daily "Bee," which began its career in November, 1875, and remained so connected for one year. Not having full control of the paper he withdrew from it, and since has had no interest in newspapers. Brought the second cylinder press to the State in 1871, that of the Daily "Oregonian" being the first, and was the first in Oregon to use steam in driving job printing machinery. Has always kept rather in advance of the times in providing himself with facilities for doing the best grades of job printing, and now has twenty-five employes on his weekly pay roll. Has published numerous books on his own account, the ninth volume of Reports of the Oregon Supreme Court being the largest and most important. At the age of twenty-two years and seven months, he was married to Miss Anna F. Riggs, youngest daughter of D. L. Rigg, of Salem, Oregon, by Rev. O. Dickinson, on December 24, 1866. She was born in New Haven, Connecticut. She, also, descended from Puritan stock. At the age of fourteen he united with the what is known as the Christian or Disciple church. Internal discussions, caused by political differences, destroyed the organization in 1863. In March, 1867, he and his wife became members of the First Congregational Church in Portland, Oregon. He held the offices of Deacon and Clerk in that organization for many years, and delegate to the State Association and Assistant Clerk for six years. Was made a Mason by Harmony Lodge No. 12, Portland, Oregon, in February, 1867, and has held the office of Secretary for two years. Holds membership in other organizations, Odd Fellows, Workmen, Knights of Honor, and has served as Secretary for many terms. Has decided views upon all leading questions of the day, being an ardent Republican; has never sought political preferment but once, and that was the position of State Printer in 1878. While he had a strong support, he had not votes enough to secure nomination, and caused his followers, after the second ballot, to throw their votes for W. B. Carter, who was nominated and elected. Has been appointed by the Governor State printing expert twice, in 1879 and 1882. Mr. Himes' job printing establishment in this city is a very extensive one, and he has, by the correctness, dispatch and artistic appearance of all work done, acquired the name of being "the" printer of Portland. Personally, George is a fine-looking man, with just a tinge of pale delicacy in his complexion, caused, no doubt, by his constant application to business; is popular among the printers and enjoys the esteem of a very large circle of warm personal friends.

WILLIAM S. JAMES,

Of the Columbia Commercial College, Portland. This gentleman was born in Lee county, Iowa, August 3, 1843, and after attending school for a few years, entered a printing office at Albany, Gentry county, Missouri, where he served a regular apprenticeship and came out a thorough mechanic. In the year 1860 young James came to the Pacific Coast, and in 1864, during the civil war, he joined Company I, Sixth Regiment Infantry, famous California volunteers, in which command he served with distinction to the end of the war. Mr. James came to Oregon in the fall of 1867, and his first situation was foremanship on the Corvallis "Gazette." Having by attentive study and assiduous application obtained a thorough commercial education, and became an artistic penman, Mr. James gave most of his attention to self-cultivation and instruction of these studies, working at printing as a means of obtaining the funds necessary to perfect himself, and he soon acquired quite a reputation as a master and became generally known. Since that time Mr. James has been connected with the foremost institutions of this State, and he was the first gentleman to inaugurate the Commercial Department of the Willamette University. The Professor was married December 29, 1869, to Miss Mary E. Bird, an estimable young lady of Portland. In the winter of 1872-'3 the Commercial College, with which he was connected, was burned to the ground and he lost all of his most valuable specimens of penmanship. Misfortunes seemed to follow, and in the following year Mrs. James was called away from earth. This last calamity, coming as it did when he was in the midst of other troubles, induced him to give up teaching for awhile. He was then offered the control of the Baker City "Herald," and he retained the management of that journal from October, 1874, until October, 1875, and met with unqualified success. Although in politics Mr. James was a Republican, on account of his liberal views on all questions of general interest, his paper received an equal amount of Democratic support. After this he was one of the incorporators of the Portland "Bee," with which paper he was connected for a year or more. Like many other new enterprises, this venture did not promise brilliant success, and he finally drifted back into his profession of teaching, for which he seemed so eminently well fitted, and in the year 1881 founded the well-known Columbia Commercial College of Portland. Professor James has made this institution a success from the very beginning, and to-day it occupies the foremost position among the commercial institutions of the Northwest. The system of studies is so well arranged, and the method of teaching so thorough, that it affords the most superior advantages for imparting to young men and ladies a commercial education, and, more than this, Mr. James has the esteem and confidence of the business community, a matter which is of no small advantage to his pupils. He is a member of the I. O. O. F., K. of P., I. O. G. T. and P. O. S. of A., and a past officer in each. He served as Grand Secretary of the I. O. G. T. for two years, and has always been a strong advocate of the temperance cause.

J B. CONGLE

Is one of the solid business men of Portland, and has by close application to business, and by some judicious investments in real estate, amassed quite a respectable fortune. He was born December 9, 1817, in Chester county, Penn. In the year 1832 he went to Philadelphia to learn the harness and saddlery trade with Mr. William S. Hansel, and in the spring of 1838 he removed to Virginia, thence to Missouri, and in the year 1841 we find him in Lafayette, Indiana, where he resided for ten years. On May 21st, 1844, Mr. Congle was married to Miss Ellen H. Gray, a young lady of Lafayette. Catching the gold fever, he went to California in the "days of '49," remaining two years in the gold mines and returning to Indiana in 1851. He came to Oregon in 1853 and located in Corvallis, then Marysville, head of navigation on Willamette river, no boats going further up the river, where he lived eight years and of which town he was the first Mayor. He was elected Sheriff of Benton county in 1857, a position he held three months and then resigned. In 1861 Mr. Congle changed his residence to Portland, and has since continued to live here. He was elected Councilman from the Second Ward in 1870, and in 1872 he was elected a Representative from Multnomah county to the State Legislature. He became a member of the Masonic order in Indiana in 1847, and in the years 1874-5 was Grand Master of that order in Oregon; in 1879 '80 he was Grand H. P. of the same order. Mr. Congle is a married man, and has a wife and two daughters, one of whom is the wife of Hon. Richard Williams, ex-member of Congress, and the other Mrs. J. B. Wyatt. It will be seen that Mr. Congle has lived in Portland twenty-one years, that he has been honored time and again with public office, that he is a member of the most respected private organization and a successful business man. He is at present the senior partner of the firm of J. B. Congle & Co., manufacturers and importers of saddlery hardware, etc.

LIEUT. FREDERICK SCHWATKA, U. S. A.

Here we have another young man who enjoys a national reputation and who, from his long residence in Oregon and the interest Oregonians have taken in his success, ought by rights to be claimed by us as a native Webfoot, although circumstances are against us. He was born in Galena, Illinois, September 29, 1849, and with his parents, both of whom are still residents of Salem, immigrated to Oregon in 1853. It will therefore be seen that the Lieutenant is not Sucker enough to hurt him much. His early life was spent at Astoria, Albany, Eugene City and Salem, mostly at the latter point, with the early history of which he was more or less intimately connected, his boyish pranks being still recounted with interest by those who participated in them, he being the acknowledged leader. He was naturally bright and intelligent, attracted the attention of Salem's best citizens, and when he expressed a desire to attend West Point Military Academy he had no difficulty in securing a powerful influence to back him and was fortunate enough to secure the Oregon appointment through Hon. J. H. D. Henderson, their own Representative in Congress. He joined that institution in June, 1867, having passed a successful examination and continued his studies unremittingly until 1871, when he graduated and was assigned to active service as Second Lieutenant in the Third U. S. Cavalry, then serving in Arizona. He was afterwards transferred to the Department of the Platte. He meanwhile turned his attention to the study of law and was admitted to the U. S. Circuit Court for the District of Nebraska, in May 5, 1875. He then studied medicine and surgery and graduated at the Bellevue Hospital Medical College, in New York, March 1, 1876. Rejoining his regiment he served in the Sioux war of 1876, participating in the actions of Tongue River (June 9, 1876), the Rosebud (June 17, 1876,) and Slim Buttes (Sept. 9, 1876). As a soldier, his record for gallantry and bravery is excelled by none, and as a commanding officer he has always succeeded in winning the confidence and esteem of those under him. Long and active service in the very outskirts of civilization imbued him with an ambition to distinguish himself in new fields of labor, and at his own request was detailed to command the Franklin Search Party in the Arctic ocean, in which he was employed from June 19, 1878, to September 22, 1880, the object of the expedition being to find the records and relics and determine the fate of the British Northwest Passage Expedition of Sir John Franklin, which sailed from England in the "Erebos" and "Terror" in 1875, and of which but very little had ever been ascertained. The expedition under Lieut. Schwatka's command, made the longest sledge journey in the world, a distance of 3,251 miles, being absent from its source of supplies eleven months and twenty days, subsisting off of the game of the country, the trip having been undertaken with but one month's rations provided, the party living on the same food as did their Esquimaux allies and guides. It encountered the lowest temperature ever recorded by white men, viz.: 71 degrees Fahrenheit or 103 degrees below freezing point. It discovered and buried many of the skeletons of Sir John Franklin's lost party, secured numerous relics, and otherwise cleared away much of the mystery connected with that ill-fated expedition. On March 20, 1879, Lieut. Schwatka was promoted to a first lieutenancy in the Third

Cavalry, and in October, 1881, was appointed Aid-de-Camp on the staff of General Nelson A. Miles, commanding the Department of the Columbia, and is at present stationed at Fort Vancouver on that duty. He has received numberless honorary distinctions since his return from the North, and is at present corresponding member of many European and American Scientific especially geographical—societies, and has by special request delivered lectures in many of the principal cities of the East. The Lieutenant is a very ordinary looking person, being of about regulation height, heavy built, with full ruddy face, indicative of good health and a hearty, robust constitution, smooth face, with the exception of a short mustache, a keen eye, its effect enforced by the use of glasses, prominent nose and an intellectual forehead. His disposition is genial and his character among men unsullied. He was married September 6, 1882, to Miss Ada J. Brackett.

S. E. JOSEPHI, M. D.,

A resident of East Portland and a gentleman well and favorably known by reason of his long continued connection with the Oregon Hospital for the Insane, was born in New York City, December 3, 1849, where he received his early education, entering the Free Academy, now known as the New York College, in 1863. Possessing a desire to establish himself in some new country and avail himself of the advantages to be derived from growing up with it, in 1866 came west and stopped for a short time in San Francisco, and the year following pressed on towards Oregon and at once entered in the employ of Dr. J. C. Hawthorne as book-keeper at the Hospital for the Insane at East Portland, and at the same time studied medicine in the institution and prepared himself for entering medical college. In 1869 he returned to New York with the intention of so doing, but adverse circumstances prevailed and he again returned to Oregon and entered the employ of Stephens & Loryea, bankers, and renewed his connection with the asylum. By judicious management and strict economy he succeeded in saving sufficient from his earnings to support his family while absent and pay his expenses through college. He at once resumed the study of medicine and finally graduated at the Medical Department of the University of California in 1877. In November of that year he was appointed Assistant Physician to the Oregon Hospital for the Insane, under the Superintendency of the late Dr. J. C. Hawthorne, and upon his death was appointed Superintendent of that institution, which position he still occupies. In 1879 he was elected to the Chair of Psychological Medicine in the medical department of the Willamette University at Portland, and in 1880 to the Chair of Anatomy in the same college. He is also a member of the Oregon Medical Society and of the American Association of Medical Superintendents. He is an honored member of the Orient Lodge No. 17, I. O. O.F., which he has represented in the Grand Lodge of Oregon several terms. He was married in 1871 to Miss Hannah M. Stone, of Portland, and they have four children living. Dr. Josephi is what we call a good-looking man. He is of about ordinary height, of graceful form and figure, jet black hair and whiskers, with a mild brown eye, pleasant voice and suave manner, a good talker, intelligent, with quick perceptive faculties, always faultlessly dressed, and every inch a gentleman. He is a keen business man and guards with zealous care the interests of those he represents. His genial disposition makes him friends everywhere, and it is a safe prediction when we say that he has just caught a glimpse of what Dame Fortune has in store for him when in due time she deals out her favors.

HON. JAMES C. FULLERTON.

One of the representative men of Southern Oregon, was born in Butler county, Ohio, December 16, 1818, coming to Oregon with his parents in 1853 and locating on a farm in the Umpqua valley. He was favored only with a common school education. He read law and was admitted to the bar in 1881. In 1873 he was appointed Receiver of Public Moneys at Roseburg, the duties of which office he has discharged with such unswerving integrity that he has had no difficulty in retaining his position up to the present time. As a public officer he has proved courteous and accommodating, and has made friends with the patrons of the place. He was married in 1874 to Miss Clara Bunnell of Roseburg, their family consisting of one child. He is a prominent member of the A. F. and A. M., Odd Fellows and Workmen. In the former fraternity he holds the position of G. J. W. of the R. W. G. L. He is tall and slim and quite good-looking, light brown hair, straight and pliable, with a light blonde mustache. His personal appearance is on the whole quite prepossessing.

HON. JAMES K. KELLY.

The subject of this sketch has held most of the places of honor and trust at the disposal of the people of this State, and now that old age is creeping on it is befitting that he be relieved of the irksome duties of public life and devote his entire attention to the practice of the high and and honorable profession in which he occupies so prominent a position. He was born in Center county, Penn., in 1819, and until he attained the age of sixteen years his life was spent upon a farm. He entered Princeton College, New Jersey, in 1837, and graduated in 1839, soon afterwards commencing the study of law at Carlisle Law School in Pennsylvania under Judge Reed, and was admitted to the bar in 1842. He opened an office in Lewiston, Penn., where he remained until 1849, when he started for California via Mexico. He remained in the mines for a short time and came to Oregon in 1851 and settled at Oregon City. He was appointed one of the Code Commissioners in 1853, and in the same year was elected a member of the Territorial Council, of which he was a member for four years, during which time he was President of the Council two sessions. He was appointed Lieutenant-Colonel of the Volunteer Infantry in the Yakima Indian War of 1855-6. In 1857 he was elected member of the State Constitutional Convention from Clackamas county, and in 1860 was a member of the State Senate. In 1864 he was the Democratic candidate for Congress, but was defeated by Hon. J. H. D. Henderson. He was also candidate for Governor in 1866, at the time Governor Woods was elected. In 1870 he was elected United States Senator, when he served his full term. In 1878, on the formation of a separate Supreme Court, he was appointed Chief Justice, which position he held until the general election of 1880, when, although the Democratic party candidate, he suffered defeat. Since that time he has settled down to private life and enjoys a lucrative practice in his profession. He is a hard worker and has been a deep student and is thoroughly versed in law. He is tall, somewhat stoop-shouldered, wears only a mustache as a facial ornament, his eyes are set well back in his head, and he has a broad, expansive forehead.

ADDISON C. GIBBS, L. L. D.,

Ex-Governor of Oregon, was born at East Otto, Cattaraugus county, New York, July 9, 1825. He was educated at Griffith Institute in Springville, New York, and at the Albany, New York, State Normal school, of which he is a graduate. He spent several years as a teacher, during which time he studied law, and was admitted to practice in the highest courts of New York at Albany in 1849. Since that time he has been admitted to practice in the Supreme Court of the United States. He practiced law in Jefferson county, New York, for one year and came to Oregon in 1850, which has been his home ever since. In 1851 he was a volunteer under Major Kearney in the first Indian war in Southern Oregon. He took a land claim in Umpqua (now Douglas) county, on which now stands the town of Gardiner, where he resided for over four years. In the winter of 1851-2 he was a member of the House of Representatives, and took an active part in having the Code system of practice and pleadings adopted, he being the only lawyer in the Legislature who had practiced under the Code. He was nominated as one of the first Code Commissioners but declined to serve. He was also selected and served as one of the Code Commissioners of the second revision in 1853. He was then offered the position of Collector of Customs for the Southern District of Oregon, a position he desired, provided he could be permitted to continue the practice of law. He went to Washington and got such permission on condition that he appointed a deputy at his own expense. He then filed his bond of $50,000, and was prepared to enter upon the duties of his office. Before returning to Oregon he married his school mate, Miss Margaret M. Watkins, a graduate of Griffith Institute. For a young man, Gov. Gibbs in New York took quite an active part as a member of the "Free Soil party," and cast his first vote for Martin Van Buren as President, and Charles Francis Adams, Vice-President, for whom he made a number of speeches in New York. In 1848 Gov. Gibbs was, against his wish, elected Prosecuting Attorney for the first Judicial District, for which position he did not qualify, and the vacancy was filled by appointment of the Governor. Upon the adoption of the Constitution of Oregon, he took a decided stand against slavery, and opposed it on the stump. In the fall of 1858 he moved to Portland and opened a law office in company with Ex-Attorney General George H. Williams, with whom he remained as partner for five years. Upon the breaking out of the rebellion, he took an active part in organizing the "Union Republican party" and in public speeches frequently advocated the Union cause. In 1862, unsolicited and without attending the Convention, he was nominated for Governor. Immediately upon his nomination he challenged his opponent to public disenssion, made over sixty speeches, and was elected by the largest majority of any man that has ever been elected to office in the State. He held the office for four years, the first two of which he was also Superintendent of the Penitentiary. During his administration he purchased seventy-five acres of land, including a water power, for the State, which is the present site of the Penitentiary and Insane Asylum; also located four hundred and eighty thousand acres of school lands for the State, in all of which transactions neither party has ever at any time in the least called in question the integrity and skill with which any of these acts were done. At the close of his term Gov. Gibbs received the nomination of the Republican party for United States Senator. Andrew Johnson was President and his policy conservative, and as between him and Congress Gov. Gibbs was a "Radical" under the opposition of Johnson's appointees and two rival candidates, after 19 ballots, during which time he came within one vote of an election, he did not succeed in securing it and withdrew and allowed another Republican, Hon. H. W. Corbett, to be elected. Gov. Gibbs returned to the bar and for two successive terms was elected and served as District Attorney. He has also served as U. S. Deputy District Attorney for four years, transacting all the business of the office during that time, and was also United States District Attorney for two years. During every Presidential campaign since 1860, Governor Gibbs has responded to frequent calls upon him to make stump speeches. As a speaker, he is ready, argumentative and forcible. He is a member of the Methodist Episcopal Church, and has been President of the Board of Trustees of that church in Portland for several years.

HON. P. H. D'ARCY,

Who, as a young attorney, stands in the foremost ranks of the profession in this State, was born in Brooklyn, N. Y., March 6, 1854, and with his parents came to this coast in 1856. They remained in San Francisco but about one year, and moved to Oregon in 1857 and settled in Portland. In 1859 they moved to Salem, where they have resided ever since. The subject of our sketch early made up his mind to secure an education, and appreciating the fact that he must carve his own fortune, he left no stone unturned that in any way would aid or assist him in securing the same. At the early age of twelve he commenced working at the printer's trade and served his apprenticeship in the "Statesman" office. By working nights and Saturdays he managed not only to earn means of pursuing his studies at the Willamette University, but also to assist his brother and sisters in the same laudable efforts. In 1873 he commenced reading law with Boise & Willis, and was admitted to the bar of the Supreme Court of Oregon in 1876. In 1878, when the act was passed creating a new Supreme Court, Mr. D'Arcy received the appointment of Clerk, which position he held until 1880, when a new court was elected, and, being of different politics, he was succeeded by the present incumbent, since which time he has been practicing law in Salem, and, for a young man, is succeeding admirably in securing a lucrative practice. He is a Democrat in politics, and represents Marion county in the Democratic State Central Committee. Mr. D'Arcy is destined to become an able advocate of the law. He has a ready command of speech and good rhetorical ability, and by his earnestness and force rarely fails to make a lasting impression on a jury. He is still a deep student, and when not otherwise engaged applies himself to his books. Personally his manners are pleasing and he has many warm friends.

GENERAL JOHN F. MILLER.

Prominent among the Democratic politicians of this State, and one who has served his party with earnestness and fidelity, is Gen. John F. Miller, of Salem. He has been intimately associated with the party successes of the past and is to-day an honored representative of its silent minority. His personal appearance is such as would attract the attention of any one in a crowd, being tall and commanding, with full face, free from whiskers, and a clear, penetrating eye. He was born in Hardin county, Kentucky, near the birth place of the immortal Lincoln, and received the advantages only of a common school education. He was raised on a farm, and in 1841 moved with his parents to Howard county, Missouri, where he resided until the breaking out of the Mexican war of 1846, when he enlisted as a private in the "Chihuahua Rangers," under Capt. Tom Hudson, which company was attached to Col. A. W. Donaphan's regiment. He participated in the battles of Sacramento and Brasito, and received an honorable discharge at New Orleans in June, 1848. Returning to Missouri, he was, on the 25th day of March, 1849, married to Miss Zerelda Jackson, daughter of Gov. Hancock Jackson, of that State. He came to Oregon "the plains across" in 1851 and settled in Jackson county, where he took up a donation claim. Was elected Captain of Company A, First Regiment of Volunteers under Gen. Joseph Lane. After several sharp skirmishes with the Indians at Evans creek and elsewhere, his company was ordered back on the plains to protect immigrants, making their headquarters on Lost river, among the afterwards famous Modoc tribe of Indians. He represented Jackson county in the lower House in 1853 and 1854 and was afterwards appointed Indian Agent at Grande Ronde under President Pierce, and was re-appointed by President Buchanan. Moved to Salem in 1862, and, with other capitalists, interested himself in the organization and erection of the Willamette Woolen Mills, being President of the company for two years, and closely identified with its interests for some fifteen years. He received the nomination for Governor at the hands of the Democratic State Convention in 1862, and made a stirring canvass of the State, but was defeated by the Republican, Hon. A. C. Gibbs. In the Legislature of 1866 he received his full party vote for the honorable position of United States Senator, his successful competitor being Hon. Geo. H. Williams. Was also Vice-President of Willamette Falls and Lock Company at Oregon City, and was actively interested in its construction and completion. Was appointed by the Legislature in

1870 one of the commissioners to select the 90,000-acre grant of Agricultural College lands, which were by them located in Southern Oregon. Was by Governor Grover appointed one of the Capitol Building Commissioners and was elected Chairman of the Board. It was under their supervision that by far the greater portion of the work on this building was performed, and its general character is commended by all who have given it a careful examination. During the last few years Gen. Miller has been actively engaged in the stock business, with his headquarters on the range in Lake county, his family meanwhile living on his farm near Salem. He has five children, all daughters, two of whom are married and have families of their own.

HON. JOHN BURNETT.

There are few names more familiarly and favorably known to the old residents of this State than that which heads this paragraph. He was born in Pike county, Missouri, July 4, 1831. He came to California in 1849 and engaged in mining, and in 1858 came to this State and settled in Corvallis, and in the year following was married to Miss Martha Hinton, of that place. He soon afterwards commenced reading law with Judge Kelsey, and was admitted to practice in 1860. He took an active part in raising the first company in the regiment of volunteers called for in Oregon in 1864, and in the same year entered into partnership with the late Judge Thayer in the practice of law, which continued five years. In 1868 he was elected Presidential Elector on the Democratic ticket, and in 1870 was elected County Judge of Benton county. In June, 1874, he was elected Associate Justice of the Supreme Court to fill the unexpired term of Judge Thayer, deceased, which expired in September, 1876. In 1878 he was elected State Senator from Benton county, which position he resigned in 1880, to accept the Democratic nomination of Judge of the Supreme Court. Gov. Thayer afterwards appointed him Judge of the Second Judicial District to fill the unexpired term caused by the resignation of Judge Watson, which term expired July 1, 1882, since which time he has been engaged in the active practice of his profession at Corvallis, where he still resides. Judge Burnett's early educational advantages were very limited, his mother being left a widow with small means and a large family. He labored hard to assist in the support of the family and obtain an education. His love for home and mother was very strong, as his affections were very deep-rooted. He is a plain, every-day sort of a man, just such a one as commands the respect and esteem of all who know him. He is of ordinary height, ruddy features, sandy hair and whiskers. As an attorney he stands high in the profession and is universally considered the very personification of honor and integrity.

HORACE CARPENTER, M. D.

The subject of our sketch is one of the oldest and most successful physicians in the State, and his name is a household word in many parts of the Willamette valley, where he has practiced for years. He was born in Connersville, Indiana, December 19, 1826. His literary education was received at academical institutions in Indiana, Michigan and Iowa, and his medical education at Keokuk, Iowa, also at Long Island College Hospital, Brooklyn, N. Y., he receiving the degree of M. D. in 1856. He began practice in Scott county, Iowa, in 1855, remaining there until 1865, when he came to Oregon. Was Assistant Surgeon in First Oregon Cavalry and Surgeon in the First Oregon Infantry, serving until close of the rebellion, then locating in Salem, where he remained some time, and then opened an office in Portland and soon established a lucrative practice. His specialty is surgery, and he is accredited with having performed some extremely intricate and successful operations. He has twice been a delegate from the medical department of the Willamette University, of which he is the principal founder, to the American Medical Association. During 1870 and 1871 he was associate editor of the "Oregon Medical and Surgical Reporter," and from 1866 to 1870 was visiting physician at the Oregon State Penitentiary. He was for seven years the dean of the faculty of the Medical Department of the Willamette University, and is at present Professor of Hygiene. He was President of the Oregon State Medical Society in 1879 and fourth Vice-President of the American Medical Association in 1881. Since the commencement of the new insane asylum building, Dr. Carpenter has, under the direction of the Board of Building Commissioners, superintended the arrangement of ventilation, light, etc., with the view of having the details of each department complete. As such officer he has shown a deep interest in the work, and has rendered valuable assistance to the Board, his suggestions being more valuable, in that he, at his own expense, visited all institutions of this character on the coast, for the purpose of more thoroughly posting himself on this subject. He was married in Iowa in 1850 to Miss S. A. Coshow, of Blue Grass, Scott county, and they have raised an interesting family. Politically speaking, the Doctor is a Republican, and takes a lively interest in politics.

LUZERNE BESSER

Is a gentleman who has distinguished himself more particularly in the municipal affairs of Portland, and who, it is generally conceded, has but few superiors as a successful politician. He has, it is true, received an occasional back-set, although he has always managed to give his opponents a lively contest. He was born in the city of Buffalo, New York, on the 25th day of October, 1833, his parents being there on a visit at the time, their home being in Clark county, Illinois, where his father settled in 1818. His early days were spent on a farm and he had the advantages then afforded of attending a public school. He applied himself more especially to the study of civil engineering, and taught school about three years, when his health failed and he was compelled to resign. Catching the western fever, he in 1852 married a most estimable lady in the person of Miss Sarah Lake, and at once started for Oregon with a view of making the then almost unknown country his future home. He arrived in Portland November 25, 1852, and in time assumed charge of the books in Mills & Blodgett's saw mill and afterwards acted as foreman for Lewis Love, who became owner of the property. Mr. Besser then rented the mill himself and run it very successfully for about three years. He then entered into partnership with Levi Estes and John Gates and erected a mill on Front street between Madison and Jefferson, where they continued in business until the great fire of August 21, 1872, wherein Mr. Besser sustained a personal loss of over $50,000, without one dollar's insurance. His indomitable energy, however, never forsook him, and we find him again struggling to retrieve his lost fortunes. His personal interest in municipal affairs induced the residents of the Third ward in 1868 to nominate and elect him as a member of the Common Council, which position he held for nine consecutive years, and discharged the duties of his office with faithfulness and integrity, serving as a member of some of the most important committees of that body. He was mainly instrumental in establishing the grades of the Third ward, and was the originator of the oil lamp system of street lighting in this city. He met great opposition in this last mentioned scheme, and was allowed but five lamps as an experiment. It proved successful, however, and the demand has increased to over three hundred lamps, which are in use at the present time, the saving to the tax payers of the city being over $3,000 annually. He was employed as book-keeper in the U. S. Custom House in Portland, under Collector Kelly, from 1875 to 1877 inclusive, and here, as elsewhere, proved an efficient officer. In July of 1877 he was tendered and accepted, at the hands of the Board of Police Commissioners, the office of Chief of Police, and in that capacity served the public most satisfactorily for nearly three years. During his term of office the writer of this sketch was connected with the daily press of Portland, and as a representative thereof, was oftentimes compelled to call upon him for facts connected with his office as Chief of Police, and always found him willing to impart information, courteous and accommodating, but none the less circumspect and careful to avoid any disclosures that would in the end defeat the ends of justice. He possessed many, if not all, of the qualifications of a detective, and his term of office was marked with the arrest and conviction of an unusually large number of desperate characters, who are now paying the penalty of their crimes in the reformatory institutions of our State. In fact there were no grave or serious crimes committed in this city during Mr. Besser's term of office without the ultimate arrest and conviction of the guilty parties, he sparing no pains or expense to secure the arrest of fugitives from justice, be their temporary residence in Oregon or any of the adjacent States or Territories. Prominent among his arrests was that of Brown, Johnson and Schwartz, who were afterwards convicted of the murder of young Joseph and the robbing of O'Shea's pawn-broking establishment, and the former two executed and the latter consigned to imprisonment in the penitentiary for life. During the last two or three years the subject of our sketch has been engaged in private enterprises of various kinds, including the improvement and speculation in city property, and interesting himself more or less in the political questions of the day. Politically speaking, he is of strong Republican proclivities. In public or private life he is genial, pleasant and courteous, and is exceedingly fond of narrating incidents of territorial life in Oregon. He is of medium size and weighs about two hundred pounds, thrifty and sober, and consequently robust, healthy and strong. He is a plain, good-natured, pleasant gentleman, who will in the future, as in the past, make his power felt in the circles of public life.

PROF. J. T. GREGG.

Among the rising young attorneys of our State, the subject of this sketch stands prominent and although young in years is rapidly gaining an experience that will prove invaluable in years to come. He has energy and ambition and will succeed where other men would fail. He was born in Allen county, Indiana, September 20, 1847. He immigrated to California in 1855, where he resided until 1864, when he first came to Oregon. His early education was received in the public schools of California. He taught school in this State until 1868, when he returned to California, and in 1870 entered the State Normal School in San Francisco for the purpose of thoroughly preparing himself for the profession of a teacher. He remained there two years and returned again to Oregon. In 1874 he was elected principal of the East Salem Grammar School, which position he held for eight consecutive years. In this position Prof. Gregg gave universal satisfaction to the patrons of the school, the pupils under his charge having made excellent progress in their studies. In 1876 he was appointed City Superintendent of the Salem public schools; and in 1878 was elected County Superintendent of Schools for Marion county, both of which positions he still holds. While engaged in school-work he devoted his spare time to the study of law, and was admitted to the bar in 1881, and he is now engaged in the practice of law in Salem. He is a P. G. of Olive Lodge No. 18, I. O. O. F., of that city. Politically he is a Republican, and takes an active interest in politics, and during the session of the Legislature just closed he has acted as Clerk of the House Judiciary Committee. He is considered pretty good-looking, ordinary height and build, full whiskers, brown hair, clear-cut features and pleasant brown eyes. He is unmarried, and by the young ladies is considered a desirable catch.

HON. W. CAREY JOHNSON.

Prominent among the self-made men of Oregon is he whose name heads this sketch, and who has been a prominent character in business and political circles for many years past. He first saw the light of day in Ross county, Ohio, October 27, 1833, and received the benefits of a common school education, when with his father, Rev. Hezekiah Johnson, he came to Oregon in 1845 and settled in Oregon City, where he has resided ever since. He commenced learning the printer's trade and worked on the case in Oregon City for several years. In 1854 he commenced reading law with Wait & Kelly, and was admitted to the bar September, 1855, which in view of the fact that he worked at the case four days each week and taught an evening school a good portion of the time to earn money to pay his expenses, may be considered a very judicious outlay of time and talent. On arriving at the age of maturity he gave all of his hard-earned savings, with the exception of twenty dollars, to his then aged father, and started in anew to earn a name and fortune for himself. He was elected City Prosecuting Attorney in 1858 and City Recorder in 1859. He was meanwhile establishing a lucrative practice in the profession of law and steadily advancing to the front rank of the legal fraternity. In 1862 he was elected Prosecuting Attorney for the Fourth Judicial District. In 1865 and 1866 he held the highly responsible position of special attorney, under the venerated Hon. Caleb Cushing, to investigate and settle the affairs of the Hudson Bay and Puget Sound Companies. He was elected State Senator in 1866 to fill a vacancy, and during that session rendered valuable service as Chairman of the Judiciary Committee. He is now the senior member of the well-known legal firm of Johnson, McCown & Macrum, with offices at Oregon City and Portland. As an attorney at law Mr. Johnson stands high in the profession. He is an earnest student, a careful reader and a deep thinker. He is a fine-looking gentleman, of ordinary height and build, very black whiskers and mustache, prematurely bald, a clear black eye and always neatly dressed. He has been several times honored with the complimentary vote of his party friends for U. S. Senator, and during the exciting contest just closed received the votes of the "solid sixteen." He was married on Christmas of 1868 to Miss Josephine De Vore, a graduate of the Willamette University and one of the most intelligent ladies in the State. They have a family of three children who are already developing minds of far more than ordinary brilliancy. Mr. Johnson has a beautiful residence in Oregon City, and his home life amid such surroundings cannot be otherwise than pleasant.

WILLIAM R. WILLIS.

The well-known attorney of Douglas county, whose success as a member of the bar is second to none in the district in which he resides, is a native of the Buckeye State, having been born in Boone county, Ohio, on the 22d day of June, 1825. His parents moved to Putnam county, Illinois, in 1827. He was raised on a farm and was favored with but comparatively few facilities of procuring an education, but he assiduously improved those offered him, and thus gained a foothold to other advancement. He arrived in Oregon in 1853, having accompanied his mother on the trip around the Horn, his father and the remainder of the family having come across the plains. He commenced reading law and was admitted to the bar in 1864, having originally settled in Douglas county, where he has resided ever since, his parents having died there within a few months of each other and at the ripe old age of seventy-eight years. He was married in 1866 to Miss Caroline Haines, of Douglas county. He was elected County and Probate Judge in 1860 and served four years in that position, and in 1869 was appointed Registrar of the United States Land Office, which position he held for nine years. He then devoted his entire attention to the practice of law, and stands high in his profession. He is a prominent Odd Fellow, with the rank of P. G., and a member of the Encampment. He is of low build, wiry frame, bright eye, sharp features, black hair and whiskers, and an excellent pleader.

HON. LOUIS T. BARIN

A well-known and highly-esteemed resident of Clackamas, is an active, energetic citizen and a gentleman that takes a lively interest in the welfare and prosperity of our fair young State, of which he has been a resident for over a score of years. He was born in Providence, Rhode Island, in 1842, and came to Oregon when he was twenty years of age and settled in Oregon City, where he took up a piece of government land and for the first few years interested himself in improving it. He enlisted in Company E of the First Regiment Oregon Cavalry, and was elected First Sergeant, which position he held for three years, receiving an honorable discharge at the end of his term of service. Returning to Oregon City he commenced the study of law in 1869, in the office of Johnson & McCown, and was admitted to the bar in 1872, and in the same year was elected a member of the House of Representatives from that county. His wedding took place during the session, the bride being Miss Josephine H. Harding, of Oregon City. He was elected City Prosecuting Attorney in 1874, and was re-elected in 1875. During the years 1877 and 1878 he was Mayor of Falls City, and was considered an efficient officer. He received the appointment of Register of the United States Land Office in January, 1878, under President Hayes, and was re-appointed by President Arthur in February, 1882. He is of the average build, rather heavy set, and an active politician. He prides himself on being an uncompromising Republican, and has stood by his political principles in times and places that try men's hearts. He is still in the prime of life and has a bright future before him.

SOLOMON ABRAHAM, ESQ.

In this, our republican form of government, men who earn a national reputation, as a general thing, indulge in a greater or less degree in the politics of our country. There are some men, however, who possess remarkable business sagacity, and as such acquire an enviable reputation among their fellow men, and who, although you never hear their names mentioned as aspirants for public office, nor would they accept one were it tendered them, are none the less interested in the political welfare of their country and wield a powerful influence in their respective neighborhoods, their work, although quietly performed, being none the less effective. Such a man is the subject of this sketch. He was born in Russia-Poland in 1832 and came to this country in 1850. Landing in New York City, with the enterprise characteristic of his race, he resolved on becoming a merchant. Possessed, however, of scant means, his stock in trade consisted of such only as could be carried in a basket and peddled from door to door. Industry and frugality combined, however, soon gave him a little start in the world, and he came to Oregon and in 1852 opened a small retail establishment in Oregon City. He was dissatisfied, however, with his success, and in 1854 he went to Roseburg, in Douglas county, where he has resided ever since. The new mercantile firm of Abraham & Brother flourished prosperously. The firm paid strict attention to business, catering carefully to the wants of trade, and their custom increased rapidly. The firm sold out in 1875 to A. F. Brown, for the purpose of taking a brief respite. With his characteristic energy, however, he soon wearied of a life of ease and inactivity, and in 1877 we again find him at the head of a magnificent mercantile house, the firm then being Abraham, Wheeler & Co., which firm is today doing the leading mercantile business of Southern Oregon. Their sales during the present year will no doubt aggregate $200,000. His business connections are not confined to the mercantile trade by any means, he being at present right-of-way agent and a heavy contractor, furnishing large amounts of lumber and material to the O. & C. R. R. Co., to be used in the extension of their road through Southern Oregon. He also owns large tracts of land in Douglas county, which he is rapidly improving. He takes a lively interest in politics and in a quiet way is a powerful faction. His integrity is unquestioned and his credit is unlimited. He is undoubtedly one of the most sagacious business men on the Northwest coast, and evinces unusual enterprise, tempered with judgment in the management of his affairs. He was married in 1861 to Miss Julia Hinkle, of Douglas county, and is an honored member of the Masonic order and of the Odd Fellows. Would that Oregon had a man like Sol. Abraham on every square mile of her broad domain.

PROF. J. H. BRENNER,

"Mine host" of The Esmond, the leading hotel in Portland, was born in San Francisco, Cal., November 7, 1854, and two years afterwards was brought to Oregon, where for many years the refreshing dews of Webfoot imparted to him beauty, health, strength and wisdom, until he now deservedly ranks amongst the foremost of the distinguished men of this State. Almost from infancy he gave evidence of remarkable musical taste. At the age of six years he received his first instructions in harmony, and after a few years' close application became wonderfully proficient on almost every instrument string, reed and brass. At the age of eleven he was sent to the Lyceum at Strasbourg, and from thence to a noted Parisian college. During the few years spent in Europe he not only perfected his musical education, but also acquired a thorough knowledge of the French and German languages, both of which he speaks fluently. Returning to Oregon in 1870, he entered active life as Professor of Music, established classes in Portland and in nearly every large town throughout the State, and soon became known as the most popular and thorough teacher in the profession, which honorable distinction he retained until he gave up that occupation in the spring of 1880, to assist his father in the hotel business. Six weeks after The Esmond Hotel was opened to the public Mr. H. Brenner died, leaving his son to assume the responsibility of a new and important business. With that persistent energy which characterizes all of the young man's undertakings, he soon surmounted all the difficulties that loomed up before him, and made The Esmond what his worthy sire had designed it to be—the leading hotel of the Northwest. In doing this, he has been materially aided by the solicitous attentions of his respected mother and his accomplished sister, Miss Rose Brenner, both of whom leave nothing undone to make guests feel entirely "at home" under their roof. Mr. Brenner is courteous and attentive to everyone; but he deserves special praise for the filial affection shown to his mother, and for the many thoughtful attentions shown to her and his sister. Other young men of his age, courted and flattered as he is, would be apt to overlook these little amenities, which, after all, speak louder than words in stamping the truly affectionate disposition and noble character of the man. Mr. Brenner is still unmarried. As to his personal appearance, it is only necessary to state that at social gatherings he is always at the highest premium for the "ladies' choice," to know that he is young, handsome and accomplished.

REV. P. S. KNIGHT.

There is, perhaps, no minister on the coast that stands higher in the community in which he lives than does the popular divine whose name heads this sketch. For years past he has been a pastor of the people and a friend to all. He is not hedged in by sectarianism, and is confined to no single line of thought or purpose, save to do that which his Master has given him to do, and to perform such work in a manner dictated by his own conscience, irrespective of what others may think or believe. His sermons are practical and he clothes his thoughts in plain terms. His flights of imagination, while eloquent, are none the less easily followed by the unlearned as well as the student. Mr. Knight was born in Boston, Mass., on the 21st day of October, 1836, becoming an Iowa pioneer at the early age of six months. Here he resided until 1853, when, with his parents, he came across the plains with an ox team and settled near Vancouver, W. T. He served a full apprenticeship at the carpenter's trade from 1854 to 1857, in which latter year he came to Salem and attended the Willamette University in 1858 and 1860. He read law under Smith & Grover in 1861 and 1862 and was admitted to the bar in 1863. That year and the year following he edited the Salem "Statesman." Having always evinced an adaptability for the ministry, he during all these years was preparing himself for a ministerial career, and in 1865 and 1866 he served as pastor of the Congregational Church at Oregon City, returning to Salem in 1867 in response to a call from the Congregational Church in that city, which he accepted, and which pulpit he has occupied continuously since that date. In 1870 he interested himself in the organization of a State institution for the education of deaf mutes, and has done more than any other one man to ameliorate the condition of this unfortunate class of our citizens. By personal and persistent effort, he succeeded in securing a small appropriation from the State, and in organizing the school overcame difficulties that would have discouraged most men. He has had personal supervision of the institution since that time, and has, in addition to his ministerial labors, served as one of its teachers, in which work he has been assisted and encouraged by his wife, nee Miss Eleanor Smith, to whom he was married April 21, 1861, the wedding taking place at the M. E. Church in Salem. Although never taking an active part in politics, Mr. Knight is a true blue Republican, and feels a just degree of pride in its progress as a political party.

WILLIAM F. BENJAMIN,

A man of sterling worth and a well-known citizen of Douglas county, was born in Brown county, Ohio, April 2, 1827, and with his parents moved to Illinois in 1834, settling in Du Page county. He received an ordinary common school education and taught school several winters at the minimum price of $12 per month. He was married in 1851, moved to Iowa in 1859, and returned to Illinois in 1866. He came to Oregon in 1870 and settled in Douglas county, where he has since resided. In 1876 he was elected a member of the House of Representatives, and in 1878 was appointed Register of the United States Land Office at Roseburg, a position he still holds. By studious and temperate habits, strict adherence to correct principles and a due regard for the rights and opinions of others, he has secured the esteem of his neighbors and friends. His aim in life has apparently been to do right because it was right, and he ever appears just what he is, a quiet, unassuming citizen. Temporary advantage at the expense of principle found no sympathy in his make-up. He united his fame and fortunes with the Republican party many long years ago, and, to quote his own words, "purposes to stay with it until life's changeful scenes are ended."

HON EARL C. BRONAUGH,

Who stands to-day as one of the most prominent attorneys in the State, was born in Abingdon, Virginia, March 4, 1831. He was early imbued with the principles of the South, but was never strictly partisan in his views. He was never in sympathy with slavery, but was none the less a firm believer in the rights of State Sovereignty, and when his native State seceded young Bronaugh went with her, heart and soul, enlisted in the hopes and destinies of the new Confederacy of States. He secured his educational advantages prior to his reaching the age of twelve, when, with his parents, he moved to Shelby county, Tennessee. They founded a new home in the woods and suffered all the privations of the pioneer life of that early day. Here Mr. Bronaugh spent six years of his early manhood, when becoming imbued with a desire to read law, he entered Hon. J. W. Clapp's office, at Holly Springs, Miss., in 1849 and in 1852 was admitted to the bar. He taught school in Tennessee and Arkansas for a couple of years. He was married at Jacksonport, Arkansas, in 1854, to Miss Araminta Payne and opened a law office in a log cabin, of which he was architect and builder, aided only by a strapping colored boy. He was elected Judge of the First Judicial Circuit of Arkansas in 1860, which office he held until the close of the civil war. He was a volunteer in the rebel line, serving as scout and sharpshooter. He was broken up during the war and in 1868 came to Oregon, and has at different times been associated as partner with R. E. Bybee, Esq., and Hon. John Catlin, and was a few years since invited to become a partner in the well-known and leading law firm of Dolph, Bronaugh, Dolph & Simon. Mr. Bronaugh is really a fine-looking gentleman, tall and commanding statue, well-proportioned, with pointed features, a fine forehead, well-shaped head, dark auburn hair and beard, the latter being very heavy and sprinkled with gray hairs. As a pleader he has very few superiors, and is thoroughly at home in all branches of his profession.

WILLIAM H. HOLMES, ESQ.

Oregonians naturally feel an increased interest in the ambitions and aspirations of a young man who was born and raised right here in our own State. To such we are prone to give a helping hand and an encouraging word, to the detriment, perhaps, of an equally worthy young man whose nativity was elsewhere. This fact, however, is not the only reason why Mr. Holmes is so popular among those who know him. He has won, and fully deserves every iota of esteem and regard in which he is held by his industry, integrity and enterprise. He has stepped outside the ruts of routine life in town or country, and is making for himself a reputation that will, in time, give him prominence and honors among his fellow men. He was born in Polk county in May, 1850, and received his education at La Creole Academy, most of his early life being spent on a farm. He read law with Thayer & Williams, of Portland, and was admitted to the bar in 1874. He soon afterwards opened an office in Salem, where he has since resided. He was nominated by the Democracy in 1880 as their candidate for Representative, and accepted his defeat in a strong Republican county very gracefully. In 1882 he was nominated for Prosecuting Attorney for the Third Judicial District, which, while nearly 1,100 Republican in 1880, gave Mr. Holmes 16 majority, his friends in Polk standing solidly by him regardless of politics. He will make an efficient officer and gain friends daily in his official capacity. He is a Royal Arch Mason. He was married August 13, 1875, to Miss Josephine Lewis, of Polk county. Mr. Holmes is highly esteemed by all with whom he is intimately acquainted.

COLONEL WILLIAM P. MILLER.

Here, too, is an Oregon pioneer, although his locks are not yet whitened with age, as are the majority of those who away back among the '40s braved the danger and endured the hardships attending a trip across the plains. Mr. Miller rarely alludes to the incidents of his early life in Oregon. He lives and acts in the present, and it requires no small amount of "reportorial pumping" to induce him to open the flood-gates of incident and romance with which his memory is stored. We cornered him a few days since, however, and from him learned that he was born in Missouri March 12, 1836, his early life being spent on a farm, during which time he attended the common schools, in which he secured such education as he now possesses. He came to Oregon in 1845, and in common with emigrants of that day was subject to many hardships in crossing the plains with their ox teams. With his parents he settled in Washington county, where they remained about a year and then moved to Sauvie's Island, where they remained until 1853, going from there to Jackson county and engaged in farming and stockraising. In 1856 returned to Yamhill county and in 1858 moved to Wasco county and was engaged most of the time in stock-raising and running pack trains. In 1861 there was a company of seventy-five organized to prospect for gold, and Col. Miller was elected captain, and they were the first discoverers of the John Day, Burnt River and Powder River mines, which afterwards turned out very rich. Moved to Yakima valley, in Washington Territory, in 1869, where he resided until 1877, when he returned to The Dalles. Served in Capt. John F. Miller's company during the Rogue river war of 1853, and was commissioned as Colonel and took an active part in the Umatilla war of 1877-8. He was appointed Warden of the Oregon State Penitentiary in 1878 by His Excellency Gov. Thayer, and it is due to his careful management that the institution has been run so economically during the past four years. He is an excellent manager, a careful financier, and in his general supervision of the work has been as careful of the State finances as he would have been of his own. He is well liked by the inmates of that institution, and is strict, without being harsh or cruel. He was married to Miss Sarah E. Raffety on the 21st day of September, 1864, and one child, a bright, intelligent little girl, has thus far blessed their union.

MARION F. MULKEY.

The subject of this biographical sketch has led an active life, both as a public man and as a private individual. He is one of our self-made men, and from obscurity in early life has attained a prominence in the legal fraternity highly flattering to a gentleman of his age. He was born in Johnson county, Missouri, November 14, 1836, and with his father, Johnson Mulkey, came to Oregon in 1847 and settled on Oak creek about three miles west of Corvallis. They there took up a donation claim and lived a pioneer's life in every sense of the word. Among the teachers in the traditional log school house of that early day who wielded the birch over young Mulkey's shoulders were Hon. James H. Slater, our present United States Senator, and Hon. Philip Ritz, now a prominent fruit grower near Walla Walla. Endowed with more than ordinary ambition, and with a view of getting outside the ruts of routine life on the farm, he, in 1854, entered the Pacific University at Forest Grove, and, under the venerated Dr. Marsh, commenced fitting himself for college. In the fall of 1858 he entered Yale College, at New Haven, Conn., from which he graduated as one of the class of '62. He returned to Portland and read law with Hon. E. D. Shattuck and was admitted to the bar in 1864. He was appointed Deputy Provost Marshal in 1863 and helped make the enrollment of that year. In 1866 he was elected Prosecuting Attorney of the fourth Judicial District, and in 1867 represented the citizens of the Third ward in the Portland City Council. In 1872 he was elected City Attorney and re-elected in 1873, since which time he has been associated in the practice of his profession with Hon. John F.

Caples, who is now serving his third term as Prosecuting Attorney of the Fourth Judicial District. As an attorney, Mr. Mulkey has few superiors. As Deputy Prosecuting Attorney is a terror to evil doers, and once on their trail never flags until they are brought to the bar of justice. In his profession he ranks with men who are, by many years, his senior. As a speaker none are more forcible, and his flights of oratory are frequently such as hold an audience spell bound, while his cool and logic reasoning has great influence with a jury. His face is clear-cut, with beard and mustache, his eye being keen, o'ershadowed with an expansive forehead. He is an unswerving Republican and an active worker in the party, and as an attorney and politician, he has a bright future before him. He was married in 1862 to Miss Mary E. Porter, of New Haven, Connecticut, and has a family of two children.

AUSTON MIRES, ESQ.,

Stands high among the young attorneys of Southern Oregon and has established a foothold in Douglas county, from which it would be difficult to eradicate him, possessing, as he does, talent, energy, ambition and industry, qualifications that entitle him most conclusively to the place he has won. He was born in Des Moines county, Iowa, in 1852, and came to Oregon in 1853, and with his parents settled in Douglas county, where they have resided ever since. He was raised on a farm and attended the common schools and is a graduate of the Umpqua Academy. He was for three years employed as route agent on the Oregon & California Railroad between Portland and Roseburg, during which time he laid by money enough to pay his expenses through the Law Department of the University at Ann Arbor, Michigan, from which he graduated in 1882, and returned to Oregon, where he gained admission to the bar of this State and was then admitted to partnership with Hon. W. R. Willis, of that city, During the session of the Legislature just closed he has acted as Chief Clerk of the Senate, the laborious duties of which position he has performed with promptness and precision, and has thereby gained a host of new and enthusiastic friends. He is considered fine-looking, being of rather low stature, well-built, full face, ruddy complexion, well-defined features, heavy mustache and light brown hair. He is unmarried, but is very popular among the ladies, a red hot Republican, and a prominent young member of the Masonic fraternity. His career promises to be a brilliant one in the profession he has chosen.

ALFRED KINNEY, M. D.

Of Salem, is one of those jovial, good-natured men that we are always glad to meet. He is active and energetic, and what he does he does with a will, and infuses humor and good nature into all with whom he comes in contact. He is an Oregon boy, and made his debut on this world's stage in Yamhill county, near the town of West Chehalem, on the 31st day of January, 1850, and when ten years of age moved with his parents into the town of McMinnville, where he attended school until he was eighteen years of age, working meanwhile in his father's flouring mill and mastering the miller's trade. At an early age he displayed a fondness for the medical profession and in 1868 he went east and entered the Bellevue Medical College in New York City, being at the same time a private student under Dr. Lewis A. Sayre, who is undoubtedly as fine a surgeon as America can boast of. After attending two courses of lectures, he applied for a position in the Charity Hospital on Blackwell's Island, and ranked first in the class at the special examination, only six of about one hundred applicants passing successfully. He was at once appointed first surgeon and remained there about two years and a half, the average number of patients meanwhile being over 1000. At the end of his term of service he was presented by the Board of Commissioners of Public Charities and Corrections with an elegant case of surgical instruments as a recognition of his skillful attention, which testimonial he still keeps and highly prizes. He graduated with high honors and received his diploma in 1872, returning to Oregon in the fall of the same year and locating at Portland, and at once entered into a lucrative practice. Desiring a change, however, he went to Umatilla county in 1878 and entered the stock business. He moved to Salem in 1880 and resumed his practice, which he is still following with marked success. He has devoted himself especially to the study and practice of surgery, and has, since his return to Oregon, performed some operations that are indeed astonishing in their nature, and bid fair to add a still greater amount of knowledge to the store now possessed on that wonderful branch of medical science. His skill and intelligence is conceded and honored by the profession. Sincerity of purpose and largeness of sympathy for the sufferings of the unfortunate, beam forth in every feature on his visits to the sick room. During his residence in Oregon he has performed upwards of sixty successful amputations, and has three times successfully performed the intricate operation of tying the subclavian artery. Dr. Kinney has never but once aspired to political honors. At the last general election he was one of the Democratic nominees for State Senator in Marion county, and, although the county usually gives a Republican majority of from 500 to 700, Dr. Kinney's popularity was so universal that he was beaten by but seven votes. His canvass of the county was a "still hunt" that his opponents will long remember, but his political ambition is satisfied, and surgery and the practice of medicine will attract his entire attention hereafter. He was married in Portland January 28, 1874, to Miss Louisa P. Dickinson, and one child has thus far blessed their union. He is a well-built man, slightly rotund, with pleasant facial expression, and a keen, penetrating eye, with nerves as steady as clock work.

HON. JAMES C. TOLMAN,

Our present Surveyor-General, is a man to whom much credit is due for the industry and application he has displayed in working his way onward and upward to places of honor and trust. He was born in Washington county, Ohio, in 1813, and moved to Champaign of the same State in 1821, where he resided until 1839, when he moved to Iowa. From there he immigrated to

California in 1849, where he worked in the mines with some success until 1851. Desirous of seeing "The girl he left behind him," he returned to Oskaloosa, Iowa, in 1851, and shortly afterwards married Miss Elizabeth E. Coe, with whom he recrossed the plains in 1852, and coming direct to Oregon settled on a farm in Jackson county, where he has resided ever since. His early education was obtained under great difficulties, but he availed himself assiduously of such as he had, and by judicious reading in later life he has made himself well posted on all general subjects, and in many ways is a leader among men possessed of greater literary abilities. Stock raising and agricultural pursuits are his main forte, but he has branched out in merchandising and running a tannery with no indifferent success. He was an uncompromising Whig up to the breaking out of the rebellion, and since then a stalwart Republican, and has always taken an active interest in politics, although he has never urged his own claims for political honors with any degree of persistency. He was nominated for Governor on the Republican ticket in 1874, but the formation of a third party gave the administration into the hands of the Democracy, and he accepted his defeat with becoming resignation. He was appointed Surveyor-General in 1878, and has made a very efficient officer. General Tolman is a low built man, rather spare, of a quick, nervous disposition, sharp features, full whiskers and short thick hair, well nigh whitened with age. He has an interesting family and enjoys home life. He is a man of strict integrity and unsullied reputation. He appreciates his friends and has few, if any, enemies.

PROFESSOR THOMAS VAN SCOY,

Now President of the Willamette University, is one of the leading instructors of our State, and is rapidly increasing his popularity among the students and patrons of the institution of learning over which he presides. He is a gentleman of rare literary ability, and as chief executive of the University has surprised even his most ardent admirers. He was born in White county, Indiana, February 13, 1848, his father, William Van Scoy, having emigrated there from West Virginia the year previous. Thomas was the youngest of a family of fourteen children. He worked on the farm with his father, attending school in the winter months, till eighteen years of age, when he entered school at Battle Ground Collegiate Institute, where General Harrison fought the Indians in 1811 on the Tippecanoe river. After spending two years in this school he attended Brookston Academy in his native county for about a year, and in 1869 he matriculated at the Northwestern University at Evanston, Illinois, from which institution he graduated in a class of thirty in 1875. Leaving college he entered the ministry of the Methodist Episcopal Church, and was stationed at Rensselaer, Indiana, where he spent three years in preaching, having received into the church during that time three hundred members. At the close of the ministry in this place, he again entered school at Garrett Biblical Institute. In 1880 he graduated from this school and immediately came to Oregon to take the chair of Greek in Willamette University, which position he occupied for a little more than one year, when he was elected President of the same institution.

At the close of the Sophomore year, while in college, Prof. Van Scoy was called to the Principalship of Brookston Academy. He taught here three years and then resigned in order to resume his studies. Prof. Van Scoy is a pleasant-appearing gentleman and one well calculated to make friends with all with whom he is intimately associated. He is highly esteemed by his pupils who, while they realize his power of discipline are none the less cognizant of the fact that he is deeply interested in their personal advancement in study, and in order to aid them in their literary pursuits willingly devotes hours of time which rightfully are his own. We have often seen him with his coat off and hammer and nails in his hand repairing the University fences, engaged in setting out shrubbery, or in some way adding to the beauty of the campus, thus evincing an interest in the general appearance of the surroundings, in appreciation of the fact that all tended towards making the students more interested in their studies. Mr. Van Scoy is rather tall and slender, with a pleasant face, mild blue eye, auburn hair and whiskers and a high forehead. He always dresses with taste and keeps up the good old-fashioned style of literary gentlemen, wearing a white vest. He was married September 22, 1875, to Miss Jennie E. Thomas, their family consisting of one child. Politically speaking he is a Republican, and takes a lively interest in the success of that party. In connection with Prof. Van Scoy, who takes so active an interest in the success of the institution, we consider it but just to give a short sketch of the

WILLAMETTE UNIVERSITY.

In 1844 a building which had been constructed at a cost of $10,000 on the same grounds, where now the Willamette University stands, for the use of the Oregon Mission Manual Labor School, was purchased and a school established under the name of Oregon Institute. This school began the same year with twenty pupils. It was incorporated as Willamette University in 1853, and began its career in college work. It has sustained a degree of prosperity, in some respects, unexcelled by any other institution of learning on the coast. A building in the form of a Greek cross, four stories high and eighty feet square was erected in 1867. The old building was destroyed by fire in 1871. In the new building are a chapel, seven recitation rooms, two halls for literary societies, a library and apparatus room, president's room, besides several rooms occupied by students. There are four well organized literary societies, in connection with which are two small libraries. The library of the University contains 2,500 volumes. The departments of the University are: 1, College of Liberal Arts; 2, Medical College, organized in 1866; 3, Woman's College, organized in 1880; 4, Conservatory of Music, organized in 1881; 5, Art Department, in 1881; 6, University Academy, organized with a three years' preparatory course in 1880. The present value of property belonging to this institution is estimated at about $90,000, $63,000 of which is in real estate and buildings, and $27,000 in cash endowments. From 1850 to 1860 Rev. F. S. Hoyt, D. D., was President; 1860 to 1865, T. M. Gatch, Ph. D.; 1865 to 1867, Rev. J. H. Wythe, M. D.; 1867 to 1868, Rev. L. T. Woodward, A. M., was acting President; 1868 to 1870, Rev. Nelson Rounds, D. D.; 1870 to 1879, T. M. Gatch, Ph. D.; 1879 to 1880, Rev. Charles E. Lambert, A. M., B. D.; Since 1880, Rev. Thomas Van Scoy, A. M., B. D., has been President. The degrees conferred in Willamette University on examination are, Bachelor of Arts, Bachelor of Philosophy, Bachelor of Science, Mistress of English Literature and Doctor of Medicine.

HON JOHN KELLY.

The name of the subject of this sketch will be long remembered in the annals of this State. His positiveness of character and disposition have become proverbial, and when once his mind is made up on any subject it is next to an impossibility to change it. Like all pioneers to this coast who have emerged into public life, Mr. Kelly understands himself thoroughly, and dares to pursue a course consistent with his ideas of right, in the face of any and all opposition, be it of a political or personal character. He was born in Dublin, Ireland, May 3, 1818, and came to Canada in 1838 and to Vermont in 1840. He went to Wisconsin in 1843, where he resided until 1846, when, the Mexican war breaking out, he enlisted in a Missouri cavalry company and served during the war. At its close, in 1849, he accompanied the Mounted Rifles to this coast in the capacity of wagon master. In January, 1853, Mr. Kelly was married to Miss Elizabeth Parker, and settled on a farm in the Umpqua valley. In 1861 he was appointed Register of Public Lands at Roseburg, which position he filled with credit to himself and the government he represented for a period of eight years, and, declining a re-appointment, he returned to his farm. He afterwards moved to Lane county, where he continued to reside until 1876, when he was appointed Collector of Customs at Portland, which position he held until 1880. He proved a very efficient officer and gave very general satisfaction to the business men of this city with whom the business of his office brought him in almost daily contact. Mr. Kelly is a man something below the medium height, rather heavy built, and a ruddy, healthy complexion. He is a very sociable gentleman and a pronounced Republican, and, as such, has always taken a lively interest in politics. He is the personification of industry and activity in whatever he undertakes, and, as a friend or neighbor, he stands high with his fellow-men.

DR. S. R. JESSUP.

A well-known and popular physician of Salem, and one whose kind, attentive treatment of the sick and geniality of manner towards the well have made him deservedly the favorite of all classes, was born in Stillisville, Indiana, April 23, 1839, where he resided until he was about eleven years of age, when with his parents he moved to Iowa and worked on the farm. By dint of teaching through the summers he was enabled to attend school during the winter months. He came to Oregon in 1863 and settled in Yamhill county. He studied medicine at Fort Yamhill until 1866, and afterwards attended lectures at Toland College, San Francisco. He then went up to the Warm Springs Indian Agency, where he spent a year as "medicine man" among the aborigines. He returned to Salem and graduated from the Medical Department of the Willamette University in 1868. He settled in Dallas, where, on August 26, 1868, he was married to Miss S. Coshow. He went East and in 1871 graduated at the Bellevue Hospital and Medical College in New York City, and returning to Oregon he settled at Salem, where he has since resided. He occupied the chair of Professor of Anatomy in the Medical Department of the Willamette University for several years. In 1879 he received the unanimous vote of his ward as a member of the Common Council, which compliment was again paid him in 1880. The Doctor is a short, thick-set gentleman with pleasant features, a bright, keen eye, face well covered with whiskers of a dark brown, and a good-shaped head. He is an indefatigable worker and very attentive to his patients. He is considered one of our most successful physicians and enjoys a lucrative practice. Always genial, courteous and good natured, he imbues cheerfulness to those around him, and is respected and esteemed by all who know him. He is a pronounced Republican, though liberal in his views, but is not a candidate for office, being too much attached to his profession.

VAN B. DE LASHMUTT, ESQ.,

A well-known resident of Portland, is now in the full prime and vigor of manhood, having first seen the glorious light of day in Burlington, Iowa, July 27, 1842. "Van," as he is familiarly known, came into this world with a whoop and a yell, and, to tell the truth, he has been making things lively ever since. With his parents he came across the plains to Oregon, and the family located on a farm in Polk county, where he remained until he was fifteen years of age, when, farm life proving burdensome to "Van," who was naturally of a stirring disposition, and an adventurous, enterprising turn of mind, he struck out for Salem, where he entered the "Statesman" office as an apprentice at the printer's trade. The paper was then edited by Hon. A. Bush, who was making things generally tropical. In September, 1861, young DeLashmutt enlisted as a private in the Third California Volunteer Infantry, and, with his company, served three years on the plains, the life proving decidedly irksome and monotonous at times. The regiment was under command of Gen. Connor. In the winter of 1863-4 Mr. DeLashmutt published the "Union Vidette" in Salt Lake City, and, as a Gentile paper, threw hot shot into the camps of Mormonism for several months. The excitement of this enterprise proved acceptable to DeLashmutt, but he finally disposed of his interest in the paper and was next heard of at Washoe City, Nevada, in 1865, where he purchased the "Times," and, for a few months, showed the residents of that part of the country how to run a newspaper. The enterprise, however, did not "pan out" very well, so "Van" packed his collar box and took a bee line for Oregon, the country of big wheat fields, webbed feet, pretty girls, and big red apples. He reached Portland in the winter of 1865-6 and accepted a case on the "Daily Oregonian." He applied himself closely to his work and managed to lay by some money, with which, in 1868, he went into partnership with H. B. Oatman, Esq., in the grocery business. We do not doubt but that "Van" sanded his sugar and watered his vinegar as faithfully as any of his competitors, but even then the business was too slow for him, and he began looking around for new fields to conquer. The inauguration of the railroad system in Oregon about that time created a boom in real estate in Portland, and in 1871, having disposed of their grocery business, we find the firm of DeLashmutt & Oatman branching out into the real estate and general brokerage business. This was just the business for a live, enterprising man like Mr. DeLashmutt, and, within a very few months, they had in their hands property for sale and rent aggregating in value many thousands of dollars, and some of their real estate transfers netted the enterprising young firm a handsome margin. "Van" is chuck full of business and knows no such word as fail. He is judicious in his speculations and is willing to take fair risks. From an obscure firm they have arisen to a level with any real estate firm in Portland, and their business is rapidly increasing, and, from a poor boy, who in 1856 was willing to, and did for sometime, wash dishes for his board at Bethel, in this State, Mr. DeLashmutt to-day stands as one of the solid men of Multnomah county, a man whose word is as good as his bond, and one thoroughly esteemed by all who know him. He has recently interested himself in the organization of the Metropolitan Savings Bank, and has just been elected as its President, another mark of the esteem and confidence reposed in him by the public. He has never taken a very active interest in politics, although he is a strong Republican. No man in Portland affords a better example of what pluck and industry will do than does Mr. DeLashmutt, and Dame Fortune has not yet forsaken him by any means. "Van" is a friend in need to those who are or have been a friend to him.

PROFESSOR THOMAS CONDON

Was born near Fermoy, on the river Blackwater, in the South of Ireland, sixty years ago. When he was ten years old his father migrated with his family to America, and found a home on New York Island, a few miles north of the city. The family was poor and the children at an early age left home to support themselves. The subject of this sketch was the oldest of the children, and employment was soon found for him with a gardener in the neighborhood, who raised flowers for the New York market. The boy's evenings were always spent in study, a habit soon noticed and kindly encouraged by his employer's family, until it became plain that an earnest student's habits had taken fast hold of his life. This led to the selection of a new situation for him, that of office boy in the office of a distinguished physician in Broadway, New York. Here the fullest opportunity was given him for study, the fine library of the family was at once and kindly opened to his use. Private lessons in drawing and mathematics were added, and after two or three years of this drill and culture, a place was secured for him in a surveying party on the survey of the New York and Erie railroad, then in progress. The commercial disaster of 1837 broke this up, and he found employment as a clerk in a New York tea store. Two years of this work varied his experience of life, and he next moved out West to Michigan, with his father, to find there a home for the family. The father returned to New York, a few months later, and the son remained in Onondaga county, New York. Here he continued for several years, alternately teaching to earn means, and then attending some neighboring academy or seminary to continue his own progress. It was during this period 1840 to 1849—that the Geological Report of the State of New York was published. The study of the successive volumes of this report gave a new and earnest energy to his pursuit of natural science; and the stone quarries of Onondaga, Cayuga and Madison counties, to whose examination every hour of leisure was devoted, furnished materials to intensify his increasing love of the study of geology. Occasional lectures and frequently published articles from his pen at this time gave public expression to his interest in this special line of study. In 1849 he entered the Theological Seminary at Auburn, N. Y., from which he graduated in 1852. In the fall of 1852 he was married to Miss Cornelia Holt, of Niagara county, N. Y., and with his bride started for Oregon. They located at St. Helens, on the Columbia, in the spring of 1853, when the young preacher became a missionary to the people and a teacher of the town school. Ague impaired Mrs. Condon's health, and a call to preach at Forest Grove was cheerfully accepted as a means to reach a less malarial climate. St. Helens, Forest Grove and Albany became successive fields of labor. In 1862 a new field opened at The Dalles, and into this Mr. Condon entered with fresh zeal. Dalles people still remember how much of earnest work and cheering fruits clustered around twelve years of earnest effort here. It was during this period that Prof. Condon published to the people of the Pacific coast those interesting discoveries he made in the geology of the John Day valley and the valley of the Crooked river, especially those of the fossil horse. The first of these fossil horse bones was brought to Prof. Condon by our present Governor Moody, who found some men digging a well in 1866, half way between the Touchet river and Palouse Landing. They had dug sixty-eight feet without finding water, but at that depth struck some bones. Mr. Moody brought these to Prof. Condon, who found them to be horse bones, and so published soon after in a lecture in Portland. This was some time before Prof. Marsh's discoveries, but inasmuch as the facts were only published in a public lecture instead of through a scientific journal or society, Prof. Condon was not scientifically entitled to the credit. After this discoveries in the geology of Oregon rapidly multiplied, and Prof. Condon's frequent public lectures have for years continued to keep the people of Oregon posted on their results. In 1872 Prof. Condon was made State Geologist of Oregon, which office he resigned on accepting the chair of Geology of the State University. In 1874 he was elected Geological Lecturer and soon after Professor of Geology in the college at Forest Grove. In 1876, at the organization of the Faculty of the State University at Eugene, Prof. Condon was chosen Professor of Geology and Natural History, which post he still occupies, spending as of old his vacations in new geological researches, and thus adding to the scope and scientific value of a fine cabinet which has grown under his hand. The Professor is an active, wiry little man of low stature and untiring industry. He is an enthusiast on the subject of geology. As a personal friend he is invaluable and cannot do too much for those he likes. As a man and neighbor none excel him, and he is universally esteemed by all who are acquainted with him. Genial, suave, polite and courteous, he wins his way at once to the hearts of those with whom he comes in contact, and stands to-day a man honored, esteemed and revered among men. Although a teacher, he is still a student and ever will remain one. Nature is constantly revealing her secrets to him, and his ambition is to be the first to reveal and simplify her mysteries to the world at large. His cabinet of minerals, etc., is indeed a valuable one and should be purchased of him by the State and Prof. Condon himself employed at a liberal salary to continue his interesting researches and in published reports inform the world at large how rich we are in mineral resources. The cabinet is the result of years of labor, and were it destroyed in any way could never be replaced. The Professor would hesitate long before parting with it, but he would sooner dispose of it in this way, no doubt, than to sell it to parties outside of the State, he having received many offers for it already. As a traveling companion, although a man of sober thought and dignified at times, he is none the less fond of a joke, and is a wit in his quiet, serious way. He is a good talker and is prepared with anecdote for one, theology for another, politics for the third, fish for another, mirth for another, sentimentality for those who desire it, and at all times and under all circumstances is brim full and running over with natural history and geology. In a word, Prof. Condon is one of God's noblemen, and no pen sketch written by us has so utterly failed to convey our estimation of the man's true worth than has the one completed at this point.

C. B. WATSON.

Was born at Time, Pike county, Illinois, on the 25th of November, 1849, and is therefore 33 years of age. In 1860 his parents removed to Logan county, where in 1862 his father enlisted in the 106th Illinois Volunteers, and remained in active service until the close of the war. This left the boy at the age of 13 to support a family of nine, all younger than himself except one sister. His father was a farmer and in the cornfield the boy passed his time until 20 years of age. This portion of his life constituted one of the severest trials that an ambitious youth could well bear. He could not attend school, and the small, still hours of night found him wrestling with a meagre supply of books and no teacher, while from daylight till dark the winter's storms and summer's heat found him toiling for the support of the family. At the end of the war his father returned to the family, reduced by the hardships of such a life to a wreck of his former self, from which, though he lived until 1878, he never recovered. Young Watson's task as head of the family continued without intermission until 1870, when he borrowed $100 and came to California. He reached Sacramento City October 1st with one dollar and fifty cents. He secured a job of wood chopping on Cache creek, near Woodland, for seven months, losing but seven days in that time. He then came to Oregon, stopping in Rogue river valley, where he spent the summer of 1871. In the fall of the same year and during the winter he attended school at Ashland, where he paid board by cutting wood and "doing chores." In the spring of 1872 he commenced teaching school. After teaching for a short period he and six others started for Boise City with a band of horses. Returning in the fall of that year he again attended school at Ashland Academy. The summer and fall of 1873 was spent in teaching and in surveying. In May, 1874, he received the nomination for Representative by the Republicans of Jackson county, but was defeated. He was married September 1, 1874, to Miss Ella J. Chitwood, daughter of J. H. Chitwood. From 1874 to 1876 he was connected with Dr. Chitwood in a drug store, and during that period studied law. In 1875 he became a candidate for Prosecuting Attorney for the First Judicial District, and was beaten by 185 votes. In 1877 he took charge of the "Oregon Sentinel," which position he held for nearly a year. In December of that year he was admitted by the Supreme Court of Oregon. In March, 1878, he went to Lake county and opened an office and in November with his brother, W. W. Watson, established the "State Line Herald." In this year his name was again placed on the Republican ticket as a candidate for District Attorney of the First District, but he declined to run. In the early part of 1880 he enlarged the "Herald" and made it a stalwart Republican paper. In April, 1880, he was placed on the Republican ticket as a candidate for Presidential Elector, and received the highest vote on the ticket. During this canvass his newspaper office was burned with all in it. In November, 1880, he changed his residence to Portland and during the last campaign made a canvass of a portion of the State in behalf of the Republican party.

FRED PAGE TUSTIN, ESQ.

The old countries of the Eastern continent have contributed largely to the talent of this, our own free America, and, generally speaking, those who have received their education in the schools of old England and come hither and adopted our manners and customs without forcing upon us, as many do, taunts and sneers of superciliousness, rarely fail to make warm and lasting friends and to meet with the business success they so deservedly merit. Their educational training, when rigidly followed, is perhaps superior to our own, and, when preparing for a profession the English student is, beyond a doubt, put through a better course of preparatory study than is he who pursues the same profession under the American system of preparation. The subject of this sketch was born and raised on English soil and did not leave his native land until along in 1872, at which time he was about twenty-four years of age, having been born in the city of Oxford, England, November 7, 1848. He studied law with Edward Vere Nicoll, at Shipston, in the county of Worcester, England, from 1864 to 1872. In the spring of the latter year he started for Oregon, reaching Roseburg on July 3d of the same year. While in Roseburg he was engaged in various pursuits, in all of which he succeeded in gaining warm and steadfast friends by his quiet, industrious habits and gentlemanly deportment. As soon, however, as he had been in Oregon a sufficient length of time to gain a citizenship he again applied himself to the study of law, having meantime moved to Albany and entered the office of Weatherford & Piper. He was admitted to practice before the Supreme Court of this State, in December, 1877, in the latter part of which month he moved to Pendleton, in Umatilla county, where he has since resided, devoting his attention to the practice of law and engaging somewhat in agricultural pursuits. Mr. Tustin is a young man of rare educational talent and is destined to become one of the leaders in the legal profession of Eastern Oregon, where he is making friends rapidly and building up a lucrative line of practice. He has always been a strong Republican and a firm believer in the doctrine of the majority rule, and has since 1878 been an active member of the Republican State Central Committee and has been a regular attendant at its meetings and also at the State Republican conventions. He is a communicant in the Protestant Episcopal Church, and has been largely instrumental in advancing its interests in that new country. He is also an influential member of the Knights of Pythias. Mr. Tustin is a gentleman of low and heavy build, slightly obese, with full, ruddy face, covered with brown whiskers, a well-shaped head, eyes of blue, and deep-set brown hair, and of a genial, courteous disposition. He was married at Roseburg, August 25, 1874, to Miss Annie Sanderson, granddaughter of the late Captain Hembree, of Yamhill county, who died and was buried in the cemetery at Albany, in March, 1875. By the way, Mr. Tustin's name is prominently urged by citizens of Eastern Oregon for the Executive appointment as Circuit Judge of the recently organized Sixth Judicial District.

RALPH M. DEMENT.

The profession of law has among its followers many young men possessed of the necessary qualifications which, if judiciously administered, will within a few short years earn for them a prominent place in the ranks of the legal fraternity, there being to-day, as there has been for centuries past, "plenty of room at the top." The subject of this sketch is one of that number who has it in his power to become a leader, having been favored by circumstances, and being possessed of energy, industry and ambition sufficient to nerve him to the contest and carry him onward and upward toward the very summit of legal fame. He was born in Oregon City July 27, 1856, his parents being classed among the pioneers of this State. He received excellent educational advantages, having attended the public schools of San Francisco, Cal., and graduating in 1875 with the degree of B. S. in the Collegiate Department of the Columbian University at Washington, D. C., and subsequently, in 1877, with that of L. L. B., in the Law Department of the same institution. He was officially connected with the U. S. War and Interior Departments for several years. In 1879 he removed to Portland to enter upon the active practice of his profession, and formed a partnership with Hon. John H. Mitchell, ex U. S. Senator, and has since that time been in constant practice. He is active and industrious and is destined to become one of the most prominent attorneys of the State. He has as ye hardly reached the prime of life, is of medium height, slight build, brown hair and eyes, and of a social, genial disposition. He made a host of friends while in Salem during the Legislative session just closed, where he was a prominent and enthusiastic supporter of Mitchell for re-election to the U. S. Senate. He is unmarried.

HON. J. L. COLLINS,

Now a resident of Dallas, Polk county, was born in Warren county, Missouri, May 9, 1833. He acquired a general knowledge of the rudimental principles of an education in the imperfect subscription schools of that part of the country. In 1846 he crossed the plains with ox teams, in the first company that ever came by way of the Klamath lakes, and across the Siskiyou, Umpqua and Calapooia mountains into the Willamette valley, often driving the foremost team that broke down the thick sage-brush upon the trackless waste. He left the place of his birth on the 20th day of April, 1846, and after suffering a multitude of hardships and privations almost incredible for a boy of thirteen years, arrived on the Luckiamute, in Polk county, on the 5th day of March, 1847, having remained during the greater part of the winter in an unoccupied cabin built by Eugene Skinner, near Eugene City, where, in company with Harrison Turnedge, who agreed to remain with him, he endured great hardships. The winter was a severe one, and having in compassion received into their camp an old sailor named Samuel Ruth, who was badly crippled, and Mr. Turnedge being sick and unable to leave camp a good portion of the time, it devolved upon young Collins, then a mere boy, to shoulder his gun and with its breech breaking the ice in the sloughs and streams, wade through them waist deep in order to reach good hunting grounds on the other shore and secure game in sufficient quantities to meet the necessities of himself and his unfortunate companions. In the spring of 1847 his father settled in the southern part of Polk county. He worked hard every day helping to erect and improve their rude but nowise uncomfortable home. Being too poor to procure lamp oil or candles, he pursued his studies at night, by the rude fire-place lighted with pitch wood. After a few years, when the family could manage to get along without his assistance, he was permitted to go to the institute at Salem, where, by working hard at whatever his hand could find to do mornings and evenings and on Saturdays, he made his way through a few terms of that school, then under the management of Prof. F. S. Hoyt and his excellent wife. While at Salem he read law for a time under Hon. B. F. Harding and Hon. L. F. Grover. In 1853 he went to California, where he made and lost a considerable fortune in mining. Returning home in 1855, the Legislature being in session at Corvallis, he was employed by Hon. Alonzo Leland to report the proceedings for the "Democratic Standard," then published at Portland. The capital was removed during the session to Salem, and a few days before the adjournment Capt. B. F. Burch organized Company B of the recruiting battalion First Regiment of Oregon Mounted Volunteers, for service in the Yakima Indian war. Mr. Collins at once enlisted, and after the adjournment of the Assembly he joined the troops in the field on the Columbia river, just above The Dalles, and was with Col. Thomas R. Cornelius throughout his famous "horse-meat campaign." These volunteers pursued the Indians during March and part of April, being often reduced to the extremity of subsisting upon the horses captured from or abandoned by the Indians in their flight. He was in several smart skirmishes, and bore a part in the battle of the Simcoe, where the gallant Capt. Hembree fell, that won for him the respect of his officers and the confidence and esteem of all his comrades in arms. On returning from the war he engaged in teaching in Polk county, diligently pursuing his studies. In November, 1859, he was admitted to the bar and began the practice of law. He was a Democrat in politics until the beginning of the rebellion, when he abandoned that party and was a member of the State Convention at Eugene City, and aided in organizing the Republican party for its first effective campaign in Oregon. In 1861 he married Miss Mary Whiteaker. His practice grew rapidly, and he soon acquired a comfortable home, and was supremely happy in the prosperity of his affairs. His wife died in 1864, leaving one child. In the autumn of 1864 he was elected Chief Clerk of the House of Representatives, which office he also filled during the special session of 1865. In 1867 he was again married to Miss Mary E. Kimes. In 1869 he was appointed Judge of Polk county by Gov. George L. Woods, to fill a vacancy occasioned by the appointment of Judge W. C. Whitson to the bench in Idaho. Judge Collins filled this office with such distinguished ability, fairness and justice that not a murmur of disapprobation has ever been heard against him, even from his political opponents. He is still pursuing his profession at Dallas, in the enjoyment and esteem of all who know him. He is a man of positive character: tenacious, obstinate and fearless in pursuing whatever he believes to be right; and has by his own exertions acquired an education superior to that of many persons who have enjoyed the blessings of wealth and the aid of colleges. He is a forcible speaker and a graphic writer. He is warm-hearted and true to those who win his confidence, and has suffered more, perhaps, from adhering to his friends in their adversity than from any other cause.

HON. STEPHEN FOWLER CHADWICK.

The subject of this sketch is a native of Connecticut, where he received his education. He studied law in the city of New York and was admitted to the bar in that State. Immediately after his admission to the bar he came to Oregon, arriving here in 1851. He settled in Southern Oregon, where he followed his profession with success and honorable distinction. He was elected to represent Douglas county in the Convention that framed the Constitution of Oregon. He was Presidential Elector in 1864 and 1868, and was the messenger in 1868 to carry the vote of Oregon to Washington. In 1870 he was elected Secretary of State and served eight years. The last two years he became Governor under the Constitution, on the resignation of Gov. Grover, who was elected to the U. S. Senate. During Gov. Chadwick's term as Governor the State was inflicted with the Indian wars of 1877 and 1878; that of 1878 being more threatening to the peace of our

State east of the mountains than any war that had preceded it. In this war the Governor served in person and was at the front during the continuance of the war. It is but just to state that it was owing to his personal presence at the point of outbreak, when the Snake Indians made their descent on the settlements and burnt Cayuse Station, that the fatal blow was averted. Gen. Howard, the day this attack was made, had ordered his troops, at an early hour, to move to a point east of the Blue Mountains, believing that the Indians were in advance of him. Gov. Chadwick, at the council held by Gen. Howard with Gov. Ferry, of Washington, and Gov. Chadwick at Weston, on the same day, was convinced that the Indians were behind Gen. Howard and so stated, but the General, feeling that his information was reliable, ordered his troops to go in search of them in the direction indicated. Gov. Chadwick returned to Pendleton that night to learn, as he had supposed, that the Indians were behind General Howard and were threatening the settlements with destruction. He also learned that the house where he nooned was burnt in an hour after he left it by the Indians, and that, on leaving the station, that he and his escort passed the Snakes, concealed in ambush, not over one hundred and fifty yards from the road. He gave his attention at once to the wounded and to the safety of the inhabitants that were gathered into Pendleton for protection, and despatched a courier after night to Gen. Howard, or any officer found, to return with the troops that were taken away. This courier overtook the troops near Walla Walla. They returned while the Snakes were digging rifle pits and preparing for a general attack as well as for defence. The prompt action of the Governor in procuring these troops, and their immediate attack on the Indians that followed, was the means of driving the savages from the State, and saved the lives and property of the people of Eastern Oregon. During the entire war the Governor gave his personal presence to his duties, and was most fortunate in his efficient conduct of that war. Though one of the most serious and threatening to our State and Territories of Indian wars, it was conducted and closed on behalf of the State by the executive, with great economy and activity. The Governor, at the great council of the friendly chiefs and the military officers under and including General Howard, demanded the outlaws that were responsible for this war, and who were known to the chiefs. General Howard assented to this. The names were given, and the Governor had them arrested and they were tried, convicted and executed. But this was not the case in the Modoc war. The demand of Gov. Grover for the outlaws who were the cause of that war was wholly disregarded by the military who tried them, permitting some of them to escape punishment. Gov. Chadwick has received distinction as a Mason, having filled every station in the Grand Lodge of Masons, including that of Grand Master, seven times Master of a lodge, Grand Master in the Lodge of Perfection. He has received the thirty-third degree in the Scotch Rite. As Chairman of the Committee on Foreign Correspondence of the Grand Lodge of Masons, of Oregon, he is now serving his seventeenth year. This would suggest efficiency and ability, and he has also received marked distinction as an Odd Fellow. In early life he obtained a knowledge of the art of printing, and was for a season during his studies a writer for the newspapers. Gov. Chadwick is a gentleman of low stature and heavy set, slightly inclined to corpulancy. He is of very pleasing address and a man of great geniality of character. As a public officer, he made friends rapidly, and the vote he received on the occasion of his re-election to the office of Secretary of State was a flattering testimonial of the esteem in which he was held by the public. As a speaker, he is forcible, earnest and persuasive, and possesses a vast fund of what has been termed personal magnetism. Although now turning fifty years of age, he is in excellent preservation and bids fair to live for another quarter of a century. Gov. Chadwick held many minor and important offices in early life. He was Deputy U. S. District Attorney and acting Prosecuting Attorney under our Territorial existence in Southern Oregon, and was the first judge of Douglas county and first postmaster of Scottsburg. He has contributed largely by his valuable writings and addresses on various occasions, especially those delivered at the laying of the corner stone of the State Capitol building, and at the pioneer re-union, to the history of our State. He was married in 1856 to Miss Jane A. Smith, a most estimable lady and a native of Virginia and of an excellent family. By this marriage there are four children, two daughters and two sons. The elder daughter became the wife of W. T. Long, Esq., of Salem. The Governor is very fond of good society, and, like all genial men, is fond of good plain living, which he enjoys as much as any gentleman with whom we ever met. His genial manners, liberal and charitable disposition, and his many acts of kindness have won for him a host of friends, of whom he must feel justly proud. He prizes highly his annual feast that comes off on the first day of January, when he makes his yearly round among his acquaintances, and he is credited with ample capacity for this treat. He is a good and trusty citizen of the olden time in Oregon and a resident of Salem, in our State.

GEORGE HUMPHREY.

No man is better or more favorably known in Linn county than is he whose name heads this sketch, and who is at present the Sheriff of that county. He was born in Jefferson county, Ohio, January 23, 1833, and with his parents moved to Illinois in 1835, and a year later moved to Iowa, where he resided until 1865, when he moved to Oregon and settled in Linn county, where he has resided ever since, and where he has made a host of friends who have every confidence in his honesty, efficiency and integrity, and that they have not mistaken their man is evinced by the fact that he has never betrayed them, and by his obliging and accommodating disposition has ever shown a willingness to do anything in his power to show his appreciation of their regard. Mr. Humphrey never had many educational advantages, but he has managed to pick up considerable information, and is today better posted on general subjects than many who, in early life, enjoyed facilities for securing knowledge of which he was deprived. Mr. Humphrey was for eight years prior to 1880 Deputy Sheriff of Linn county, and in 1882 he was nominated and elected Sheriff of that county by a handsome majority. Mr. Humphrey is a prominent Mason, with the rank of Past Master in the Blue Lodge and P. H. P. in the chapter. In 1854 he was married to Miss Martha Wills, of Monroe county, Iowa, and their family at present consists of three children. Mr. Humphrey is a plain, every-day sort of a man, of a little more than ordinary height, ruddy complexion, broad-shouldered, and a lover of the good things of this world. He is an exponent of the eternal principles of the unterrified Democracy, and is a successful politician. His generosity and good nature are greatly in excess of his income, and were it not for the will power of the man over himself, he would be poverty-stricken to-day. He is plain and unassuming and makes friends rapidly.

HON. J. C. MORELAND,

One of the leading attorneys of Oregon, and a well-known resident of Portland, was born in Tennessee in 1844, and with his parents came to Oregon in 1852 and settled in the woods in Clackamas county, where they endured the hardships and privations of a pioneer's life. He was raised on the farm and followed the plow until along in 1860, when he went to Portland and commenced learning the printer's trade and worked for about three years and a half on the old "Oregon Farmer." He succeeded in laying by sufficient money to pay his expenses during his somewhat protracted attendance at the Portland academy. He commenced reading law in 1866 under the late Hon. David Logan, and was admitted to the bar in 1868. He was a member of the Portland City Council from 1872 to 1875, and in 1877 was appointed City Attorney, which office he held until the Common Council accepted his resignation in 1882. During his incumbency in this office, his official acts never failed to receive the unqualified endorsement of all good citizens, as he was ever zealous and conscientious in the discharge of his duties, acting ever without fear or favor, and enforcing to the utmost of his ability the strict letter of the law. He, since his resignation of that office, has actively resumed the practice of law and has at once stepped back into the prominent position heretofore held by him. As an attorney, he has few superiors on this coast, and a client's case in his hands receives and secures at the hands of the court all the merit it demands. Mr. Moreland is a Republican and takes an active interest in politics. He was married in 1867 to Miss Abbie B. Kline, and they have three children. Mr. Moreland is a pleasant-appearing gentleman, slight build, of medium height, prominent features, brown hair and whiskers, and a clear, expressive eye. He has not yet reached the meridian of life and his era of usefulness has but barely commenced.

HON. JOHN C. PEEBLES.

The subject of the following sketch was born January 23, 1826, in Westmoreland county, Penn. In 1838 he removed to Elkhart county, Indiana, and in 1850 he came to Oregon, arriving at Oregon City, October 7th, and remaining there until the following March, when he removed to Marion county, settling at Fairfield, his donation claim embracing the present town site.

In 1852 Mr. Peebles entered public life as Assistant Clerk of the House of Representatives, and in 1853 he was elected to the Legislature, serving in the House with Hon. L. F. Grover and Hon. E. F. Colby as colleagues. In 1854 he was elected to the Council, where he served three years and was afterwards elected a member of the Constitutional Convention, serving as Chairman of the Committee on Education. In 1860 he was elected State Librarian, also serving as Chief Clerk of the Senate at that session. In 1862 he was elected County Judge of Marion County, and re-elected in 1866, and again in 1874, serving in that capacity twelve years. In 1880 Mr. Peebles was Chief Clerk of the Senate. He also served as Chief Clerk of the Senate the last time the Republicans had control of the Senate prior to 1880. In all the various positions which Judge Peebles has filled, he invariably closes his term with the plaudit of "Well done" from his constituents. In politics Judge Peebles assisted in the organization of the Democratic party in the, then, Territory of Oregon, and acted with that party up to the inception of the civil war. At the commencement of the war he unhesitatingly cast his influence in favor of the Administration of President Lincoln, and circulated the first paper to obtain signatures for a Union meeting in the City of Salem. Since then Judge Peebles has been an unswerving member of the Republican party and was honored with the position of Chairman of the Republican State Conventions of 1878 and 1880. Mr. Peebles read law for two years prior to coming to Oregon, but never sought admission to the bar. His tastes inclined to agricultural pursuits, and he now resides three and a half miles south of Salem, in a pleasant home, on a farm on the line of the O. & C. R. R. He was married in 1851 to Miss E. J. Mark, of Clackamas county, Oregon. Five children, two sons and three daughters, are living, the eldest son, George A., is a graduate of Willamette University, attorney-at-law, and now principal of the Salem public schools. He is a fine-looking gentleman of ordinary height, a well-shaped head, slightly bald, sharp and prominent features and gray hair and whiskers.

JOHN M. PITTENGER, ESQ.

It is perfectly natural to admire pluck and ambition in a young man, and this, no doubt, is one reason why he whose name heads this sketch has won so many friends during his residence in Oregon. He is of that class who are opposed to leading the routine life of an unambitious citizen, but with the energy and enterprise characteristic of Young America when untrammeled with restraint, he seeks higher and nobler spheres of life and looks forward to securing fame and fortune before being overtaken by old age. Mr. Pittinger was born in Medina county, Ohio, August 18, 1855, and attended an academic course at Oberlin in that State. Although raised on a farm he applied himself to his studies with the laudable purpose in view of adopting some one of the leading professions. He taught school in Ohio and Michigan and came to Oregon in 1878, and during the winter of 1879-80 was Principal of the Sheridan Academy. He then went to East Portland and has speculated some in real estate, and acted as Deputy Prosecuting

Attorney in that city. He has recently entered the law office of Caples & Mulkey with a view of completing his studies and applying for admission to the bar at the March term of the Supreme Court. Mr. Pittenger is a young gentleman of fine personal appearance, light built, regular features, smooth face, with the exception of a mustache, and dark brown hair. He is of a genial disposition, enjoys a joke and has the happy faculty of making friends of all with whom he comes in contact.

W. LUNDBERG

Was born in the city of Copenhagen, Denmark, on September 6, 1836. He received his early education until the age of fourteen under the direction of private instructors, and was confirmed according to the rites of the Lutheran Church. Besides his mother tongue, he became master of German, French and English, and having a great taste for mechanical work, was apprenticed to a manufacturer of philosophical and mathematical instruments. His uncle, P. Faber, who was then Director General of the government telegraph, instructed him in the use of the instruments, and through him the youth acquired a fondness for electrical experiments. When young Lundberg's term of four years as apprentice had expired, he traveled for a short time through Germany, France and England, and not feeling satisfied with the information he received there in regard to electricity, made up his mind to go to the very fountain head of electricity and liberty, and arrived in New York in the early part of 1855, when he immediately went to work for the firm of Charles T. and J. N. Chester, then the most prominent manufacturing electricians of the United States. When the rebellion broke out, in 1861, a brother of the above firm, S. Chester, was appointed Captain of Company I, of the Fifteenth New York Regiment, under Col. John McLeod Murphy, with the intention of making his company a telegraph corps. Mr. Lundberg received the appointment of First Lieutenant of this company and was sworn into the United States service, but when the government would not recognize the company as a telegraph corps, they were, after sixteen weeks' service, mustered out. He then received a call from the California State Telegraph Company as manufacturing electrician, and arrived in California the latter part of 1861. After remaining in their service two years he started an establishment of his own, and met with great success, sending instruments all over the world. In April, 1870, Mr. Lundberg superintended the electrical department under Col. Von Schmidt in removing Blossom Rock in San Francisco harbor, exploding twenty-three tons of powder in one charge. In 1871 he sold out his establishment and took a trip to Japan, where he remained four months, and then returned to San Francisco, where he lived until 1875, when he came to Oregon, arriving here the latter part of November. The following January he received appointment of Superintendent of Fire Alarm Telegraph and has held that position ever since. In 1881 Mr. Lundberg associated himself with J. Dilg in a manufacturing establishment for electrical, surveyors' and optical goods. In 1879, together with a few others, he organized the Natural Science Association, before which he has delivered several lectures on the phonograph, electricity and other scientific subjects. Mr. Lundberg became a member of the Masonic fraternity in 1866, and has so continued ever since.

JAMES R. BAYLEY, M. D.

The subject of this pen sketch has been a resident of our State for almost thirty years, during which time he has been closely identified with its progress, and to-day, although he is aged and gray, and his footsteps totter somewhat, he is a man who commands the esteem and respect of all who know him, and one who stands high in his profession. He was born in Clark county, Ohio, in 1819, receiving an academic education at Springfield, his younger days being divided between town and country life. He commenced the study of medicine in 1841 and was admitted to practice three years later, being a graduate of the Ohio Medical College. He at once commenced practice at his old home in Springfield, where he remained for four years, afterwards locating in Cincinnati, where he enjoyed a successful practice for seven years. In 1852 he was married to Miss Elizabeth Harpole, of Green county, Ohio, and moved to Oregon in 1855 and settled at Lafayette, remaining there two years and moving to Corvallis, where he has resided ever since. He was a member of the Territorial Council in 1856 and 1857, and has been twice elected Judge of Benton county. He was a member of the State Senate in 1866 and 1868, and was appointed Supervisor of Internal Revenue in 1869, serving until 1873. Since that time he has devoted himself to the practice of his profession in Benton county. He is a thirty-two-degree Mason and Past Grand High Priest and Past Grand Master of the Masonic jurisdiction of Oregon; has been a prominent Odd Fellow and is of Presbyterian religious belief. He is the father of six children and the grandfather of one. He is tall and slender, with pleasant face and an agreeable temperament.

HON. C. W. FULTON,

An esteemed citizen of Astoria, and one of the most prominent young attorneys in the State, made his appearance on this mundane sphere August 24, 1853, at Linn, Ohio, where he remained until 1855, when with his parents he removed to Harrison county, Iowa, where his early boyhood was spent on a farm. In May, 1870, they moved to Pawnee county, Nebraska. His father served as Second Lieutenant in Co. A, Twenty-First Iowa Regiment. The subject of our sketch received a liberal education, attending the common schools in Iowa during the winter months of his residence there and the High School at Pawnee City for a couple of years. In 1873 he commenced the study of law in the office of Hon. A. H. Babcock, of Pawnee City, Nebraska, and was admitted to the bar in 1875. He started for Oregon the same year and landed in Portland nearly broke. Nothing daunted, however, he went to Albany, where he heard of a vacancy in a school near Waterloo, about eighteen miles distant. Mr. Fulton walked there, secured the school, walked back to Albany, passed his examination, secured his certificate and taught for one term at $40 per month and board around. He then went to Astoria and commenced the practice of law, where he has since resided, and has succeeded in building up a lucrative business. In 1878 he was elected State Senator and served his constituents and the State at large faithfully in that capacity for the term of four years. He is rather above average height, spare built, smooth face with the exception of a mustache, light hair and whiskers and a pleasant eye. He stands well in business, legal and social circles and has hosts of friends throughout the State. He is married and is said to make a model husband.

D. L. MOOMAW,

At present a prominent citizen of Baker City, was born in Eastern Virginia, in 1837 and came to Oregon in 1858. He settled in Oregon City, where he was engaged in teaching school until the spring of 1861. The gold excitement caused by the discovery of that coveted commodity in Northern Idaho induce him to emigrate hence and he remained in the mines for several years. His success was not brilliant in amassing a fortune of any considerable magnitude, and he returned to Oregon in the spring of 1870, locating at Baker City, where he has resided ever since. He has become closely identified with the interests of that section of the country and is enthusiastic in its praise. He has always been an active politician, but is not a candidate for political honors. He is a gentleman of pleasing address, a little below medium height, heavy set, full beard and hair of dark brown. He is unmarried; in fact, he is considered by many a confirmed old bachelor, but he is still in market and is very popular among the ladies. He is an uncompromising Republican and represented his county in the last Republican State Convention.

H. F. ADAMS, M. D.

Was born June 23, 1836, in Sheldon, Vt. When fourteen years old he was sent to St Albans Academy and later to North Hampton Institute. His early religious training was in the Congregational Church. When scarcely nineteen years old young Adams attended his first course of lectures at the Medical Department of the University of Vermont. During the following summer he read with Surgeon O. S. Searles, M. D., and in the fall he entered the Medical Department of the University of New York, a private student of Prof. Valentine Mott, M. D. The next year he entered for his third course of lectures at Albany, New York, but while there his health failed and he was compelled to seek rest, he having already been troubled with hemorrhage of the lungs. He soon after began the practice of medicine in Oakland county, Mich., where he was united in marriage to Miss Lavinia Perry. This union was brief, as his devoted wife soon fell a victim to that dread disease phthisis pulmonalis. Soon after this event the Doctor entered the volunteer corps of surgeons in the United States army. His health, however, became again impaired and he was compelled to resign his position and go north. In the fall of 1862 he settled in Jo Davis county,

Illinois, where he married his present estimable companion, Miss Louisa Wilkerson. As the result of this union, the Doctor has three daughters, each of whom is receiving, or has already received, the benefits derived from a collegiate course of instruction. In 1864 the Governor of Illinois offered Dr. Adams a commission as surgeon in a cavalry regiment which he accepted and again entered the army work. His health continued poor, and as a sanitary measure he came to the Pacific Coast, where he has gradually improved until he is now robust and hearty. Dr. Adams holds a diploma in regular graduation from the Missouri Medical College, and several State diplomas, and is now United States pension surgeon by appointment of the Secretary of War. He is building up a lucrative practice in Marion county, where, by his strict attention to the requirements of the profession, he has won the confidence and esteem of a large circle of friends. The Doctor is hale and hearty, weighing over two hundred pounds, and his geniality and conviviality are proverbial.

ANDREW LOCKHART.

This young gentleman is the clerk of the Senate Judiciary Committee. Although this clerkship is by far the most important among all the committees, Mr. Lockhart is well qualified to discharge its arduous duties in a satisfactory manner. He is well educated, and has the great advantage of being a printer by trade. He was born in Coos county in the year 1861, attended the county schools and afterwards graduated from Heald's Business College, San Francisco, thus obtaining a thorough commercial education. After leaving the college he entered the office of the "Coos Bay News," where he learned his trade as a printer, and was afterwards associated with Messrs. G. Webster and J. Harker in the publication of the "Coast Mail," in Marshfield, Coos county. In 1881 he was appointed Deputy U. S. Collector for the southern district of Oregon. He is at present studying law and will soon be admitted to practice.

ROBERT NEWCOMB.

The present Grand Recorder of the Grand Lodge of the A. O. U. W. of Oregon and Washington Territory, was born in New Orleans, Louisiana, November 4, 1842, and with his parents came to California where "Bob," as he is familiarly known, completed his education in the San Francisco High School, and afterwards learned the book binder's trade. In 1864, owing to failing health, he visited the Sandwich Islands, where he was married to Miss E. S. Whitens September 29, 1868. He settled in Douglas county in 1873, where for several years he was interested in the newspaper business. In 1877 he went into law partnership with Hon. L. F. Lane, afterwards member of Congress from Oregon, and opened a law office in Roseburg, where he continued in business until elected Grand Recorder in July, 1881. Mr. Newcomb is prominently connected with several fraternal organizations, being Grand Senior Steward Grand Lodge A. F. and A. M. of Oregon, Grand Vice Chancellor of the Grand Lodge Knights of

Pythias of Oregon and Washington, Past commander of the American Legion of Honor, and is a member of both branches of the I. O. O. F. Being naturally of a genial, whole-souled temperament, he makes friends rapidly and has no difficulty in retaining them. He is one of those jolly, soul-invigorating men whose very presence in a crowd instills in those around him a spirit of ease and conviviality, and hence his popularity. He is rather above medium height, spare built, well-defined features, dark hair and whiskers, black eyes and a pleasant smile. He is just in the prime of life and has a bright future before him.

HON. THOMAS M'F. PATTON

Was born in Carrolton, Ohio, March 19, 1829, and in 1838 moved with his parents to Findlay, Ohio. He attended school at Martensburg Academy and the Ohio Wesleyan University, Delaware; read law and was admitted to the bar in 1850. He started for Oregon overland in 1851, and settled in Yamhill county, where he remained a few months and moved to Salem in December of the same year. In the spring of 1853 he went to Jackson county and was shortly afterwards elected County Judge, which position he resigned in 1854. During the Indian war of 1853 he served as orderly sergeant in Company A, commanded by Captain John F. Miller. He returned to Salem, and on August 3, 1854, was married to Miss Fannie Cooke, only daughter of Hon. E. N. Cooke, afterwards State Treasurer. He served as Chief Clerk of the House in 1860 and was appointed Chief Clerk in the office of Superintendent of Indian Affairs in 1861 under W. H. Rector, Esq. He was for several years secretary of the People's Transportation Company, and was again elected Chief Clerk of the House in 1866. In 1872 he was elected a member of the House from Marion county, and on the 26th of March, 1876, he was appointed Appraiser of Merchandise for District of Willamette, which position he still holds. He was elected Grand Master of Masons in 1872 and was re-elected in 1873. Mr. Patton is a gentleman of about medium height, spare built, with sharp-pointed features, eyes set back well into his head, with full beard and hair of a dark brown color. He is a good business man, cautious in his investments and therefore more or less successful in his business enterprises. He owns considerable real estate in Salem and is considered comfortably well-fixed in worldly matters. His family consists of three children, two sons and one daughter, the latter married to John D. McCully, Esq., of Joseph, Union county, Politically speaking, Mr. Patton is a Republican, and his religious tendencies are cast with the Congregational Church.

DR. JOHN BLAKIE PILKINGTON,

A well-known occulist and physician of Portland, was born near Providence, R. I., in 1834, of an English father and a mother of Scotch and Irish nativity. His father was the youngest of three brothers brought over by American manufacturers to run the first four color calico print works in this country. He was a man of boldly inquiring mind, enterprising and of sterling honesty qualities which his son has inherited to a marked degree. The doctor spent five years of his early life on a farm and fruit nursery, and at the early age of seventeen became a school teacher. He began the study of medicine with his uncle, a Scotch physician, in 1856 and worked his way through college. He came to California in 1860, and for three years superintended a silver mine, and in 1867 filled the position as assistant assayer on the celebrated Comstock lode. He shortly afterwards returned to his profession and took the honors of the Medical Department of the University of the Pacific in 1870, and came to Oregon in 1871, settling in Portland, where he has since resided, having built up a large and extensive practice and established an infirmary and sanitarium, which, in the future of the Northwest, promises to be to Portland all that the hosts of such institutions are to metropolitan cities elsewhere. He served for two years as Professor of eye and ear diseases in the Medical Department in the Willamette University. The doctor is a man of original ideas, of thorough fearlessness of character, science-loving, and a liberalist in medicine, religion and politics. In the relation of husband and father, no man in the State is more happily placed. Five sons give fair promise of perpetuating the name and making it honored in the future history of our State. As an occulist Dr. Pilkington is gaining an enviable reputation throughout the State. During his residence here he has performed all of the great operations upon the eye, such as the modified Linear extraction, cneuclcation, artificial pupil, etc., as performed by the great masters of the old world with remarkable success. Over eighty per cent. of his cataract operations have been successful. The doctor is one of the most genial men in his profession and is universally esteemed and respected by a very large circle of friends and acquaintances. He is of ordinary height, rather slight build, a face fairly beaming with good humor, full beard and brown hair. He has never sought political honors, being literally wedded to his profession, the practice of which occupies his entire attention.

FRANK G. ABELL,

The popular and artistic photographer of Portland, was born in Roscoe, Winnebago county, Illinois, September 20, 1844. He went with his parents to California in 1857, and finished his education in the Methodist College at Santa Clara. After leaving this institution he remained with his parents at their home in Petaluma, Sonoma county, for a few weeks, and then joined the Lloyd Magruder mining expedition to Powder river. He was then but sixteen years of age, and not taking kindly to mining, returned home in the following fall, 1862. Having taken a fancy to the photographic business, and being possessed of talent in that line, he proceeded to San Francisco, and entered the well-known establishment of William Shew, on Montgomery street, where he remained four years, becoming master of the art in all its branches. In 1863, at the age of nineteen, Mr. Abell was married to Miss Kate Lauder, daughter of George Lauder, Esq., a prominent hay and grain dealer of San Francisco, and has now two children, the oldest of whom, Emma May, aged eighteen, is at present perfecting her musical education in the Bay City, under the direction of Mrs. Marriner-Campbell, and the youngest, George L., aged sixteen, is attending the State University at Eugene, from which institution he will soon graduate. In 1866 Mr. Abell paid a visit to his old home in the East, where he remained one year, and upon his return was again engaged by Mr. Shew, where he held forth until 1871. In that year he started out on his own account and took a business trip through California, taking in San Diego, Grass Valley and all the towns of importance throughout the State, Mrs. Abell accompanying him on the entire journey. His venture proving so successful, Frank concluded to pay a visit to Oregon, believing that his work would commend itself to the residents here, and he arrived at Ashland in November, 1876; he spent the winter there and in Jacksonville, and then moved on to Portland, stopping in Roseburg two months and in Eugene three months, reaching here in November, 1877. On his arrival Mr. Abell saw at once that this city afforded a superior opportunity for a photographer of ability and, after paying a very short visit to his home in San Francisco, returned and bought out the establishment of D. H. Hendee commencing business January 10, 1878. Since his arrival here Mr. Abell has brought his business to a high degree of perfection, and obtained an extensive and well-merited patronage. During the last session of the Legislative Assembly he visited the capital and obtained single photographs of each member, and also a grouping of all together; likewise the State officers. The enterprise was the first one of the kind ever attempted, and gave general satisfaction.

REV. EDWARD R. GEARY, D. D.,

Who to-day stands as one of the most eminent divines upon this coast, and who is so universally beloved and respected by all who know him, was born in Boonsboro, Maryland, April 30, 1811, and was one of the distinguished graduates of Jefferson College, Pa., in the class of 1834, having made his way by teaching as his sole pecuniary resource. He spent three years at Alleghany City as a student of theology, and then went to Alabama and was successively principal of the academies of Mt. Hebron and Livingston. Several of his pupils became men of note in the civil and military service of their sections. He remained there about two years and a half, when he returned to Pennsylvania and entered the ministry of the Presbyterian Church. He became the pastor of the church of Unity at Fredericksburg, Ohio, where he remained for a period of thirteen years. He was married to Miss Harriet R. Reed at New Berlin, Pa., and some years after her death to Miss N. M. Woodbridge, of New York. He came to Oregon in 1851 and settled in Yamhill county, and was appointed Clerk of the United States Circuit Court by Judge Pratt. He was afterwards elected County Clerk of Yamhill county and Superintendent of Public Schools. He was then appointed Chief Clerk in the office of Gen. Palmer, at that time Superintendent of Indian Affairs, and was present when the treaties were made with all the Indian tribes in Oregon west of the Cascades. He also assisted Generals I. I. Stevens and Palmer in drawing up the treaties with the tribes of Washington, Idaho and Montana Territories, and, pending the negotiations east of the Cascades, was in charge of the Oregon Superintendency. He then moved to Linn county and resumed preaching. In 1859 he was appointed Superintendent of Indian Affairs to succeed Gen. Nesmith, and while in office paid the Mott claims and inaugurated the treaties alluded to above. He remained in this office about two years. He then returned to Linn county and was appointed Probate Judge, which office he held two years. He has been repeatedly urged to accept nominations for places of high public trust, but has declined a life of such publicity, preferring rather to serve as an humble laborer in his Master's vineyard. He moved to Eugene City in 1876 and assumed pastoral charge of the Presbyterian Church of that city, where he has resided ever since. He is a prominent member of the Masonic fraternity, and member of the Scottish Rite, and a thirty-second-degree Mason. He is at present a member of the Board of Regents of the State University, and as a citizen, honored and respected by all. He is a man of remarkably striking appearance, tall, and well proportioned, with hair and whiskers of silvery white, and a face fairly beaming with kindness and good nature. His voice is pleasant and his manners genial. He at once creates a good impression and he improves on acquaintanceship. He has a family of seven children, one of his sons being a graduate of West Point Military Academy, and is now a lieutenant in the army. Two others are physicians.

HON. BENJAMIN F. BURCH.

This gentleman's career in life is one of which he should justly feel proud. It is a well known fact that in early days the great majority of men who came to this coast did so under the excitement which the discovery of gold had created in the Eastern States, and on arriving here all hastened to the mountains with the anticipation of making a fortune within a year or two, and returning to their Eastern homes to spend the remainder of their lives in ease and luxury. Such, however, was not the case with the subject of our sketch. The pursuit of agriculture, rather than that of mining, appears to have been his ambition, and he to-day resides near Independence, in Polk county, on the same donation claim located by him in 1848. Mr. Burch was born in Chaiton county, Missouri, May 2, 1825, and obtained an ordinary common school education. On the 25th of April, 1845, he left the home of his parents and started across the plains for Oregon, reaching here in October of the same year. In 1846 he assisted Hon. Jesse Applegate and others in viewing and locating the Southern Oregon wagon road, and conducting the straggling parties of immigrants over the same. During the Cayuse Indian war of 1847-8, Mr. Burch served as Adjutant in both Col. Gilliam's and Col. Waters' regiments, preparing all of their official reports. He was married September 6, 1848, to Miss Eliza A. Davidson, daughter of Hezekiah Davidson. She, too, is an honored pioneer, having came to Oregon in 1847. Mr. Burch also was captain of a volunteer company during the Yakima Indian War of 1855-6. In 1857 he represented his county in the Constitutional Convention, and was a member of the standing committees on Military Corporations and Internal Improvements, rendering valuable assistance in framing both of these important clauses in our State Constitution. He was a member of the first State Legislature and represented Polk county in the Senate of 1868 and again in 1870, serving as President during the former session. He was also a member and the Chairman of the Investigating Committee, appointed by the Legislative Assembly of 1870 to examine and report upon the condition of the executive, administrative and financial departments of the State government. During the administration of Gov. Chadwick, Mr. Burch served as Superintendent of the Penitentiary. Such was his management of that institution that the joint committee appointed by the Legislative Assembly to investigate the affairs of that institution recommended in their report his continuance in office. He is now an honored citizen in private life, taking such interest only in public affairs as every man should who is interested in the welfare of our country. Mr. Burch is a Democrat in politics and has, heretofore, taken an active interest in political matters. He is a man of strong executive ability and is generally a leader in any enterprise he may be interested in. He rarely follows, as he has a mind and will of his own, and his opinions are generally considered worthy of careful consideration. He is of ordinary height and build, plainly dressed, genial and courteous to his friends, and is honest, sincere and earnest in everything he undertakes. There is a vein of good humor in his composition, and a disposition to relish a good joke. He has always endeavored to do his duty honestly and faithfully in the discharge of his official duties, and has won and well merits the confidence and esteem of his neighbors and friends.

DR. ARTHUR INGRAHAM NICKLIN

Is one of the leading physicians and surgeons of the State, and now resides in Eugene City, in Lane county. He at present holds the important position of United States Examining Surgeon for pensions. He was born in Tyler county, West Virginia, on October 4, 1828. When he was fourteen years of age his parents with their children moved to Iowa, where they resided for eight years, and then (1850) took a long westward course across the plains, by the old wagon-train means of transportation, to Oregon, arriving in Portland about the middle of November of that year, and a few months afterwards the family located in Polk county, where they resided six years, and thence moved to Salem. While yet in Virginia, Dr. Nicklin had begun the study of medicine under the tutorship of his uncle, Dr. I. T. Nicklin, an eminent physician of that day, and in Iowa and Oregon he lost no opportunity of devoting his spare time to the pursuit of this study, which he had heartily embraced while a mere boy. In the meantime he had not neglected his other studies and when, in 1857, he became a resident of Salem, he was a well-read physician. However, he concluded to become even more thorough and proficient, and for this purpose he took a regular course of three years in the Medical Department of Willamette University, whence he graduated with distinction. In 1862 he was married to Miss Lavina C. Draper, sister to Mrs. Rev. N. Doane. A few years previously he had taken charge of a large mercantile house, in which his father was interested, and to which he gave his attention until sometime about 1872, when he began to give his whole attention to the practice of medicine and surgery. In 1873 he moved with his family to Eugene City, and in the same year he was appointed physician at Klamath Indian Reservation, but he soon found the salary allowed much less than the profits of the practice which he had abandoned, and he resigned the position and returned to Eugene City, where he has since resided. In 1876 he was appointed United States Examining Surgeon for pensions, which position he still holds. Dr. A. I. Nicklin has had marked success in his practice as a physician and Surgeon, and enjoys the esteem and confidence of all with whom he has come in contact.

DR. JOHN A. CHILD,

Of Portland, is a gentleman well and favorably known in the ranks of the profession, and as the Grand Master of the A. O. U. W. is gaining an enviable reputation throughout the State and adjacent Territories. He is an Englishman by birth, having been born in London in 1836, and is consequently forty-six years of age. His parents came to America when he was five years of age, and settled in Cincinnati, Ohio, where he was educated. He is a graduate of St. John's College, of Cincinnati. He moved to Portland January 3, 1877, and has been a resident of this city ever since. He has been a druggist for thirty-two years, and has a fine store on the corner of Second and Morrison streets, where he carries a stock of goods that would do credit to a city of even larger dimensions than is the metropolis to-day. The Doctor is an excellent business man, watches the market carefully, purchases advantageously, and is prompt and obliging in his dealings with his customers. He is an old army surgeon, having enlisted during the war, serving three years; enlisting as a private, he was promoted to the position of hospital steward, and mustered out of service at Baton Rouge, La., as assistant surgeon of volunteers. He was in the campaign of the opening of the Mississippi, capture and fall of Vicksburg, and also in Gen. Bank's campaign up Red river. Dr. Child has been a member of the Masonic fraternity for twenty-five years, having passed through the Ancient York Rite, Master Mason, Royal Arch, Council and Knights Templar, and has held office continually in one or more of them for nineteen years. The Doctor is a genial, pleasant gentleman, and numbers his friends by platoons. None know him but to respect him, and having once made a man his friend he has no difficulty in retaining his friendship.

HON. D. C. IRELAND.

"In prosperity prepare for a change, in adversity hope for one." This is a favorite adage with him whose name heads this sketch, and we never see or hear it without having pleasant thoughts of him. He is a warm friend to those whom he likes, and will, as the saying is, "do to tie to." He was born in Rutland, Vermont, July 4, 1836, and with his parents moved to Indiana in the year 1840. They lived there a number of years and then moved to Michigan. Mr. Ireland commenced learning the printer's trade in the office of a newspaper published at Mishawaka, by Hon. Schuyler Colfax, afterwards Vice-President of the United States. He established the "Free Press" in that city in 1855, and shortly afterwards moved to Minnesota. In 1860 he was sent to Red river of the North by Burbank & Co., of St. Paul, Minn., with the machinery for the first steamboat ever built on that stream. In 1861 he was Clerk of the Semple Commission, appointed by Congress to settle troubles growing out of liquor selling and timber stealing on the various Indian reservations in Minnesota. From Minnesota he moved to Oregon and established the "Enterprise" at Oregon City in 1866, and for some time was the city editor of the "Daily Oregonian." In 1870 he was the local editor of the "Daily Bulletin," and remained on that paper until 1872, when he went to Astoria and started the "Daily Astorian," which he managed very successfully until 1881. He was for three years Mayor of that city, and made a host of warm, personal friends during his official career. He was elected one of the delegates to the National Republican Convention, which met at Chicago in 1880, and is at present the member from this State of the National Republican Committee. He disposed of his interest in the "Astorian" in 1881, and moved to Portland, where he is now engaged in the management of one of the best conducted job printing offices in this city, under the firm name of D. C. Ireland & Co. Mr. Ireland is an active, energetic business man, and is fast building up a trade that promises success and competency within a few years. As a writer, Mr. Ireland is forcible and accurate; as a reporter, he is considered one of the best in the State, "brevities" being his specialty, and as a printer, he is thoroughly competent. He is strong in his friendship and bitter in his animosities. Fearful lest some of our lady readers may become too much interested in him, we might add that he is a married man and the father of several bouncing girls and boys.

M. L. CHAMBERLIN.

No young man in Marion county is better known or has more warm personal friends than he whose name heads this sketch. He is literally a self-made man, and what little of success he has met with in life has been the result of his own efforts, and he has had much to contend with. In face of adverse circumstances, however, and without being peculiarly favored by any freaks of fortune, he has succeeded in placing himself above probabilities of want, and, above all, he has earned and well merits the confidence and esteem of an unusually large circle of friends. Mr. Chamberlin was born at Dryden, Mich., May 17, 1847, and with his parents immigrated to Oregon in 1858. He settled in Yamhill county, and in 1867 moved to Salem, where he has resided ever since. Being the only boy in a family of eight children, adverse circumstances placed him at their head at an early age, and manfully has he discharged his trust, having denied himself much to aid and assist his sisters in securing an education, and his reward has been a liberal one, in that the family to-day stands among the highest in social, literary and musical circles. He was elected City Treasurer in 1879 and in 1880 was elected County Clerk of Marion county by a very flattering majority, and in 1882 he was the unanimous choice of the Republican County Convention for renomination, and his election followed, as a matter of course. He has surprised his most enthusiastic friends by the efficiency he has displayed in his official duties, and is universally respected as a faithful and obliging officer. The details of his office are carefully watched after, and the public interests have never been more carefully guarded in that office than they are under Mr. Chamberlin's careful management. Mr. Chamberlin is a man of about ordinary height, well-proportioned, with a face betokening good nature, partially protected by a beard of dark brown. He is still unmarried, although he has been in the matrimonial market for years. Having at a very early age started in life as a bachelor, he has from the force of habit kept it up, and his lady friends are fearful lest he will never reform and adopt habits more in keeping with his natural love for the ease and luxury of a quiet home among loved ones. As a friend, he is as true as steel, as a neighbor he is much respected, and as a man his character is above reproach.

W. SHOWERS.

This gentleman is the present County Treasurer of Multnomah county, and as an instance of his popularity let it be known that he is now serving his sixth year in that position. He was born in Zanesville, Muskingum Co., Ohio, in 1830, and received his education in his native town. In the year 1855, attracted by the visions of gold, he went to California, and remained in Trinity county and points adjacent for five years, digging for the precious metal. At the breaking out of the war, Mr. Showers, then but thirty years of age, joined the Fourth Infantry, California Volunteers, and served in that command until 1864, when he was mustered out at Wilmington, Los Angeles. He then came to Portland and was in the employ of the railroad company for a number of years. In the year 1878 he was elected by the Republican party County Treasurer of Multnomah, and has since been honored with a re-election twice. He is well known throughout the county, stands well in his party and is secure in the friendship of our very best citizens.

HENRY C. BOYD,

Of Portland, Oregon, was born in New York in the year 1854. He came with his parents to Oregon in 1860, and was educated in the common schools of this city. Since he has arrived at the age of maturity he has been engaged in the fire insurance business, and is at present the local agent for the Hamburg-Bremen Insurance Company. He was married to Miss Josephine Glenn, of Columbus, Ohio, in the year 1881. Although a young man, Mr. Boyd has been remarkably successful, and is at the present time doing a most flourishing business. He is socially a pleasant young gentleman, and has made numbers of friends in our city, and has a fine prospect in the future. His knowledge of underwriting was acquired under the severe tuition of his father, Hon. Hamilton Boyd, whose knowledge of that art is second to none North of San Francisco. Mr. Boyd, Jr., has the record of standing among the first on the list of underwriters, and we bespeak for him a long and successful career. We can cheerfully recommend him as one who will be fair and impartial in settling his losses, as a manager of his branch; he is also the adjuster, and parties deal direct with him, both in effecting insurance and in getting their money should they be so unfortunate as to require it.

HON. JOHN C. CARTWRIGHT,

Collector of Internal Revenue for the District and State of Oregon, is one of those quiet, unassuming gentlemen, whom we sometimes meet in the walks of public life, and realize the fact that in his case at least the office has sought the man, not the man the office, as is too generally the case. He is a native of Michigan and was born in 1837. He came to Oregon in 1853 and read law with Hon. Jos. G. Wilson, afterwards Representative in Congress from this State. He was admitted to the bar in 1860 and opened an office at Salem. He was a member of the House from Marion county in 1864, and in 1866 was elected State Senator from the same county. In 1867 he received the appointment of United States District Attorney. At the expiration of his term of service in this capacity in 1871, owing to failing health, he removed to Eastern Washington Territory, and there engaged in the stock business until 1873, when he moved to The Dalles, and, in partnership with Hon. R. O. Dunbar, resumed the practice of law. In 1876 he was elected Presidential Elector on the Republican ticket and was a participant in the memorable Electoral College of that year, when poor Cronin —peace to his ashes was so prominent a factor, and when Oregon's vote elected President Hayes. In May, 1877, he received his present appointment. Mr. Cartwright is a gentleman who is highly esteemed by all who know him and is regarded as a man of sterling integrity. He is tall and spare built, smooth face, save the mustache, sharp features, clear peaceful eye, and black hair. He is a warm personal friend and one that never forgets a favor. He is courteous, genial and generous. As a public officer, he is attentive and obliging and in every way efficient. He was married at Salem on Christmas, 1861, to Miss Mary Helm, only daughter of Rev. Wm. Helm, of the M. E. Church.

JAMES HENDERSHOTT.

This gentleman is a son of David Hendershott, Esq., one of the most eminent lawyers of old Kentucky. He was born in St. Clair county, Illinois, in the year 1829. His parents moved to Iowa when young James was but six years old, and there he spent the years of his boyhood and received his educational training. In 1852 he set out for Oregon, and, after driving the historic mule-team five months, he had the happy satisfaction of setting his foot in our beautiful little city of Salem, where he remained one year. Like every other young man of nerve and ambition, Jim took the mining fever and used the pick and shovel with good success in the northern part of California and in Southern Oregon. He became known among his companions as a good, whole-souled, jolly fellow, having a kind heart and possessed of a dauntless spirit, and in the year 1856 he was elected to the position of Sheriff of Josephine county, being re-elected at the expiration of his term of office. Previous to that time he had been County Clerk, and had become a general favorite, and as soon as his second term of Sheriff had expired he was elected Assessor. In 1862 he went to Idaho Territory and staid in Florence a short time, from whence he removed to Grand Ronde valley, Union county, where he has since resided. In 1866 the Democrats of that county sent him to the Legislative Assembly as a Representative, and in 1868 he was returned as a Senator. Since that time Mr. Hendershott has remained at home, engaged in farming and stock-raising and has made for himself a beautiful valley home, and amassed a fortune that his industry certainly merits, but which would be much larger but for his princely liberality. In 1848 Mr. Hendershott was married to Miss Harriet J. Vincent, who was born in Georgetown, Ohio, in 1831. He comes from an old and well-known family, and is a cousin of the late Geo. D. Prentice, who was for years recognized as one of our most brilliant journalists and was editor of the Louisville "Courier-Journal."

LEHMAN BLUM.

In our journey through life we occasionally run across a young man who in business, social and political circles, has fairly distanced competitors, endowed with greater advantages perhaps, but still lacking some qualifications possessed by the young man who so soon outstrips in the race. That qualification may be embraced in a single word, ambition! Without it life loses half its charm and wealth its attendant pleasures. The young man whose name heads this sketch is endowed with ambition, coupled with industry, integrity and good business sagacity. Success has therefore crowned his efforts thus far, and Dame Fortune smiles approvingly upon him. He was born in New Orleans, Louisiana, December 13, 1847, and came to this coast with his mother in 1853, she passing away in 1861. In 1865 he came to Oregon and commenced clerking for Jacobs Mayer, of Portland. He remained there seven years and secured a thorough knowledge of the dry goods business. He then went into business on his own account, the firm name being Harris & Blum. While a resident of Portland he was interested in the advancement of the city and was considered one of its most enterprising young men. He was for nine years Secretary of the Hebrew Benevolent Society, and for six years one of the Board of Directors of the Portland Library Association. Disposing of his interest in the dry goods business at advantageous figures in 1874, he accepted the position of traveling salesman for the well-known firm of Jacobs Bros., in Portland. He remained with them until 1878, when he went to Pendleton and engaged in the general merchandising business, and has already built up a lucrative trade, and will, we feel confident, within a few short years rank as one of if not the leading merchant in Eastern Oregon. He is a red-hot Republican and takes a lively interest in politics. He has never aspired to the honors of office, but whenever he does, he will be very apt to succeed, as he is very popular wherever known. He was married in San Francisco in June, 1878, to Miss Etta Hoehheimer, a most estimable young lady. Mr. Blum is rapidly assuming the position of influence and competency, and a man of his energy and ambition knows no such word as fail. He has been his own master since his sixteenth year, and his success since that time is but a forerunner of what the future has in store for him.

A. W. WITHERELL,

The present accommodating Deputy Sheriff of Multnomah, was born in Eastam, Massachusetts, in the year 1837. When but three years of age he removed with his parents to Jersey City, where he passed his earlier years and received his education. At the age of fifteen years he went to Troy, New York, and secured employment with B. F. Thompson, wholesale dealer in fruits, where he remained until he was eighteen years of age. He then went to California, and after remaining there two years came on to Oregon. On arriving here he secured the agency of the Pacific Steamship Co. at St. Helens, which he retained for three years. Having a desire to see the country, he then traveled our Pacific States and Territories for awhile, and concluding that Portland afforded the greatest opportunities for a young man of grit and industry, settled down in our little city in the year 1867. He immediately secured a position in the retail dry-goods house of Mrs. C. Levy, now Levi & Strauss, in which position he remained fourteen and a half years. Last July, after the sweeping Republican majority in Multnomah county, Mr. Witherell received from Sheriff Sears the appointment of Deputy Sheriff, in which position he still continues, and gives the utmost satisfaction. He was married in 1869 to Miss M. V. Chapman, daughter of John Chapman, Esq.

CLAIB. H. STEWART

County Clerk of Linn county, and one of the most popular young men in that vicinity, was born at Knoxville, Iowa, December 29, 1852. His father, Dr. Wm. Q. Stewart, was a successful practitioner of medicine in that city. He afterwards moved to Monroe county, where his father engaged in the general mercantile business. Having met with reverses, he immigrated to Oregon in 1865, just at the close of the war. The subject of our sketch entered the office of the "State Rights Democrat," at Albany, in June, 1867, and remained connected with that paper in the varied capacity of "devil," compositor, foreman, business manager, proprietor and editor, until October 1st of the present year, when he disposed of his interest to Chamberlain & Stites, the present publishers. Mr. Stewart was a pleasant writer and the paper under his editorial management was spicy and interesting at all times. He has held various positions of public trust, such as Alderman, Treasurer, etc., of that city, and as the Democratic nominee for the office of County Clerk was elected by 362 majority, running over one hundred votes ahead of his ticket. He has been an active worker in politics for many years and was Chairman of the Democratic County Central Committee for two campaigns. He is a genial, whole-souled young fellow, and wins, not only the friendship, but the confidence and esteem of all with whom he comes in contact. He was married to Miss Cora J. Irvine, daughter of Rev. S. G. Irvine, D. D., of Albany, January 4, 1877, and four interesting children have already blessed their union.

HON. JOHN W. CRAWFORD

The present Mayor of Salem, was born on a farm in Muskingum county, Ohio, January 6, 1835. He remained at home until he was of age, when he entered Monmouth College, Ill., from which institution he graduated in 1859. He studied law for about two years and was admitted to the bar by the Supreme Court of Illinois in March, 1861. The war of the rebellion breaking out that year, Mr. Crawford enlisted in the Seventeenth Illinois Regiment of Infantry and served over three years with the Army of the Mississippi and with his regiment participated in the fights at Fredricktown, Mo., Fort Donaldson, Shiloh, and before Corinth and Vicksburg, when those places were invested by Generals Halleck and Grant. Mr. Crawford came to Oregon in 1866, and by his indomitable energy has succeeded in building up a large and profitable business in Salem. He is a clear-headed, conscientious citizen, and has taken more than ordinary interest as a member of the Common Council and of the Fire Department in making Salem a moral, law-abiding city and a delightful place of residence.

HON. JOHN F. CAPLES.

Standing among the leading members of the legal fraternity of the State, and holding the responsible office of Prosecuting Attorney of the Fourth Judicial District, Hon. John F. Caples, both by virtue of his official position and his acknowledged professional acquirements, ranks among the representative men of Oregon. He is a native of Ohio, in which State he was born January 12, 1831. In 1832 his father removed with his family to Seneca county, Ohio, where he died in 1835. There were ten children in the family, of whom the subject of this biographical sketch was the youngest. He remained with his widowed mother on a farm until fifteen years of age, receiving such advantages of obtaining an early education as were afforded in a country school. He then began clerking in a variety store, which avocation he pursued for three years, when he went to Delaware, Ohio, and attended school until he attained the age of twenty-one. Removing to Bellefontaine, in his native State, he read law with Hon. Ben. Stanton and C. W. B. Allison, and was admitted to practice in 1854. On the 24th of May of the same year, he was married to Miss Sarah J. Morrison, daughter of F. A. Morrison, of Champaign county, Ohio. Mr. Caples practiced his profession in northern Ohio until 1858, when he removed to Warsaw, Indiana, where he continued attending to legal business until 1862. Returning to Ohio he remained until 1865, when he removed to this coast. He located at Vancouver, W. T., and resided there until 1866, when he removed to

Portland, where he soon acquired a lucrative practice. Mr. Caples is a Republican. During the war of the rebellion he was actively engaged in the recruiting service for the government in both Ohio and Indiana. His first active participation in politics in this State was in 1872, when he was elected a member of the lower House of the Legislature. After serving one term he retired from political life, until 1876, when he was elected for the first time to the position he now holds. On the 4th of December, 1877, death invaded his household and took from his side his amiable wife, and he still remains a widower. In 1878 he was again elected Prosecuting Attorney, and he has been re-elected successively to the same position at each recurring election ever since, and, without disparagement to others, it may be stated that at his third election he received a higher number of votes than any other candidate on his ticket. Mr. Caples is a man of vigorous constitution and active mind, bidding fair to insure him many more years of active life.

J. A. CHAPMAN, M. D.

Prominent among the men who have made the Northwest famous as a rendezvous for enterprise, talent and industry, may be mentioned the gentleman whose name is the title of this brief biography. Dr. Chapman was born in the town of Friendship, Alleghany county, New York, Sept. 4, 1821. He resided at that place until he was sixteen years of age, enjoying the advantage of a common school education. He then went to Cuba, in the same State, and attended the Academy two years and then studied medicine and surgery with Dr. Griffin, a prominent physician of that section, and with whom he remained for three and a half years. He then attended the Geneva Medical College, of New York, and graduated from that institution in the winter of 1845-6. He began the practice of his profession in Cuba, and continued in the business at that place for several years. He then went to Dundee, Yates county, New York, where he practiced until 1861, when the war of the rebellion burst upon the country, at which time he volunteered in the military service and was appointed surgeon of the Fiftieth New York Regiment, with the rank of colonel. He went South and served with his regiment until the latter part of 1862, when he was transferred to the overland expedition, for this coast, under Captain Crawford. He came as surgeon of the expedition with the rank of major. He left New York, May 19th, and arrived in Portland, Oregon, November 1, 1862. Hon. J. N. Dolph, U. S. Senator elect, and Cyrus A. Dolph, accompanied the expedition. Arriving in Portland, he again began practice, with the late Dr. J. C. Hawthorne, with whom he remained until Dr. Hawthorne obtained the contract for keeping the Insane of the State. In 1867 Dr. Chapman was elected Mayor of the City of Portland on the Democratic ticket. In 1868 he was elected Chairman of the Democratic State Central Committee, but resigned upon the endorsement of Horace Greeley for President by the Democratic National Convention of 1872. He was re-elected Mayor, on the Republican ticket in 1876, and served one term. Prior to this he was appointed Surgeon-General of the State Militia, by Governor L. F. Grover, with the rank of colonel. In June, 1882, Dr. Chapman was again elected Mayor for the third term, in which position he is now serving. During his long official career in Portland he has held the confidence of the people by his strict integrity, uniform courtesy and honest dealing with all whom he has been brought in contact with, either in a professional or official capacity.

HON. J. C. HUTCHINSON

Is one of the most active and best known Democrats of Douglas county. He was born October 10, 1835, in Henderson county, Illinois, where his father was one of the oldest pioneers. Young Hutchinson's parents died in 1851, and the orphan boy did not receive the advantages of youth which he would have had they lived. He, however, after attending the district school, spent one winter at Knox College, Galesburg, Illinois, and made the very best use of his time there, coming out with a very fair education. He came to Oregon on July 11, 1859, and pitched his tent on a farm in Douglas county, where he has since resided, engaged in raising stock and farming. Mr. Hutchinson was elected by the Democrats of Douglas county to the Legislative Assembly of 1870, and while there secured the passage of a bill changing the time when county assessors commence their work, which was the means of saving several thousand dollars annually to many of the counties, and which also saved a large amount of money to the State. Mr. Hutchinson's work in the Legislature was unfortunately cut short by his falling a victim to the small-pox, and he was taken to his home, where, after lingering for a few weeks, he entirely recovered. Mr. Hutchinson favored the road from Roseburg across the mountains east by way of the North Umpqua to the pasture country east of the Cascades, and also stood by the Coos Bay Wagon Road Company, of Oregon, when in the Legislature, and secured its construction. Mr. Hutchinson was married in February, 1865, to Miss S. A. Copeland, and they now have four fine children, and are surrounded by the comforts of this world. In 1871 he paid a visit to his home in Illinois, and in a few days will again undertake the same journey. We wish him a pleasant trip.

WILLIAM R. SEWALL

Is a retiring gentleman, of pleasant face and courteous demeanor. You would never think that he was destined to figure in the political arena, but rather that he was fitted for the life of the careful and successful business man. And yet this quiet personage is one of the most popular and at the same time powerful factors in the politics of Multnomah county, a truth which was clearly demonstrated during the last municipal election, when he was nominated by the Republican party for the position of County Clerk, and to which office he was elected by the largest majority ever given to a candidate in this county. He was not supported by the adherents of his own party simply, but hundreds of Democratic voters recognizing his ability and sterling integrity, gave him their unqualified support, believing that by so doing they were subserving the best interests of the tax-payers.

Mr. Sewall was born way back in old Maryland, that grand old State which was the cradle of religious and civil liberty, in the year well, it don't matter when, because Billy is quite a young man, any way. He went to New York at the age of ten and secured a position in a mercantile establishment there, where he remained for some years. In 1853 he took his way westward and engaged in the hardware business in Sacramento, where he remained twelve years. He then, in 1862, came to Oregon, and spent two years in looking after the auriferous metal in our various gold diggings. In 1864 he settled in Portland, and conducted the Western and Cosmopolitan hotels for a number of years. He then accepted the position of clerk in the service of the O. T. Co., which position he retained until he was elected County Clerk. Mr. Sewall was married to Miss Dink Elgin, of Salem, in 1869, and they now have five children. Although he has always been an active worker in his party, this is the first time that he has held office. He is a member of Samaritan Lodge, No. 2, I. O. O. F.

HON. CHARLES A. JOHNS.

Coming to Oregon when but a little over one year of age, from Missouri, where he was born June 25, 1857, Mr. Johns can be considered as much an Oregonian, to all intents and purposes, as if to the "manor born." Although not yet twenty-six years of age, he has made his mark, and if "coming events cast their shadows before," Mr. Johns will be as well and favorably known in the councils of the State, as he is well-known in the "Heart of the Valley," where he has grown from childhood to man's estate. The early years of his boyhood were passed in the beautiful little city of Scio, nestled in the windings of Thomas creek. Here he conquered the rudiments of knowledge, preparing himself for a collegiate course in the Willamette University in Salem, which institution he entered in December, 1873, and from which he graduated an A. B. in 1878, near the head of his class. The same year he received the appointment of Deputy Sheriff of Marion county, under Sheriff J. A. Baker, which position he held until his term expired in July, 1880. Mr. Johns then commenced the study of law in the office of Hon. William H. Holmes, of Salem, now Prosecuting Attorney for the Third Judicial District of Oregon, and was admitted to practice at the March term of the Supreme Court in 1881. Mr. Johns, after receiving the degree of A. M. from his Alma Mater, the Willamette University, removed to Dallas, Polk county, where he now resides and where he immediately stepped into a fair practice, which his talent and his energy entitled him to. Since his residence there he has, upon several occasions, been chosen orator of the day, and in every instance has left his impress as a ready and eloquent speaker. During the last political campaign Mr. Johns was chosen as the presiding officer of the Polk County Republican Convention, and was elected by that body as the Chairman of the Republican County Committee. On the first of last August he entered into a law copartnership with Hon. Warren Truitt, of Dallas, and was appointed by Governor Moody on September 27th, as the County Judge of Polk county, being perhaps the youngest man that ever held the responsible office of chief executive of a county in this State. In appearance Mr. Johns is a fine specimen of manhood; his physique is of the Roman style of "architecture," and commands respect from those with whom he comes in social or business contact.

I. N. SANDERS,

The present Assessor of Multnomah county, was born in Orange county, Indiana, in the year 1840. His father was a farmer, and the boy was brought up with a practical knowledge of soil-culture, in the meantime attending the neighboring schools, until the age of twenty-two. At the breaking out of the civil war young Sanders joined the Sixty-Sixth Indiana regiment, which for a time was in the Fifteenth Corps under Gen. Logan, and again in the Sixteenth, under Gen. Dodge. He marched with the gallant Sherman from Atlanta to the sea, and participated in all the battles on the line of march. The soldier boy was watched over by a lucky star, and with the exception of being shot through the shoulder at the battle of Colyerville, Tenn., Oct. 11, 1863, received no wound. He was mustered out of service in June, 1865, in Indiana, and then went to Centralia, Illinois, where he lived five years, engaged in the profession of school teaching. In 1870 he came west to Oregon and took up his abode in East Portland, where he has since prospered. He is a true Republican and was elected City Recorder there in 1875 and subsequently re-elected four times. In 1882 the Republicans of Multnomah saw that they had to put a ticket in the field which was composed of popular men, and whom the people could place dependence on, in order to secure a victory. Mr. Sanders was nominated for the responsible position of Assessor, and although his opponent was a strong man, our hero was elected by a handsome majority. He was married to Miss Asenath Ferguson in 1864, and they have six children. He is a member of Orient Lodge, No. 17, I. O. O. F., and has received all the honors of that order, having been P. G. and Representative to G. L.; he is also a member of George Wright Post, G. A. R.

EDWARD M. WAITE,

Known among the printing fraternity of the State as the "Ben Franklin" of Oregon, was born, as he says, B. C., and judging from his patriarchal appearance, nobody will dispute his assertion. In 1841, when about eleven years of age, he left Springfield, Mass., his native city, for Westfield, where he was apprenticed in the good, old-fashioned way, to Elijah Porter to learn the art of printing. Here he remained about five years, when he went to New York and worked a short time on the "Journal of Commerce," when he took Horace Greeley's advice and "went West," and he did not stop going in that direction until he arrived in Oregon City in 1851, where he hired out to work on the "Oregon Statesman," then owned by A. Bush, Esq., Territorial Printer. Here he put in nearly two years, when he quit the art preservative business and engaged in sundry speculative schemes, among which were stock buying for the immigrant trade in Eastern Oregon, shipping produce to California, etc. In company with E. Holland he went to where Silverton now stands and built a store, being the first building erected in that now flourishing little city. There our hero soon got his fill of merchandising, and afterwards he was working at the case alongside of his old chum, W. B. Carter (deceased), in the "Christian Advocate" office, in Portland; at the same time, as an outside speculation, he and Carter were runing a milk-ranch near the city, furnishing the citizens of the metropolis with pure bovine fluid. We next hear of him with the "Statesman," when it was moved to Salem, and he followed it, with the Legislature, to Corvallis and back to Salem. In 1869 he founded his present book and job office, and has added to it from time to time until now it is the best selected office in the State, if not the largest one. Mr. Waite has been the "keystone" of the State Agricultural Society for many years, having been the secretary of that organization continuously for eleven terms. He is now a member of the Common Council of the city, and his vote and influence always go for advancing the interests of Salem. In personal appearance Mr. Waite is the counterpart of Washington Irving's "Ichabod Crane," and if you can catch him when he is not engaged with a rush of business he is one of the most genial and companionable persons in the world, and a good story with a point to it will "double him up" quicker than any man we ever met.

DANIEL M'KERCHER

The book and stationery dealer of Portland, was born in Canada October, 1832. He was raised there until the age of eighteen, when he removed to Clarence county, New York. He there learned the trade of carriage and wagon-making, and after a stay of four years he went to Freeport, Illinois. After working in that place for two years at his trade, he took the regulation trip across the plains, and arrived in Portland in 1856, where he remained until 1863. In that year he took the mining fever and sought the diggings of Idaho, but after remaining there a short time he went to La Grande, Union county, where he lived for seven years working at his trade. In the year 1871 he returned to Portland, and secured a position as clerk in the employ of the O. T. Co. After retaining this position two years, he engaged in his present business, which is one of the best in its line in our city. Mr. McKercher has always been an enthusiastic Republican and a good party worker, and in the year 1881 he received the nomination of his party for City Treasurer, and he was elected in the face of a strong opposition. He is a member of the I. O. O. F. and A. F. and A. M.

HARRISON B. OATMAN.

This gentleman came to Oregon in the pioneer days, made his home here, invested every cent of money which he possessed in our land, and ever since has had his interests identified with that of the State. Such being the case, he ever stood ready to contribute his share by word and act toward its prosperity, and the result has been that to-day Mr. Oatman is one of our large land owners, and possesses multifarious interests throughout our city and State. He was born in Courtland, New York, in 1826. When a child his parents moved to Bellevue, Ohio, where he attended school, and when he was at the age of twelve they again removed, this time to Rockford, Illinois, in which place they farmed for four years. At the age of twenty-one, Mr. Oatman was married to Miss Lucena K. Ross, and in the year 1852 he, with his wife and family, crossed the plains to Oregon and located in Rogue river valley, where he engaged in farming and afterwards mined and trafficked in merchandise. He remained there fourteen years and then came to Portland, where he has since resided. On arriving here, he went into the grocery business, and, becoming the owner of considerable real estate, he finally gave up the grocery trade and devoted himself solely to speculating in lands. Last October, when the Metropolitan Savings Bank was organized, Mr. Oatman was one of the first subscribers to its stock and he is now one of its heaviest stockholders. On April 4, 1865, Mr. Oatman joined the First Oregon Infantry, and after serving two years, was mustered out July 14, 1867. It was said that this company was the last one composed of white men in the volunteer service. In this company Mr. Oatman was made lieutenant and was frequently commended for gallant conduct on the field.

HON. ASA A. M'CULLY

Is one of the solid men of Oregon, and one of those to whom the early settlers of the State owe much. He was born in the province of New Brunswick in 1818, and with his parents moved to Ohio when he was but five years of age. While a young man he learned the trade of making fanning mills and worked for nine years at the business in Ohio, when he removed to Iowa, where he engaged in merchandising and trading in Burlington and New London. In 1848 he "came the plains across" with ox teams to California and for a feat it was without an equal. Although over four months on the way, the whole train, consisting of twenty-three wagons and teams, 65 men, one woman and one dog, all came through without the loss of a life or a single pound of property, with the exception of one wagon which broke down so badly that it had to be abandoned. After remaining two years mining and trading in California, he returned to Iowa and, in 1852, again started across the plains with his family by ox teams, this time to Oregon, coming to Harrisburg and taking up a claim, a portion of which that town now stands on, which he named and in which he built the first house. The same year he returned to Iowa and brought 150 head of cattle overland, shipping also around the Horn a stock of merchandise from Philadelphia. In 1863 Mr. McCully removed to Salem and, in the following year, was elected President of the People's Transportation Company, an organization that controlled the passenger and freight traffic for many years on the upper Willamette river. He occupied that position until the locks were built, when the line was sold to Mr. Ben Holliday. Mr. McCully represented Linn county in the Legislature of 1860, and has served as Councilman of the capital city several years during his residence there. Mr. McCully is a fine, hale, hearty-looking gent, and enjoys a good joke about as well as any man in Oregon.

JAMES B. STEPHENS,

Of East Portland, who is familiarly known by the appellation of "Uncle Jimmy," was born on the line of Brook county, Virginia, and Washington county, Pennsylvania, on the 19th of November, 1806. When he was eight years old his parents moved to Indiana, when that country was still a Territory, where he lived on a farm during most of the time. He learned the coopering trade and followed the business several years in Indiana and three years in Cincinnati, Ohio. He afterwards purchased a farm in Hancock county, on the banks of the Mississippi river, and established a grocery store on his place. He came to Oregon in 1844 and, taking up a section of land, located on the east bank of the Willamette river, now known as East Portland and also Stephens' Addition to East Portland. In 1846 he made 1000 flour barrels and 400 salmon barrels for the Hudson Bay Company, and in 1847 he made 400 beef barrels for shipment to the Sandwich Islands. In 1850 he laid out the town of East Portland, and, dividing it into town lots, offered them to settlers on their own terms, thus materially aiding to build up the east side of the river. Together with his aged and respected consort, he still occupies a portion—about twenty acres—of his old claim. He was married in 1830 to Miss Elizabeth Walker, and during that period they have had seven children, all of whom are dead but one. This aged couple, whose lives are fast drawing to a close, look back with pride to the many changes that the fast-fleeting years have wrought in this country, and contrast the improvements and conveniences of to-day with the dreariness and discomforts that surrounded them when they, with brave hearts, hopeful for the future, settled on the east banks of the Willamette. They have taken a prominent part in bringing about these wonderful changes, and therefore are entitled to the heartfelt interest taken in "Uncle Jimmy" and his honored helpmate by all who know and respect them.

HON. CYRUS A. REED.

The subject of this sketch is perhaps more clearly identified with the history of Salem, the lower Willamette valley and the State at large than any other single person in our hasty "Pen Pictures." Born in Grafton, N. H., in 1825, he was thrown in a measure upon his own resources at the age of eleven years by the death of both his parents. After receiving an academic education at the Northfield Seminary in that State he learned the trade of wagon and carriage-making and painting, studying the latter branch of the business with a thorough artist. Col. Reed came to California in 1849 with the first of the argonauts, but after visiting the mines, concluded to come to Oregon, which he did, landing at Astoria and coming up to Portland in a small boat, arriving here on the 1st of January, 1850. He found the embryo metropolis with less than 200 inhabitants. He "took the school," being the second school teacher that ever taught in that "p'int of timber." He helped to build the first saw-mill here and to run it; the firm being Abrams, Reed & Co., Hon. Stephen Coffin being the "Co." Mr. Reed purchased a farm in 1852, near Salem, which he ran with a paint-shop, drug and book store in Salem; was treasurer of the first agricultural society in Oregon; was one of the first stockholders and afterwards one of the directors of the Willamette Woolen Factory; was a member of the firm of Jones, Reed & Co., that built on "Boon's Island" the first door, sash, blind and labor-saving manufactory; was elected to the Legislature in 1862 and framed and introduced the present militia law of the State; was appointed, to carry the law into effect, Adjutant General of the State by Governor A. C. Gibbs and re-appointed by Governor Woods. His printed report at the close of his official career is regarded by military men as one of the best documents of the kind ever issued. In 1869, under a contract with the State, built the Opera House building for State Department offices. The administration changing and the newly-elected State officers failing to comply with the agreement, the building was turned into a hotel and opera house. The Colonel in 1874 painted a magnificent panorama of Oregon, which is considered a fine work of art, and which is now being exhibited in continental Europe. Mr. Reed was again elected to the Legislature in 1874, and during the session introduced and carried through the bill that reared the walls, enclosed and made ready for occupation the present capitol building. In 1878 was again a member and was the originator of several bills for the advancement of the State and society. Conspicuous among them was the present gambling law; the law closing saloons on election days; the act to prohibit the public execution of criminals convicted of capital offenses. It would require a volume double the size of this book to give in detail the various enterprises Mr. Reed has been engaged in during his residence in Oregon. In personal appearance the Colonel is inclined to embonpoint, but he is as active and as full of vim and energy to-day as he was when he landed in Oregon thirty-two years ago.

HON. FRANK J. TAYLOR,

Of Astoria, is one of those genial, whole-souled chaps whom it does one good to meet and who infuses new life into you with the simple shake of the hand. His affability and good nature make him a general favorite and his friends are legion. His parents came to Oregon "the plains across" in 1845, and settled first at Oregon City and afterwards moved to Clatsop plains, where Frank put in an appearance on the 11th day of May, 1851. He received a common school education, and developing a natural taste for law he commenced reading in the office of Hall, Thayer & Williams, in Portland, along in 1871 and 1872. He afterwards attended law school at Albany University, Albany, N. Y., and graduated, being admitted to the bar of that State in 1873. He returned to Oregon and opened an office at Astoria, where he has practiced law most of the time since. He was elected and held the office of Recorder and Police Judge of Astoria from August 1, 1875, to June 1, 1878, and at present is serving as Councilman in the Common Council of that city. In 1880 he was nominated and elected member of the House of Representatives from Clatsop and Tillamook counties, and served his constituents faithfully during that session. He was an active worker and proved an important factor in that body. He was a member of several important committees and frequently took an active part in debates. Mr. Taylor is considered a fine-looking man. He is rather tall and slim, stands erect, his face being smooth-shaved, with the exception of a mustache of dark brown. His head is well-shaped, with eyes well set back and fairly glistening with good humor. He is unmarried, "'tis true, and pity 'tis 'tis true." He is popular and makes friends everywhere.

DR. LANSING S. SKIFF.

Dr. Skiff resides in Salem, the capital city of the State, where he practices the profession of dentistry, and in the annals of the dental associations of this coast takes a high rank as a skillful and successful operator, having produced some of the finest and most artistic work ever made on this side of the "Rockies." He is the founder of the Oregon State Dental Society, and served one year as President and two years as Vice-President of that organization. The Doctor was born near Syracuse, Onondaga county, N. Y., somewhere in the "thirties." He came to California in 1849, where he resided nine years, from thence coming to Salem in 1858, where he still lives. He is considered one of the substantial citizens of the city, and has been elected no less than five times to represent his ward in the Common Council, and has been one of the most active men of his community in all enterprises looking to the advancement of the material welfare of the city and county in which he lives.

D. W. PRENTICE,

Of the well-known music firm of D. W. Prentice & Co., is one of our successful business men and has made a place for himself and a name for his house that is second to none other. He was born in Worthington, Hampshire county, Mass, in the year 1835. After receiving the benefits of a common school English education, he was apprenticed to the cabinet-making and stair-building trades, and became a thorough mechanic. At the age of twenty-two he traveled west to Minnesota, where he worked at his trade for a period of ten years. He came to the Webfoot State in 1867, and took up his residence in Salem, where he lived for eight years. During this time he worked at the bench and afterwards became a teacher of vocal music. Here he met with such success that he was impelled to move to Oregon's metropolis, which he did in the year 1875. In his new home he taught vocal music for one year, and then seeing an opportunity to go into business he did so, and bought out the branch store of the great San Francisco music house, Sherman & Hyde. At that time the business was very small and its connection with the outer world very imperfect. From this small beginning Mr. Prentice has, by close attention to business and a careful study of the wants of the music-loving community, made his establishment what it is to-day—the leading music house of the Northwest and a source of great pleasure to our people. Mr. Prentice was married to Miss Lizzie De Nure, in Minnesota in 1862, and they have one child. In business circles he stands in the front rank, and socially he is a pleasant and considerate gentleman.

CAPTAIN L. S. SCOTT,

The popular and efficient Postmaster at Salem, was born at Litchfield, Connecticut, October 1, 1830. In 1832 the family moved to the Canada side of the Niagara Falls, where his father kept a hotel until 1834, when he moved to Ohio, where he resided until 1843, when he moved to Illinois, and from there in 1846 to Missouri. In 1848 the subject of our sketch drove a team to Santa Fe, New Mexico, and returning home in 1850, took the gold fever and started for California, crossing the plains with the ox team of that day and age. The greater portion of the next eleven years was spent in placer mining, in Volcano, Amador county. In 1861, on the breaking out of the civil war, Mr. Scott raised Company D, Fourth California Infantry Volunteers, and was appointed captain of the organization in September of that year. They were detailed for service in this State, and were transported hither on the steamer Cortez. They were stationed at Fort Yamhill, and during the interval between 1861 and 1865 Captain Scott was at different times commander of that post, Fort Hoskins and the Siletz Block House. In July, 1865, his company was ordered to Eastern Oregon and established the post in Harney lake valley, known as Camp Curry. In December of that year the company was ordered to San Francisco, where it was mustered out of service. Captain Scott immediately returned to Oregon, and he entered the general merchandising business in Portland, where he remained but a short time, going to Salem in 1866, where he has since continuously resided. In 1868 he was elected Mayor of that city, and was re-elected in 1869. In 1872 he was elected Sheriff of Marion county, which position he filled with great efficiency. In 1874 he was elected Chairman of the Republican State Central Committee by the State Convention of that year, which position he held until 1878. In 1878 he was elected a member of the House of Representatives. As a legislator he was active and untiring and watched carefully the interests of the county he represented. In 1879 he was appointed postmaster at Salem, which position he still holds. As such officer, he is attentive, obliging and trustworthy, and gives universal satisfaction in the discharge of his official duties. He takes an active interest in politics, and is a pronounced and uncompromising Republican. He was married October 13, 1858, to Miss Eliza J. Erwin, of Volcano, Cal., and they have five children living. He is a member of the Masonic order and of the A. O. U. W. He is of ordinary height, well-built, pleasant face, well covered with a gray beard, and socially speaking is genial, jovial and good-natured.

O. F. PAXTON.

Among the young men of this State who have, within the past few years, entered the ranks of the legal profession, none have brighter indications of success than does he whose name heads this sketch. He is energetic, industrious and ambitious. These qualities, combined with the advantages derived from an excellent education, unusual natural capacities, and a high sense of honor, place him at once among the foremost ranks of his profession. He was born in Albany, Oregon, January 4, 1858, and attended the public schools and the Albany College Institute until 1868, when he went to California and attended the Lincoln Grammar school, of San Francisco, and the Grammar School of Santa Clara. Returning to Oregon in 1870, he resided with his parents on a farm near Brownsville until 1875, when he moved to Portland, where he has since resided. In 1876 he entered the Portland High School and graduated first in a class of thirteen in 1878, being selected by them as valedictorian, and he is at present the President of the alumni of that institution. He at once commenced the study of law with the well-known firm of Thayer & Williams, of Portland, and was admitted to the bar in 1880, meanwhile serving for a few months as Private Secretary to Governor Thayer, which position he resigned in December, 1878. At the general election in 1882 he was elected County School Superintendent for Multnomah county on the Republican ticket by about 1450 majority, his opponent being the joint nominee of the Democratic and Independent parties. He is now acting as the attorney in Multnomah and Columbia counties for the State Board of School Land Commissioners. He is building up a very lucrative practice in Portland, and has gained the respect and good will of a host of friends and acquaintances. Mr. Paxton is both a student and a thinker. He has great force and vigor intellectually and physically and extraordinary working ability. He is a man of pronounced and positive opinions, and is possessed of an erect, dignified bearing, and is a ready and forcible speaker. His height is about five feet ten inches, and his weight one hundred and fifty pounds. His head is large and well-shaped, with prominent forehead and deep-set blue eyes, auburn hair, and heavy brown beard and mustache. He is considered good looking and is a favorite in society. Our lady readers will be interested to learn that Mr. Paxton is unmarried.

PROFESSOR JOHN M. GARRISON,

Who during the past few years has gained an enviable reputation throughout the State as a teacher of penmanship, was born in Atchinson county, Missouri, September 25, 1845, and with his parents moved to Oregon in 1846 and settled near Amity, in Yamhill county, where his father took up a tract of land. His early life was spent on the farm, attending the district schools when at odd times there was one in session. In 1860 he entered the Willamette University at Salem and graduated from that institution in the class of '66 with the degree of A. B. During the next five years he devoted his attention to teaching school, three years of the time being spent in Salem and two years in Corvallis. In 1869 he received the degree of A. M. at the Willamette University. Having concluded to adopt the teaching of penmanship as a profession, Prof. Garrison at once set about perfecting himself in that particular department of education, which, as every intelligent person knows, has too little attention paid to it in the common school system of the present day. Prof. Garrison therefore commenced the formation of classes in penmanship in the leading institutions of learning in Oregon and Washington Territory, and success crowned his efforts from their infancy, until to-day he is scarcely able to fill his engagements. His system is a thorough one from its rudiments to the close, and scholars under his instruction almost invariably make not only astonishing and rapid, but also permanent, improvement. He possesses the faculty of imparting instruction to his pupils and encouraging them in their efforts to succeed. He manages to create a spirit of competition among them, and those who earnestly apply themselves and implicitly follow his instructions never fail to become good penmen. Prof. Garrison has a natural love for his work and takes great pride in the advancement of its benefits, whether such advancement is the result of his own labor or that of others. He is very successful in gaining the respect and esteem of his pupils and patrons, and never fails to create good and lasting impressions wherever he teaches. He was married in January, 1876, to Miss Mary Blank, of Forest Grove, where he has been residing for the last five years, and where as a citizen and neighbor he is honored and respected.

W. T. COOK

Is the leading druggist of Centerville, Umatilla county, and is a gentleman who by his courteous demeanor and considerate nature will make friends and be a success wherever he travels. He was born in Polk county, Missouri, in the year 1848. Received his education there and afterward taught school there five years. He came to Oregon when quite a young man, and on arriving here he taught school for one year in Linn and Wasco counties, after which he embarked in the drug business in Peoria, Linn county. He remained there but one year, and then removed to Centerville, Umatilla county, where he associated himself with Mr. Irvine, who is a physician, under the firm name of Cook & Irvine. The firm has prospered, and aside from their book and drug business they are the agents for Wells, Fargo & Co., the Utah, Idaho and Oregon Stage Company, and Mr. Cook is the postmaster. It probably would not be out of place here to state that when Mr. Cook first arrived here he did not have a penny, and before he secured the position as teacher alluded to above he was compelled to work at manual labor for one year and a half. By his perseverance, industry and spirit he has now become a successful business man and has amassed a comfortable fortune, and he has always been an earnest and active Democrat. Although young and handsome, our subject has not yet been captured by the fair sex, but we trust that some day soon the marriage bell will peal forth the happy announcement that Miss ——— is about to become Mrs. W. T. Cook.

CAPTAIN J. D. MERRYMAN,

An honored citizen of Astoria and a prominent representative of Clatsop county, was born at St. Clairsville, Ohio, in 1838, and received the benefits of an early common school education. At fifteen years of age he accepted a clerkship in a general merchandising establishment at Woodsfield, Ohio, where he remained until the war broke out, when he enlisted in the Twenty-fifth Ohio Volunteer Infantry and was elected Second Lieutenant of Company B, and was afterwards appointed First Lieutenant and Captain. He was discharged from the service December 29, 1862, on the surgeon's certificate of disability, having been twice severely wounded. He came to Oregon in 1863 and was engaged in selling goods at Hillsboro until 1868, when he was elected County Clerk of Washington county and was re-elected in 1870. In May, 1873, he was appointed Deputy Collector of Customs at Astoria, and served as such until June, 1881, when he was appointed Collector of the port in place of Hon. W. D. Hare, whose term of office had expired. Capt. Merryman is a gentleman of marked executive ability and as a public officer has given universal satisfaction. He was married in May, 1873, to Miss Rebecca Eagleton, of Hillsboro. Men of Capt. Merryman's stamp are a credit to any community.

HON. GEORGE H. WiLLIAMS

Was born in Columbia county, New York, on the 26th day of March, 1823. He was educated at the academy on Pompey hill, in Onondago county, where his father removed at an early day. He studied law with the Hon. Daniel Gott. At the age of twenty-one he was admitted to practice in the courts of that State. In the same year he immigrated to the, then, Territory of Iowa, and commenced the practice of his profession at Fort Madison. In 1847 he was elected Judge of the Fifth Judicial District of Iowa. He discharged the duties of that office for five years, when both political parties offered to join in his re-election, but he declined. In 1852 he was nominated by the Democratic State Convention of Iowa as one of the Presidential Electors and canvassed the State for Franklin Pierce. In March, 1853, chiefly upon the recommendation of Hon. Stephen A. Douglas, who was his personal friend, he was appointed Chief Justice of the, then, Territory of Oregon, and immediately with his family removed here. He was a member of the Constitutional Convention from Marion county, and was Chairman of the Judiciary Committee. He was reappointed Chief Justice of the Territory by President Buchanan, but resigned and resumed the practice of his profession at Portland. Many leaders of the Democratic party at the time the State Government was formed were in favor of making Oregon a slave State, and that question, separate and apart from the Constitution, was submitted by the Constitutional Convention to the people. Mr. Williams took decided ground against the establishment of slavery in the new State, speaking and writing against it, and the pro-slavery party was defeated, but his standing as a party man was greatly impaired by the contest. When the secession movement was inaugurated Mr. Williams dissolved his connection with the Democratic party and assisted in the formation of a Union party in the State. In September, 1864, he was elected by the Union, or Republican, party U. S. Senator from this State. Mr. Williams took his seat in the Senate about the end of the civil war, and when it became necessary in Congress to consider and settle the difficult and complicated questions growing out of that sectional and sanguinary struggle. A joint committee of the two Houses, consisting of thirteen members, of which Mr. Williams was one, was organized to examine and report upon matters pertaining to the reconstruction of the Union. A vast amount of testimony was taken and various propositions discussed by this committee without any definite conclusion. Meanwhile President Andrew Johnson was proceeding independently of

Congress to reorganize the revolted States by reinstating in power the leaders of the rebellion. On the 4th of March, 1867, Mr. Williams having prepared, introduced into the Senate a bill entitled "A Bill for the more efficient government of the States lately in rebellion," commonly called the Reconstruction Bill, which, after being amended, passed both Houses of Congress and was vetoed by the President. The bill was passed over the veto, and under this act the union was re-established and the States restored to harmonious relations with the Federal Government. Many other important measures, such as the tenure of office act, an act to regulate the election of Senators, were brought forward by the Senator from Oregon. Soon after the expiration of his term Mr. Williams was appointed one of the Joint High Commission to settle by treaty with Great Britain the Alabama claims and other disputed questions between the two countries. His appointment was with special reference to the northwestern boundary between the United States and Great Britain, which had been in controversy ever since the treaty of the 15th of June, 1846. In December, 1871, Mr. Williams was appointed Attorney-General of the United States. When he came into this office the Ku-Klux clan, and various other similar organizations in the South, were operating to deprive the Union and colored citizens of that section of their political rights, and the vigorous measures adopted by the Attorney-General for their suppression aroused an intense hostility to him in the party opposed to the Administration. In 1873 Mr. Williams was nominated by President Grant for Chief-Justice of the Supreme Court of the United States, but at his instance the President withdrew his name. In the Spring of 1875 Mr. Williams resigned the office of Attorney-General, and has resumed the practice of his profession in Portland.

HON. WILLIAM H. WATKINDS.

The subject of this sketch may be classed among the remarkable as well as prominent men of Oregon. William H. Watkinds was born in Greencastle, Putnam county, Indiana, December 7, 1835. Together with his mother and other members of the family, except his father, who had preceded them by two years, he came to Oregon in 1852, crossing the plains with ox teams. Arriving in the Willamette valley, the family proceeded to Soda Springs, Linn county, near the town of Lebanon, where the father had located a land claim under the donation act of September 27, 1850. There he engaged in the work of assisting in improving a farm until 1855, when he went to Salem and became an apprentice to learn the saddler and harness trade. His advantages of obtaining an education were limited, only being able to attend school at Lebanon during a small portion of the time that he remained with his father on the farm. He is a Democrat, both by nature and education, and he early began giving much attention to politics. His first vote was cast for Gen. Joseph Lane for delegate to Congress. Having perfected a knowledge of his trade, he located at Salem and began its pursuit, which he continued with success for several years. The first State Convention he attended was at Eugene City in 1860, where he was sent as a delegate, and at which time he supported Stephen A. Douglas for President. With two exceptions, he has been a member of every Democratic State Convention since the organization of the State. He has twice been a member of the Democratic State Central Committee for Marion county. In 1870 he was appointed Superintendent of the State Penitentiary by Governor Grover, and reappointed in 1874 upon that gentleman's reinstallment in the executive chair. Upon the election of Governor Grover to the U. S. Senate in 1876 Mr. Watkinds resigned the office of Superintendent. During his term of office he was appointed one of the Penitentiary Building Commissioners, of which body he was elected chairman. That elegant and substantial structure stands a monument, attesting his sagacity and wisdom in directing its construction. And his accounts of expenses, filed in the archives of the State, after the most searching investigation, prove the honesty and economy of his administrations, both as superintendent and commissioner. During his term of office there passed through his hands nearly $400,000 of public funds, and no charge of irregularity in its expenditure has ever been sustained. After retiring from office Mr. Watkinds removed to Portland, where he still resides, engaged in the saddle and harness business. The anxiety and excitement of the fierce political contests in which he has so prominently figured have left few traces upon his sanguine frame or features and he bids fair to splinter many a lance with opponents in contests yet to be.

GEORGE H. DURHAM

Is one of the able attorneys of the Portland bar, and has attained his present position of prominence by virtue of application to study and ambition to win. He was born in Springfield, Illinois, December 4, 1843. When he was four years of age his parents immigrated to Oregon by way of the plains, and after arriving here settled at Clackamas. They removed to Oswego in 1850, and young George was enabled to attend the district school a certain number of months in each year. Having made very good progress in his studies, his parents determined to give him a college course, and in 1858 he entered the Willamette University at Salem. At the breaking out of the rebellion he left the college halls and enlisted in B Company, First Oregon Cavalry. On leaving his regiment he went to Pacific University, at Forest Grove, and graduated from that institution in the class of 1866, along with Judge E. B. Watson and Rev. M. Eells. In the same year Mr Durham was married to Miss S. E. Clarke, daughter of the well-known missionary, Rev. Harvey Clarke, and he then engaged in school-teaching at North Yamhill and at Cornelius Academy. Being of a progressive nature, and believing that he was possessed of the necessary qualifications, he determined to become a lawyer, and accordingly entered the office of the late Hon. Lansing Stout, and had the gratification of being admitted to the bar in 1869. He was appointed Register in Bankruptcy by the District Court of the United States for the District of Oregon in 1871, and in 1872 received the nomination from the Republican party for the office of District Attorney of the Fourth Judicial District, to which position he was elected by a large majority, defeating Hon. C. B. Bellinger, the Democratic candidate. Since his retirement from that office Mr. Durham has been engaged in the prosaic duties of a practitioner of the law, and is at present a member of the firm of Williams, Hill, Durham, Thompson & Mays. He takes a lively interest in the workings of his party and is recognized as a good political manager.

P. B. SINNOTT.

This gentleman, who has acquired a favorable reputation throughout the State by reason of his long-continued connection with the Grand Ronde Indian Reservation, in Yamhill county, was born in Wexford, Ireland, June 1, 1829, and came to America in 1848. He followed railroading for several years in the Eastern States and came to California in 1852, and there engaged in mining, which occupation he followed for a period of ten years. He came to Oregon in 1862 and engaged in keeping hotel until April, 1872, when he received the appointment as United States Indian Agent on the Grand Ronde Reservation, which important and responsible position he has held continuously up to the present time. As a public officer Mr. Sinnott has proved eminently successful. His accounts with the government have been accurately kept and he has experienced but very little difficulty in making his settlements. He is capable, honest and efficient, and his successful management of the affairs at the agency has elicited much praise at the hands of the department at Washington City. His influence over the Indians is almost marvelous, and under his management very many of them have made rapid and permanent progress in the line of civilization. Mr. Sinnott is a married man, an uncompromising Republican, and is highly esteemed by those who know him most intimately.

JAMES M'CAIN

Is an attorney at law at Lafayette, Yamhill county, and is a gentleman of fine attainments. He is of a quiet disposition, possessing an accurate knowledge of the law and a large amount of self-reliance, having a splendid legal mind. He has always stood deservedly high as a criminal lawyer, and has been counsel in some of the most important trials in the State. Although he has for years made criminal law a specialty, he is yet regarded as a formidable adversary in any lawsuit. As an advocate he adheres to a clear and concise discussion of the law principles and facts strictly within the record of the case, and rarely, if ever, embellishes or adorns his argument by figures of speech or illustrations foreign to the subject. He comes as near sticking closely to his text in the argument of his case as the old Baptist preacher did to his when he preached from the well-known text, "And he played on a harp of a thousand strings." We do not mean by this that he has any other characteristic of the Baptist preacher except that of sticking to his text. Mr. McCain was born in Carrol county, Indiana, March 30, 1842, and with his parents removed to Oregon in 1851, living with them on a farm in Polk county till 1866, meantime attending district school. In 1867 he began the study of law with P. C. Sullivan, of Dallas, and was admitted to practice in the Supreme Court in October, 1868. After his admission he practiced law in Dallas, and in the same year was married to Miss Electa C. Sullivan, eldest daughter of the gentleman with whom he studied law, and he has now three children. June, 1871, he removed to Lafayette, Yamhill county, where he has since resided. In politics he is a Republican.

W. W. GIBBS.

This gentleman is a son of ex-Governor Gibbs, and was assistant clerk of the Senate. He is a genial, whole-souled fellow, tall, stout and extremely good-looking, fond of a joke, but never carrying it too far. In his youth he received the benefits of a good education, having graduated from the Portland Academy, and his teachers have said that his progress in that institution was not because of close application to his books, but rather to his natural ability. After completing his education Will lived the life of the jolly farmer boy for about five years, and then was called to Portland to accept a position in the county clerk's office, where he remained two years. During all this time he had studied law off and on, and was finally admitted to practice in the Supreme Court October, 1882. Mr. Gibbs, although unmarried, is not averse to the ringing of the marriage bell, and we advise him to have a care when leap year doth come round, for he may unsuspectingly be entrapped by some fair young lady.

HON. W. S. NEWBURY

A member of the legal profession and a citizen of Portland who stands high among his fellow men, was born in Ripley, New York, September 19, 1831. He received the benefit of a common school education only, but made the most of that. In 1850 he went to Chicago, where he engaged in the occupation of salesman. He returned home in 1853, and in the fall of 1854 he went to Fox Lake, Wisconsin, where he commenced the study of law. In 1856 and 1857, at Madison, the capital of Wisconsin, took a regular course of study in book-keeping, penmanship and commercial law, and afterwards held several important positions as principal book-keeper and accountant. In the fall of 1857 he took a trip for his health, visiting St. Louis, New Orleans, Havana and Cuba and New York City, and returned west via Chicago and Madison to St. Paul, Minn., in February, 1858, and in the fall or winter of 1858 took entire charge at Sioux City, Iowa, of the business of the Little American Fur Company, of St. Louis, then having trading posts along the Missouri and Yellowstone rivers and their tributaries for a distance of 3,000 miles. He remained with this company about a year, and after visiting St. Louis, he went to Iola, Kansas, in 1869, and was elected Mayor of that city in 1870. Having meanwhile studied law, he was admitted to the bar in 1865, and at once commenced the practice of his profession. He served as an officer in the United States Volunteers nearly three years, about one year of which time he was stationed at Fort Leavenworth and about fifteen months he served with the Army of the Cumberland, in both the Twentieth and afterwards the Fourth army corps. He was Assistant Provost Marshal General of the State from June, 1864, until his election as Assistant Secretary of the State Senate in January, 1865. He came to San Francisco in June, 1870, and to Portland, Oregon, the same year, and in 1871 settled at Albany, Oregon, where he was engaged in the wheat and agricultural implement business until March, 1874, when he removed to Portland, where he has since resided. He was elected Mayor of Portland in 1877, and be it said, to the credit of his administration of the city affairs, that no complaints were made of injudicious management or extravagant practices. From 1876 to February, 1880, Mr. Newbury was engaged very extensively in the sale of agricultural implements, and was the head of the house of Newbury, Hawthorne & Co. for several years. Since the latter date he has been engaged in the practice of law, under the firm name of Newbury & Grant. He has gained some prominence in the I. O. O. F., having attended the Sovereign Grand Lodge at Baltimore, Md., in 1879, as Grand Representative from this State, duly elected by the Grand Lodge of Oregon. He was married at Middleton, Wisconsin, October 11, 1860, to Miss Alzina Taylor. He is of medium height, has black hair and pleasant features and a bright eye. He is honored and respected by all who know him, and although of a retiring disposition, is none the less popular with the public. He takes an active interest in politics and is a pronounced Republican.

BUSHROD WASHINGTON WILSON

Was born in Columbia, Washington county, Maine, July 18, 1824. At three years of age he was sent to school and kept there continuously until he was twelve years old, when his father, who in the meantime had removed to New Jersey and from thence to New York City, made arrangements to send him to a preparatory school to fit him for Yale College. The idea was distasteful to "Bush," and when the day arrived for him to commence his preparatory life he turned up missing. After some considerable search his father found him employed in the office of the New Brighton Association in Wall street, New York, an institution of which Mr. Cornelius Vanderbilt was President. After quitting this place he went to work in printing offices, among which were the "New Yorker," "Courier and Inquirer," "Brother Jonathan," etc. Horace Greeley, then editor of the "New Yorker," was a good friend to the boy and gave him much instruction that has since proved of great benefit to him. His mother died in 1840, when his father removed to Illinois, taking his son with him, where he married again. "Bush's" stepmother was a good woman, but her ways were not the young man's style, so, with the consent of his father, he "struck out." With forty-three cents he started and worked his way from St. Charles, Illinois, to New York, arriving at the latter place with a few dollars earned en route. Here he shipped for a whaling voyage and went around the world, stopping at various ports. His life was a wandering one for the next few years, including eight years at sea. Tired of a nomadic life, he arrived in Oregon in 1850, and has been a resident of the State ever since. He came by the way of Cape Horn and California, and landed at the mouth of the Umpqua river, footed it across the country, swimming all the rivers and sloughs on the way to Marysville, now Corvallis. Came to the State a Free Soil Whig and an earnest supporter of common schools. Helped to organize and has been ever since a consistent and energetic worker in the Republican party. He has filled many offices of trust and honor, notably that of County Clerk of Benton county, to which office he was elected in 1864, and continuously re-elected to the present time. His present term will make twenty years of active service in the same position. While attending to the duties of hi office he has given much time and attention to advancing the interests of the State at large as well as the local interests of the county in which he resides, particularly the improvement of Yaquina harbor and the railroad connection therewith. He was the first President of the Willamette Valley and Coast Railroad Company, and gave many years' time and much money to that enterprise, now so near completion. Mr. Wilson is a clear type of the sturdy pioneer of Oregon, and in the annals of the State the future historian will often refer to his name and deeds in recording its early history.

COL. W. W. CHAPMAN

Was born at Clarksburg, Va., August 8, 1808, and now resides at Portland, Oregon. His father, who was a millwright, and of the Pennsylvania Dutch Quaker cast of people, died in 1821, leaving a family of three sons, John B., Warner W. and Wm. W., who was then thirteen years of age. Those who have known either of the three men will readily recognize the marked family characteristic of all for energy and integrity. Having been admitted to the bar as an attorney-at-law, the subject of this sketch was married in 1832 to Margaret Fee, eighth child and fourth daughter of Col. Arthur Inghram who had several times sat in the House of Delegates of the Virginia Legislature. Mrs. Chapman is still living and enjoys good health. Soon after his marriage Colonel Chapman moved westward, first to Ohio, then to Illinois and then to Burlington, in Iowa Territory. He was U. S. Attorney under President Jackson, for Wisconsin, when it comprised Iowa and Illinois. He was the first Territorial Delegate in Congress from Iowa. He was also a member of the Constitutional Convention of Iowa, under which she was admitted into the Union. By his efforts the judiciary was made elective, which was the second, if not the first, State of the Union which adopted that mode. He was several times a member of the Iowa Legislature. When a delegate to Congress he sat at a desk with the noted Tom Corwin; and he caused the appointment to West Point of a young man named Gardner, who afterwards took an active part as a general in the Confederate army. He was a schoolmate with Stonewall Jackson, the great Southern leader; and also of the late Daniel Waldo, of "Waldo hills," in Marion county in that State. In 1847 Col. Chapman and family immigrated to Oregon, where he has since resided. Early in 1849, while in California in quest of gold, he met General Joseph Lane, who was on his way, as Governor, to organize the new Territorial Government of Oregon. He, with about one hundred other Oregonians who had spent the winter in the California mountains hunting gold, returned with General Lane to Oregon, in the old bark Jeanette.

Col. Chapman has been several times a member of the Legislature of Oregon, in the days of the Provisional Government, under the Territorial Government, and since. He was United States Surveyor-General from 1859 to 1861. In 1855-6 he took an active part in the Indian wars of Southern Oregon; he, as lieutenant-colonel, and James Bruce, of Washington county, as major, having command of the southern battalion in the spring campaign of 1856, when the war was closed up. He was strongly recommended for the position of United States District Judge, when Oregon was admitted as a State, having the recommendation of nine-tenths of the Democratic members of the Legislature; but there were "methods" in those days in regard to the Federal appointments that were no less mysterious than those of the present times. In the latter part of the fall of 1849 Col. Chapman purchased a one-third interest in the Portland land claim and town site, and moved to the place on the first day of January, 1850. Early in that year, Portland proper, extending from A street on the north to near Lincoln street on the south, and westward from the Willamette river to Twelfth street was laid off in lots and blocks as it has since been built up with fine and comely structures. In January, 1850, Portland may be said to have had its whole existence before it for a future. The buildings in the town then amounted to no more, if as much, as those in the town of Albina did in the fall of 1881. There were no roads from Portland that led anywhere, except a sort of trail that passed over the point back of Amos N. Kings, near Mr. Hodge's new residence. All back of Second street was filled up with logs, stumps and trees, and the sad, dreary aspect of the first pretensions of a town was striking in a very high degree, at that time, for Portland. The three partners in the town, early in 1850, divided their town amongst themselves by blocks and lots, and as a consequence the "omnibus" deeds were executed amongst themselves that lawyers here know so much about. This division, when the Oregon donation law was subsequently passed, was found to be exceedingly impracticable. Much discontent arose among the people who had settled in the town and bought lots here, for it began to seem that the town proprietors would be unable to get title from the general government, and so could convey none to their grantees. The alarm became imminent amongst those who had lots bought here, some honestly supposing that the town proprietors could not be able to get any title, and others, while there was very little ground for alarm took a deep interest to stir up the alarm and to magnify the danger, and endeavored to induce discord amongst the proprietors themselves. Ultimately the instrument was executed amongst the proprietors known as the "Escrow," which was subsequently upheld by Judge L. D. Sawyer, of California, U. S. Circuit Judge, as a valid instrument, and the decision was sustained by the U. S. Supreme Court. By the terms of this instrument [escrow] the proprietors re-divided the town, each taking a designated tract to himself, and upon which he became a settler under the donation law of Congress. By the escrow, each proprietor covenanted, when he should obtain title from the general government to fulfill each previous contract of any of the proprietors in regard to any lots in the parts so set off to him. Some objections have been made to the instrument of March 12, 1852, (known as the escrow) but since the decision by Judge Sawyer in Lamb vs. Davenport, no doubt has been entertained of its correctness in principle and its accuracy in detail and as being well-suited to the requirement of the occasion. In one or two instances courts have pretended to discriminate of cases that did not fall within its provisions; but there is no one who openly adopts the authorship of such discrimination, and the decision was manifestly unjust. The covenants of the "omnibus deeds" were also well-suited to the circumstances and situation of titles at the time. In the formation of all of these instruments Col. Chapman always took a prominent part, and his conduct has been fully sustained by the lapse of time and the decisions of the highest courts, and by almost all of the courts. Col. Chapman has always been a man of very great energy. Where he has failed in his enterprises, others have reaped the benefit of fortunes as the result of his pioneering. In order to place Portland ahead of its rivals as the town of Oregon, he and others entered upon the enterprise of purchasing the Gold Hunter steamship, to ply between San Francisco and Portland; but being all unacquainted with nautical affairs the result was that it "busted" them, but it made Portland. Conceiving the idea of a railroad between Salt Lake and Portland as a proper counter-plot to the Northern Pacific programme, as it was developed in 1873, when the company failed, which was to ignore Portland and adopt Puget Sound entirely as a terminus, Col. Chapman spent much time and money in favor of the adoption of the Salt Lake (Short Line) route and the building of the railroad upon the south side of the Columbia river. These problems were discussed at the East by his espousal of the one, so that when railroad building was commenced, the south side of the Columbia river was adopted, as a matter of course, for the line of the railroad. Others have reaped the benefit of this work, although but for his efforts it would have been otherwise. As a politician, Col. Chapman is a Democrat; but was always anti-slavery in his views, having voted against slavery in Oregon at the adoption of the constitution. No man, probably, ever was so inherently opposed to trickery, machinations and frauds in politics as he. Having taken his political lessons from the age and teachings of such leaders as Webster, Adams, Clay, Marshall and Jefferson, he has throughout his life deprecated and refused to adopt what are termed the common feats of legerdemain in politics, always believing that what could not be done openly to inspection was unworthy. But such is the difference between forty and fifty years ago and now. Col. Chapman is as a connecting link with a past age of American manners and customs, from which the present is far more different than can be readily believed.

J. M. BOWER

Was born in Salem, Clarion county, Penn., in the year 1852, and in the historic and influential Keystone State received his elementary instructions in the English language. At the age of fifteen he "went to seek his fortune," and landed at Des Moines, Iowa, where he learned the mysteries of the art preservative, and gained the reputation of being a first-class compositor. He then struck out for Oregon in 1870 and spent two years working at his trade. Becoming anxious to see "the old folks at home," Mr. Bower started East and remained away from Oregon two years, returning to his chosen State in 1874. He settled down in Portland and turned his attention to the study of law, and after three years studious attention to his new vocation was admitted to the Supreme Court in 1879. Mr. Bower is associated with Mr. McDougall at the present time. He is a young man of neat address, logical in his arguments, and quick in discerning every item that points favorably towards benefiting a client, and we predict for him a brilliant future.

DAN HOLTON.

The genial boniface who presides over the destinies of the well-known Holton House in Portland, though not claiming to be one of our "oldest inhabitants," is sufficiently acclimated to bear the honor of being a thorough "Webfoot," having spent the last sixteen years of his life in the growing metropolis of Oregon. Dan is one of those modest men who, though always alive to a joke, jollification and to business, seeks no notoriety outside of the favorite resort that is always enlivened by his countenance; and as his pleasant temperament and popularity merit for him a position in these annals, we called upon him for the requisite data with which to adorn these pages. With that candor for which Dan is noted, he informed us that he could not boast of valorous deeds, rank or title; that he was born and reared in the accustomed, ordinary way, and came to Oregon in 1866, in order to jog along socially with the rest of mankind, without any view of meriting or claiming any distinction. This much we did glean from him, that his first insight into hotel life was obtained from Mike O'Connor, well known to all pioneers as the proprietor of the old What Cheer House, on Front and Morrison streets. After several years' experience Dan took charge of the Cosmopolitan Hotel, and afterwards established the Holton House, on Front street, near Oak. Three years ago he secured the present site for the Holton House, southeast corner of First and Alder, and under his liberal and genial management it has become the most popular resort in the State for business and professional men, and is justly classed as the commercial house of Portland, as can readily be judged from the numerous business men who can be found congregated in his comfortable rooms at all hours, day or night. Rush of business and the geniality of the companions with whom Dan has been thrown in contact have combined to keep him in the ranks of merry and mellow bachelorship; but now, whilst he is still in the full vigor of manhood, as the gray hairs are beginning to warn him that he is approaching the "sere and yellow leaf" of life, his friends think that he should make some effort to perpetuate his name and fame for the benefit of futurity.

COL. SAL. RIPINSKY.

The subject of this sketch, although still a young man, has already given signs of rare ability as an artist, scholar and linguist, and at no distant day we may expect to see him in the front ranks of polite, intelligent society. Col. Ripinsky was born July 15, 1856, in Rypin, Poland, one mile from Strasbourg, Western Prussia. He received a good European education and studied in some of the best military schools of Europe. Here he acquired a thorough knowledge of draughting and considerable skill in sketching, drawing and painting. Indeed, so skillful was he in sketching that it was the means of his receiving a handsome souvenier from the Governor of the Province in which the academy he was attending, was located, he having sketched his highness and staff while they were examining some of the higher classes during an official visit. After visiting many of the principal cities of Europe, Mr. Ripinsky came to New York in 1872 and made a partial tour of the Eastern States. Being particularly pleased with the "Sunny South," he located at Shreveport, Louisiana, where he engaged in merchandising. Here he remained until that dreadful scourge, "Yellow Jack," swept that fair land. After having and surviving an attack of the disease he came to California and opened a studio at Sacramento, where he painted several fine oil paintings, one of which, "The battle of Chevy Chase," sold for a very high price. Mr. R came to Oregon, locating in Salem in 1878, where he has since spent most of his time in various positions until recently, when he opened a fine grocery establishment upon his own account and is, by close attention, fair dealing and pleasant manners, building up a large trade. Mr. Ripinsky, in 1878, received from the State Fair Association and Mechanics' Fair at Portland the first prizes for an emblamatic Masonic chart. In 1879 he exhibited, and afterwards presented Olive Lodge No. 18, I. O. O. F., of which he is a member, an artistic chart of the emblems of that order. During the administration of Governor W. W. Thayer he was honored with an appointment on his excellency's staff as aide-de-camp with the rank of lieutenant-colonel. Salem Lodge No. 4, A. O. U. W., recently presented the colonel as Past Master a handsome gold medal for valuable services to the order, which he wears with commendable pride. He speaks fluently five different languages. In appearance Col. Ripinsky is petite in size, finely-formed, expressive countenance, active and vigorous in his style, and is really a fine-looking man, without the least trace of effeminacy in his make-up.

DR. T. F. SMITH

Is one of the most successful physicians and surgeons in the Willamette valley, and now an honored citizen of Independence. He is one of those happy, good-natured men that we occasionally find in the professional ranks, and who, when we meet them, infuse new vim and vigor into one's self by some mysterious magnetic power, not visible, but none the less effective. He was born at Smithfield, Peoria county, Illinois, August 7, 1847, and with his parents came to this coast at an early age. He enlisted in Company F, First Oregon Infantry in 1864, and served until 1866, during which time he was in several engagements with the Indians, being wounded in the fight of September 19, 1865, in Harney Lake valley. For his gallantry in that engagement he received special mention. On being mustered out of service in 1866, he was appointed Assessor and Tax Collector for Ada county, I. T. He shortly afterwards came down to the Warm Springs Indian agency, where he remained until 1869, when he went East and commenced the study of medicine, graduating with high honors from the College of Physicians and Surgeons at Keokuk, Iowa, June 16, 1874. He at once returned to this coast and opened an office at Vancouver, W. T., where he soon built up a large practice. His health failing, he accepted an appointment as Lieutenant and Surgeon in the United States Army, and was stationed at Fort Sitka, Alaska, which position he resigned in 1876, when he resumed active practice at Dallas, in Polk county. In November, 1880, he was severely injured by his horse stumbling and falling on him, the Doctor having his leg broken and sustaining other injuries. The accident was the means of laying him up for some time, and on his recovery he moved to Independence, where he still resides, and where he has already gained an extensive practice, which, as he becomes better acquainted, is rapidly increasing. During his practice he has performed many of the most difficult operations in surgery, including excision of the lower jaw, lip, upper jaw, tumors, cancers and numerous very difficult amputations, all of which have proved successful. Socially speaking, the Doctor is one of the most genial men we have ever met, and as a physician and citizen he stands high in the community where he resides. He is a staunch Republican and takes an active interest in politics. He was married March 10, 1870, to Miss M. E. Smith, of Washington county, Iowa, and they have one boy. The Doctor is at present Post Surgeon of McPherson Post, No. 3, G. A. R., which is the only fraternal organization of which he is a member.

FRANK PIERCE MAYS

Is another one of our representative men who was born and raised in Oregon, and possesses that energy and vim characteristic of the native Oregonian. He was born in Lane county on the 12th day of May, 1855. In 1858 his parents moved to Wasco county, where he has resided ever since. He was reared on a farm and attended the country schools. He went to Salem in 1872 and commenced a course of study in the Willamette University, and graduated in the year of our centennial, one of the class of '76. He early evinced a warm admiration for the legal profession, and resolved on reading law. He found a competent tutor, a good adviser and a warm friend in Hon. W. Lair Hill, a leading and influential member of the profession, and in 1877 entered his office at The Dalles as a student. He was admitted to the bar in January, 1880, and in the March following was admitted to partnership with his tutor. In 1881 the firm merged into the now prominent firm of Williams, Hill, Durham, Thompson & Mays, of Portland and The Dalles. Mr. Mays is a young man of far more than ordinary talent, and is applying himself closely to the profession of which he is destined to become, at no late day, an honored and prominent member. He is unmarried, of slight build, has a youthful though earnest expression of countenance—an expression which is proved in his conduct of professional business to be a true index of his character. He is Republican in politics, and adheres closely to the principles of the party. His future, through his own personal efforts, promises to be a brilliant one, and a host of warm personal friends wish him abundant success.

HON. GEORGE A. STEEL.

The present efficient and courteous Nasby of Portland, is a gentleman whose enterprise, energy and prominence in public life have made his name familiar from one end of our State to the other. He has been endowed with sufficient ambition to give him pride in prominence, and with ample integrity to avoid coalition with the dregs of political life which so often tarnish and ruin the reputation of less honorable men. Mr. Steel was born in Stafford Ohio in 1846. He came to Oregon in 1863, when sixteen years of age, in company with Captain J. D. Merryman, now of Astoria. He was for a short time a clerk in the Portland postoffice under E. G. Randall, but shortly afterwards accepted the position of Secretary of the old Oregon Iron Works. He was afterwards appointed accountant in Ladd & Tilton's bank, which responsible position he held for a period of five years. In 1870 he was elected Treasurer of Multnomah county, and here again he displayed his adaptability to the oft-times arduous duties of public life. In 1871, in partnership with J. K. Gill, he purchased the interest of Harris & Holman in the stationery business, and the new firm of Gill & Steel at once found favor with the public. They subsequently bought out Bancroft & Morse, another leading firm of this city, and extended their business interests accordingly, Mr. F. A. Bancroft entering the firm at that time. Close attention to the wants of trade and fair dealing with the public caused their business to increase rapidly. Mr. Steel eventually bought out his partners, and for some time conducted the business under the firm name of G. A. Steel & Co. Unfortunate investments in real estate in 1872 embarrassed him financially, but with the indomitable pluck and perseverance for which he is noted, he weathered the storm, and although he lost heavily he liquidated his debts honorably, paying dollar for dollar, and gained new friends by his manly course in so trying a period of his life. The reverse of fortune was a severe one, but it did not discourage Mr. Steel by any means. Disposing of his goods at a great sacrifice, he closed out his business, enjoying the confidence and esteem of all business men with whom he had had commercial dealings. He became an active worker in politics in 1876, was elected Chairman of the Republican State Central Committee and his management of the hotly contested campaign of that year was indicative of marked executive ability. In January, 1877, Mr. Steel was appointed Special Agent of the Postoffice Department for the Northwest Coast, and here, as elsewhere, he showed energy, enterprise and untiring industry. He resigned the position in 1879 and was at once appointed Deputy Collector of Customs at Portland, under Hon. John Kelly, where he remained until September, 1880. In March, 1881, his name was sent to the Senate by President Garfield for the position of Postmaster at Portland. Vexations delays occurring, he did not take charge of the office until some time afterwards, and he has since been reappointed by President Arthur for four years, his appointment being unanimously confirmed by the Senate. His management of the office has been highly satisfactory both to the postal department at Washington and the thousands of patrons of the office. The work has been carefully revised and systematized under his supervision, and its fast increasing business is dispatched with celerity and accuracy. Recent judicious investments have placed Mr. Steel on his feet once more in a financial point of view, and being still in the prime of life his future cannot well be otherwise than successful. He was married to Miss Eva Pope, of Oregon City, in 1869. As a man, he is universally esteemed; as an officer, he is prompt and efficient, and as a friend, he will do to tie to.

COL. JOHN KELSAY.

There is, probably, no member of the bar in Oregon more well and favorably known than he whose name heads this sketch, and a history of his career, such as it justly merits, would prove of deep interest to our readers. Having been a resident of Oregon for almost thirty years, he is familiar, by active participation, with many of the most stirring events of pioneer life in this State. Space, however, permits the mention of but the very outlines of his history at the present time. Col. Kelsay was born in Wayne county, Kentucky, October 23, 1819, and moved with his parents to Missouri in 1829. He was the recipient of only the ordinary common school advantages of that early day, and commenced the study of law in 1842. In 1844 he was elected a member of the House of Representatives of that State. He obtained license to practice law at Jefferson City, Missouri, in the summer of 1845, since which time he has been continuously in the practice of his profession. He came to Oregon in 1853 and settled in the city of Corvallis, where he still resides. In February, 1856, he enlisted as a private soldier in the Oregon Volunteers, and served during the Indian war of that year, having been promoted first to the Captaincy of his company and then to the command of the Second Regiment Oregon Mounted Volunteers as its Colonel, which position he filled until the close of the war. He was a member of the State Constitutional Convention in 1857 from Benton county, and in 1868 was elected one of the Justices of the Supreme Court to fill the unexpired term of the late Judge R. E. Stratton. In whatever capacity he has served, either in public or private life, he has ever retained the unqualified respect and esteem of all with whom he came in contact, and, as a man of unblemished integrity and unsullied character, Col. Kelsay has no superiors. He is still an active member of the legal fraternity and enjoys a lucrative practice.

WILLIAM SARGENT LADD.

Senior partner of the well-known banking houses of Ladd & Tilton, of Portland, and Ladd & Bush, of Salem, was born in Vermont in 1827. During his infancy his parents moved to New Hampshire, where at Tilton his father, who was a practicing physician, secured a very extensive practice. The subject of our sketch received the advantages only of a common school education, although he for a short time attended the Northfield Seminary. He was quick to learn, but after all did not particularly relish the routine life of a student, and he soon abandoned it. His executive, rather than his educational, ability secured him a position as a teacher in a neighborhood where unruly students had theretofore rendered the life of the teacher burdensome. He successfully completed his engagement, winning the esteem and obedience of his pupils, and then and there severed his connection with educational institutions in the capacity of a teacher. At the age of twenty Mr. Ladd turned his attention to railroading and was employed as freight and passenger agent of the Boston, Concord & Montreal railroad. His industry and careful attention to the minor details of his position won for him the confidence and respect of his employers, and rapid promotion was guaranteed him. The limits of this line of business were, however, too contracted for a man of his energy, enterprise and ambition, and in 1851 he resigned his position, and, in direct opposition to the advice of parents and employers, he started west to seek fortune and fame among the then undeveloped territories of the Pacific slope. Thinking that Oregon offered superior advantages to men of his calibre, he, striking out for Portland, reached here in the spring of the same year. While waiting for some employment more congenial to his tastes, he labored in clearing certain newly opened streets of trees and stumps in the then small village of perhaps 250 inhabitants. His business qualifications could not long remain hidden beneath the observation of practical business men, and he shortly afterwards accepted a position as clerk and bookkeeper for the firm of Wakeman, Dimon & Co., who had sent a stock of goods out here in charge of Mr. Goodkin, a junior member of the firm. This gentleman shortly afterwards returned east, and Mr. Ladd took charge of their business, and, in partnership with C. E. Tilton, Esq., subsequently purchased the interests of the firm, which partnership existed until 1854, when Mr. Tilton withdrew. Mr. Ladd continued the mercantile business until April, 1859, when he sold it to his two brothers and Mr. S. G. Reed. In April, 1859, in partnership with C. E. Tilton, Esq., his former partner, he established the first banking house on the Northwest coast. In 1854 Mr. Ladd was married to Miss Caroline A. Elliott, an estimable lady of far more than ordinary good sense and domestic qualifications, and who, during the succeeding years, has proved a noble wife and mother. Their home in Portland is one of the pleasantest in the city. Wealth and good taste have united in beautifying its surroundings, and their appreciation of the beautiful is evinced in their choice selections of statuary, paintings, etc., and those who are sufficiently fortunate to be classed among their friends, find much within their home to interest and instruct them in arts and sciences hitherto, perhaps, unknown to them. Such a home, opened as it is, to respectable citizens of all ranks, cannot fail to elevate the tastes of those around him, while Mr. and Mrs. Ladd's reputation as host and hostess insure a welcome to their friends and those who are the friends of their friends. Mr. Ladd is considered among our most substantial citizens, and evidences of wealth surround him at his home. His wealth, however, has not been all lavished on his home surroundings. He has always taken an active interest in educational matters, having served several terms as Director in the common schools of Portland. He was one of the founders, and for years a director and liberal supporter, of the Portland Academy and a warm friend of the Willamette University at Salem, of which he is one of the trustees. His liberality is proverbial and many of our young men have occasion to thank him for substantial aid in securing an education. The Presbyterian church, of which himself and family are members, has received almost princely contributions from his purse, and scarcely a church or chapel of that denomination in Oregon, Washington or Idaho Territory has been started without assistance from his liberal store. He has also rendered efficient aid to the Methodist denomination, in which his early manhood was spent. He has been a friend to the Young Men's Christian Association and the Portland Library, having for years provided them with elegant and commodious quarters free of charge. Mr. Ladd's enterprise and energy has not been wholly confined to his banking business, he having been a bold and successful originator and operator in enterprises outside of the regular banking routine. He is the senior member of the banking firm of Ladd & Bush, at Salem, was, from its early organization, a heavy stockholder and director of the O. S. N. Company, as well as a director in the Oregon City Woolen Mills and the Salem Flouring Mills Company. A gentleman of his intelligence and enterprise is necessarily sought after by his fellow citizens to fill positions of public trust. He has, however, invariably declined accepting any public office other than those involving usefulness, without regard to public honors or emoluments. He has held the position of Mayor of Portland, and his name has repeatedly been mentioned as a suitable one to place on the Congressional ticket, but he has persistently refused to enter the arena of political strife. During the war he was a staunch war Democrat, and has since exercised his right of voting his own ticket, although in national matters he has of late years sided with the Republicans. Such is a brief outline of the history of a man whose active and enterprising spirit, sound business sagacity, open-handed liberality, pronounced Christian character, and love of the beautiful and useful in nature and art, has contributed largely to mold the character of a city of 30,000 souls, and lay deep and broad in a great measure the commercial honor, political virtue, enlightened education and Christian principles of our young and growing commonwealth. A hospitable man, it affords him pleasure to entertain his friends beneath his own roof, and his acknowledged wealth does not prevent his greeting the poor man just as sincerely and heartily as he does the railroad magnate or the merchant prince. All honor to such men say we, and it is with pride that we point to Hon. W. S. Ladd as one of the "Representative men of our State," for as such he reflects credit and honor upon us, and we regard and esteem him as one of our most honorable and upright citizens.

MATTHEW P. DEADY.

In the brief space which our limits compel us to allot to sketches of our representative men, it is impossible to do justice to the life, the character or the labors of the distinguished gentleman whose name heads this article. Little more, therefore, will be attempted than to allude to the more prominent events in which he has been an actor, for these alone will illustrate a character, solid, pure, wise and energetic. Judge Deady was born near Easton in Talbot county, Maryland, on May 12, 1824. His parents were substantial and respectable people, his father being a teacher by profession. In 1828 the family removed to Wheeling, Virginia, where his father was employed as principal of the Lancasterian Academy for some years. In 1834 he had the misfortune to lose his mother, who died on her way back to Wheeling from Baltimore, where the family had gone on a visit to her father. In 1837 young Deady removed to Ohio with his father, and spent a few years on a farm. He left the farm in 1841 and went to Barnesville, where for four years he wrought as an artisan at the anvil and attended the then somewhat famous Barnesville Academy, working as well at the forge of thought as that of matter, hammering and shaping to his mind the ores of knowledge found in the mine of good books. Having completed his apprenticeship, young Deady listened to the promptings of a laudable ambition and determined to read law—a profession that reserves its rewards and honors for those alone who combine great mental power with severe application. Supporting himself by teaching school, he began the study of the law in 1845 with the Hon. William Kennon, of St. Clairsville, Ohio, since on the Supreme Bench of the State, and now deceased. In October, 1847, he was admitted to the Supreme Court of the State, and commenced the practice in St. Clairsville. He crossed the plains to Oregon in the year 1849. Here he supported himself during the winter by teaching, and in the spring of 1850 commenced the practice of his profession, and soon became a man of mark in the community. Such was the confidence he inspired that he was chosen from Yamhill county at the June election, in 1850, to the lower House of the Territorial Legislature, in which he was an active and leading member during the session of 1850. In 1851, after a severe contest, he was elected a member of the Territorial Council, from the same county, over Hon. David Logan, and served as Chairman of the Judiciary Committee of that body in the session of 1851-2, and as presiding officer during the special session of July, 1852, and the regular one of 1852-3. At this early period of his career he had already won his spurs, and was generally recognized as one of the leading men of the country, both at the bar and in the Legislature. He was strongly urged, in the spring of 1853, as a candidate for Delegate to Congress, but received the appointment of Associate Justice of the Supreme Court of the Territory, which he accepted and held, by subsequent re-appointment, until the admission of the State to the Union in February, 1859. Soon after his appointment he removed to the Southern District, then comprising the country south of the Calapooia mountains, and settled in the valley of the Umpqua upon a farm, where still may be seen the fruitful orchards and vines planted and trained by his own hands during the intervals of judicial labor. Whilst occupying this position he was elected from Douglas county one of the Delegates to the Constitutional Convention, that met at Salem in 1857, and formed the present Constitution of the State. Of this body he was chosen President and took an active and influential part in its deliberations and conclusions.

At the first ection under this Constitution Judge Deady was elected from the Southern District without opposition, one of the Justices of the Supreme Court of the State, but being upon the admission of the State in 1859, also appointed Judge of the United States District Court for the State, he accepted the latter position, and removed to Portland in 1860, where he has ever since resided, and sat in the District and Circuit Courts with marked industry, integrity and ability. In 1861-2 he prepared and reported to the Legislature of 1862 the present Code of Civil Procedure. It was adopted with two small amendments, and, with slight alterations, has constituted the Code of Civil Procedure for the State since it went into effect in May, 1863. At the request of the Legislature of 1862, he also prepared and reported to the Legislature of 1864, a Code of Criminal Procedure, including the definition of crimes and their punishments, which was passed at that session without amendment, and which, substantially, is still in force. The leaders of the bar have generally appreciated and spoken well of the preparation and provisions of these codes, but some ill-read "lawyerlings" are to be found who persist--perhaps justly--in attributing their frequent failures to win cases to their inability to understand "Deady's Codes." In the midst of his judicial and juridical labors, Judge Deady has found time to prepare and publish a large amount of correspondence and contributions in the periodicals of the country, replete with information concerning the history of Oregon and its affairs. He has also devoted much time and labor to the establishment and support of charitable and educational institutions and agencies in the community, one of which is the excellent Portland Library, of which he is President, and another the State University, in which he is President of the Board of Regents. In June, 1852, he was married to Miss Lucy A. Henderson, the daughter of Mr. Robert Henderson, of Yamhill--a lady universally respected and well calculated to preside with dignity in the Judge's household. They both occupy a high social position, and are among the best people of Trinity Church, of which the Judge is a vestryman of long standing. Judge Deady is quite six feet two inches in height, with a form and figure duly proportioned. His eyes are blue and sparkle with good humor and intelligence. His hair, originally a wavy auburn, is now sprinkled with grey, setting off to advantage his large, well-poised head, and ruddy, clear complexion. The brow is broad and massive, particularly showing what, phrenologically speaking, are denominated the perceptive and reasoning faculties. On the Bench he is urbane and courteous, but apt to require that decorum which he regards as indispensable to the dignity of the Court and the orderly transaction of its business. What are called the "Bullies" or "Buccaneers" of the bar soon find their level in his court. In practice before him it is necessary to work, neither reputation nor eloquence being sufficient to compensate for neglect or carelessness in the preparation or conduct of a case. To the young and inexperienced lawyer, just commencing the struggle of life, he is particularly kind and encouraging, and not a few who have achieved distinction during his time on the bench remember with gratitude the kind word which conveyed to others his recognition of the genius or ability displayed in their first efforts before him. Space forbids us to attempt an analysis of his judicial labors. They are interwoven with the history and commerce of the country, and have given direction and shape to the legislation, both of the nation and the State. Possessing in a preeminent degree the faculty of judicial analysis, he can select from the most complicated mass of facts, the point or circumstance on which the case must turn; and so clearly is the ground of his decision set forth in the opinion as often to evoke surprise that any other view than the one expressed could ever have been entertained. A distinguished member of the Portland bar once said: "I have never known any one who, to a greater degree than Judge Deady, sought to honor his station by being inflexibly just, nor one who held the scales with a more impartial hand. If I were to characterize him by allusion to his predominant mental traits, I would say that above most men of my acquaintance he is distinguished for what we may call mental intrepidity, and his chief ambition in the administration of his office, is to preserve inviolately spotless the ermine he wears." In conversation in the social circle, Judge Deady is correct, lively and entertaining, though in animated debate he sometimes gives the impression that, like Dr. Johnson, he argues for victory. As a speaker his merits are not generally known. His position on the bench has necessarily kept him from the public discussion of those matters by which his ability in this field would have been universally recognized. Those, however, who have met him in assemblages where mind was acting on mind, and wit and eloquence ruled the hour, remember with delight the graceful humor, elegant diction and forcible expression, which there characterized his impromptu utterances. In the lecture room he is always instructive, sound and entertaining, often giving direction to and leading the public mind in new channels of investigation. Indeed, his lectures on "Law and Lawyers," "Trial by Jury" and "Towns and Cities," are not only excellent monographs on the subjects indicated by the titles, but they abound with much original thought and curious learning. He is indeed an individual of whom the State may be proud, and I cannot, in my recollection of the public men whom I have met, call to mind one of whom it may more truthfully be said: "His aims are noble and his methods just."

HON. T. A. M'BRIDE.

The subject of the following sketch was born in Yamhill county, Oregon, in 1847. His father was the late Dr. Jas. McBride, well known to all old Oregonians, and whose memory is still venerated by all who ever knew him. He was one of the leading men in the Territory, and his daily walk was always in the direction of everything that was pure and noble, and, being a man of far above average ability, his example and teachings have been lasting in their effect. His sons inherited their father's ability and uprightness of character and all of them are a credit to our young State. His brother, Hon. Geo. W. McBride, is the leading merchant of Columbia county and speaker of the House in the Legislature of 1882, where he made a reputation that will favorably compare with any of his predecessors. The subject of this sketch was educated at McMinnville college and there received a good English education and laid the foundation for a classical course, which has been steadily built upon ever since, until his acquaintance with the dead languages will favorably compare with that of any man in Oregon. He was admitted to the bar in 1870 and has practiced law in Oregon ever since, with the exception of two years, which were spent in the same profession in Utah. He was the first Republican every elected to the Legislature from Columbia county, and that in the face of a large Democratic majority. He owed his election solely to his great personal popularity, not only among Republicans but also Democrats. In that Legislature Mr. McBride made quite a reputation as a debater, and his speeches and witty repartees are often referred to by those who heard them. In 1881 he removed from St. Helens to Oregon City, where he has practiced law to the satisfaction of his clients and remuneratively to himself. He has recently been appointed by the Governor Prosecuting Attorney of the Fifth Judicial District, a position he is well qualified to fill. He is studious and is destined to take a position in the front ranks of the members of the profession. Mr. McBride has a pleasing address, a great deal of magnetism and makes friends of all with whom he comes in contact. As a companion, he is both entertaining and instructive, and as a friend, one whose fidelity is beyond question. Few men possess as many good qualities as are to be found in the person of Mr. Thos. McBride.

HON. JOHN H. MITCHELL.

It is not possible to give a full biographical history of the man whose name is the title of this sketch in the limits within which the writer is circumscribed in this work. Though but 47 years of age, his history would fill a volume as large as that in which he is given this brief mention. Mr. Mitchell was born in Washington county, Pennsylvania, June 22, 1835. After acquiring the rudiments of an English education at the public schools of his native county, he attended for some time the Washington Institute, of Butler, Pa. He then entered the law office of Hon. Samuel A. Purviance, of the firm of Purviance & Thompson, of Butler, under whose instruction he remained for two years. After passing a most satisfactory examination, he was admitted to the bar of Butler county in 1858. There he immediately commenced the practice of his profession, but remained only for a short time. His mind was filled with the love of adventure and the Pacific Coast offered the most promising field for his young and energetic spirit. Leaving his native State, under circumstances so sad in their character that a weaker nature would have sank under their weight, he came to California. After remaining a short time in San Francisco he removed to San Louis Obispo, where he remained a few months. The fame of Oregon, as a young and growing commonwealth, had, in the meantime, attracted his attention, and in July, 1860, he took passage at San Francisco for Portland, and arrived in this city by due course of steamer. He at once turned his attention to building up a legal practice and at the same time engaged actively in local politics. So quickly did he make his influence felt that in the year 1861, he was elected Corporation Attorney of Portland. The succeeding year he was nominated and elected, by the Republican party, to the Oregon State Senate, in which body he served acceptably to his constituents four years. During the first two years of his term he was Chairman of the Judiciary Committee and the last two years he held the honorable position of President of the Senate. At the close of his Senatorial term he received every mark of approval from his immediate constituents, and in 1866 strenuous efforts were made by his political friends to secure him a seat in the U. S. Senate. They only failed to elevate him to this exalted position through lack of one vote in the caucus. He earnestly and honestly supported the caucus nominee, who was only defeated by the action of a factions few who refused to acquiesce in the decision of the caucus after participating therein. In 1865 he was commissioned Lieutenant-Colonel, by the Governor, of the State Militia. In 1867 he was elected Professor of Medical Jurisprudence in Willamette University at Salem, Oregon, and occupied the chair for nearly four years. In 1872 his name was again presented to the State Legislature as a candidate for the U. S. Senate, to which position he was elected to succeed Hon. H. W. Corbett, whose term expired March 4, 1873. In this body he at once took a leading position. He served as a member of the Committees on Privileges and Elections, Commerce and Claims, and was made a member of the Select Committee on Transportation Routes to the seaboard, of which Senator Oliver P. Morton, of Indiana, was Chairman. That Senator dying, Senator Mitchell was made Chairman in his stead. It was in this position that he was enabled to do the greatest service for Oregon, and he did not fail to make use of the rare opportunity to do his whole duty to his constituents. To him is due the credit of the location and construction of the Transcontinental railroad, on the south side of the Columbia river. He also did all in his power in favor of the construction of the locks at the Cascades. During the whole history of this government, no Senator, during his first term, ever held so many and so important positions on committees in the U. S. Senate. Mr. Mitchell is possessed of remarkable energy and rare abilities, which, together with untiring industry, enable him to accomplish a vast amount of mental labor with apparent ease. From 1868 until January 1, 1873, when he resigned all other engagements to enter upon his duties as United States Senator, he was constantly employed in positions of high honor and trust. For five years he was the attorney for the Oregon & California Railroad Company and the North Pacific Steamship Transportation Company, of San Francisco, at an annual salary of $10,000. Throughout his public career he has been distinguished for his keen discrimination and enlarged views of statesmanship. His unswerving adherence to the principles of the Republican party and his fidelity to his friends are distinguishing traits in his character. Be he rich or poor, high or low, a friend of John H. Mitchell's never had occasion to charge him with ingratitude or a want of courtesy under any and all circumstances. A quick perception and sound judgment, united with business tact, have secured to him rapid and great success, and he carries with him an influence rarely in the possession of a man so young in years. In 1882, when the Legislative Assembly of the State of Oregon convened, Mr. Mitchell, at the earnest solicitation of his friends, appeared as the candidate for re-election to the United States Senate. A caucus was held composed of thirty-six members, being exactly two-thirds of the Republican majority on joint ballot, and he was unanimously chosen as the choice of the party to fill the exalted position to which he aspired. For reasons presumed to be satisfactory to themselves, seventeen Republican members refused him their support. Such was his personal influence and popularity that five Democrats joined his Republican friends and his vote reached, for several ballots, forty-two, forty-six being the number required to elect. And, never falling below thirty-nine votes and occasionally reaching his original forty-two, he held his strength during seventy-seven consecutive ballots and until the last minutes of the expiring session. It was at this critical juncture that Mr. Mitchell manifested magnanimity and greatness of soul, which still further endeared him to his great army of friends. Realizing that he could not be elected, and having the interest of his adopted State more at heart than his own personal ambition and advancement, he besought his friends to support Hon. J. N. Dolph, his friend and former law partner, and that gentleman now holds the proud position of United States Senator for six years, commencing on the 4th of March, 1883. On Mr. Mitchell's return from Salem to Portland, after the adjournment of the Legislature, he was received by the citizens with all the "pomp and circumstance" of a conquering hero, instead of a defeated candidate. He has returned to Washington City to attend to important cases in which he is employed before the Supreme Court of the United States, but proposes to come back in a few months and again engage in the practice of his profession in Oregon, where he will be greeted with the same regard and confidence which has been accorded him from the hour he first became a citizen of "the sunset State."

JOHN P. WARD.

No politician in Oregon is better known perhaps than the subject of this sketch, who, while quiet and unobstrusive in his deportment, and in a crowd saying but little, and that in a manner not calculated to attract attention, is none the less a "full hand" in a political campaign, and one whose opinion, judgment and forethought are carefully considered as being those of one who knows whereof he speaks. He is an active worker and takes a deep interest in politics, be the question of a municipal, county, State or national character. Mr. Ward was born in Washington county, Rhode Island, June 30, 1833, and early developing a love for the sea, he shipped as a sailor at the age of fourteen years and followed the sea for about eight years, the last few of which he served as master of coasting vessels. He followed railroading in 1855 6 and at intervals until the war broke out. He then joined a railroad exploring expedition and made a tour to Mexico, pushing on to California, which State he reached in 1862, and a year later he came to Oregon. He was a police officer in Portland in 1864 6. During the latter year he was appointed Warden of the State Penitentiary, which was then located at Portland. He was afterwards appointed Deputy Sheriff of Multnomah county, which position he held for seven years under the several administrations of Sheriff Al Zieber, C. Bills and J. M. Caywood, in which office he made hosts of friends and an extensive acquaintanceship. In 1874 he was appointed Deputy Collector of Customs under Hon. H. W. Scott, which position he held until 1880, when he was appointed Inspector of Steam Vessels, which position he now holds. Mr. Ward has a legion of warm friends in Multnomah county, where he resides, and as a citizen he is universally respected. He is married and has an interesting family, one of his sons occupying a trustworthy position in the employ of the O. R. & N. Company.

EUGENE D. WHITE.

This gentleman is a native Oregonian, having been born at Oregon City in 1851. He passed the days of boyhood there, and finished his education at the University at Forest Grove, when he went east of the mountains and engaged in mining for three years. Desiring to perfect his commercial education he then came to Portland and went through a course at the National Business College, after which he was tendered a position as accountant in the house of Wadhams & Elliott, wholesale grocers. He remained with this firm three years, and was esteemed by his employers as a reliable and capable book keeper. After resigning this position, he embarked in the general brokerage business, associating himself with Mr. Ferry. The new firm has now been in business but two years, and have already taken a foremost position in that line. They deal principally in real estate, and are the agents for the Oakland Home, of California, and the Metropole of Paris, Insurance Companies. Mr. White was married to Miss Emma Giltner, daughter of Dr. J. S. Giltner, in 1876. Mrs. White is a very accomplished lady, being a graduate of the Baltimore Female Institute, in music, painting and belles-lettres. Mr. White became a member of the Masonic order in 1876, and is present Master of Willamette Lodge No. 2, also a member of Knights Templar. He is a nephew of Col. B. Jennings, who was the first G. M. of Masons in this State.

HON. GEORGE W. YOCUM

Was born at Newport, Pennsylvania, April 27, 1833. He moved with his parents to Franklin county, Indiana. While there he attended Asbury University, at Greencastle, and after leaving there he attended College at Miami University, at Oxford, Ohio, for a term of three years. Immediately after college he commenced the study of law under Hon. John D. Howland, at Brookville, Indiana, and was admitted to the bar of the Supreme Court of that State a few years later. He was afterwards elected District Attorney of the Third Judicial District, and held the office one term. He moved in 1857 and opened an office at Albia, Monroe county, Iowa, where he practiced law for nineteen years consecutively, and in 1867 he was honored by being elected Mayor of that city and held the office one term. He came to Oregon in 1874 and commenced the practice of law at Portland, where he has resided ever since. He was elected a member of the Common Council in 1877, and proved active and efficient in the discharge of his duties as such. He secured his education under adverse circumstances, having taught school at intervals to raise funds with which to carry on his law studies. He has been a very close student, and the success he has attained has been the result of unremitting application. He never has difficulties with the bench or bar, as he always endeavors to treat his fellow-man with fairness. He has never considered himself handsome or courtly in his manners, and he has consequently refrained from indulging in politics, although he is an earnest Republican. He has many warm friends and some bitter enemies. The former he appreciates and the latter he pities. His zeal for his clients sometimes causes unfriendly feelings, but he bears malice toward none who deserve his esteem. While residing at Albia, Iowa, he was married to Mrs. Josie Woolsey Craig, who had two daughters by a former marriage. These are both graduates of the Portland High School, and one of them was recently married to F. Clarno, Esq., the junior member of the firm of Yocum & Clarno. One boy completes their family circle. Mr. Yocum is of medium height, heavy built, square-shouldered, full beard and brown hair, liberally sprinkled with grey. His specialty as an attorney is said to be in cases where land titles are involved, although he is considered well qualified to act in any department. As a citizen and neighbor he is highly esteemed, and as a member of the bar he is respected.

REV. F. P. BERRY,

Of Salem, is a gentleman who, although he has resided in the State but comparatively a short time, has during his residence here acquired a leading position among the clergy, and is universally esteemed among those with whom he has become acquainted. He was born at Dover, New Jersey, February 26, 1846, and resided with his parents until he became of age, attending school meanwhile at the public and private schools of that city, and for a few years teaching in schools of that vicinity. He entered the Freshman class of Wabash College, Crawfordsville, Indiana, in 1868, spending his freshman and sophomore years in that institution, and then went to Princeton College, New Jersey, where he spent his junior and senior years, and graduated in the class of '75. His health failed him, and for two years he was unable to preach. In 1877 he went to Kansas and spent a year riding horseback and preaching in school houses, etc., in the farming districts. It was a toilsome life, but he regained his shattered health and settled in Wellington, Kansas, in 1878, where he remained for three years, during which time his congregation erected a new church edifice. He resigned charge of that church in 1881, and returned to New Jersey, spending several months there and in adjacent States. He came to Oregon in the fall of 1881, in response to a call from the Presbyterian church of Salem. During the summer of 1882 he visited Wellington, Kansas, and on August 30, 1882, was married to Miss Minnie J. Staub, of that place, returning to Salem with his bride in September following, and at once resumed charge of the Presbyterian church of that city. Mr. Berry is still a young man and, possessed as he is of far more than ordinary talent, his future gives promise of bringing him full measure of success in the profession he has chosen. He is highly esteemed by his congregation and is making friends rapidly among our citizens generally.

W. F. BOOTHBY.

The well-known arshitect of Salem, was born at Linnington, Maine, July 12, 1840. His early life was spent upon his father's farm. He commenced learning the carpenter's trade when he was sixteen years of age. He attended the Fally Seminary at Fulton, N. Y., from 1858 to 1860, when he opened a general commission house in Portland, Maine, where he remained until the war broke out. During the famine in Ireland, in 1860, Mr. Boothby loaded two ships with provisions, which reached there in due season, and in a measure relieved the suffering poor. Disposing of his business in 1861 he came to California via the Isthmus, landing in San Francisco in November of that year. He at once started for the mines and was for some time engaged in Gen. Fremont's quartz mill, then the largest in the world. During the next few years he was engaged in various enterprises, contracting for and building houses, stores, etc., running a sawmill, selling goods, etc., and came to Oregon in June, 1864, and settled in Salem. He commenced canvassing the city for the sale of Abbott's History of the Civil War, but the enterprise was too tame for a man of his energy and ambibition, and through the influence of old Father Waller, peace to his ashes, he secured a place as foreman in Jones & Reed's sash and door factory, where he remained about eighteen months. In 1866, in partnership with H. Stapleton and H. R. Myers, they bought out Sam. Bass' interest in a sash and door factory. In about one year's time Mr. Myers disposed of his interest in the business to Messrs. Boothby & Stapleton, who afterwards built a new factory, which was soon destroyed by fire involving a loss of some $20,000. They rebuilt and continued business for several years, occasionally drafting a house of some importance. In 1872 they contracted with Marion county for the erection of the elegant court-house building that is now the pride of Salem and the surrounding country, and which cost in the neighborhood of $100,000. In 1870 he associated with Martin & Allen, of Salem, and contracted with that city to furnish water for fire purposes and private use ; built works in 1870, Mr. Boothby serving as president of the company since that date. In 1879, owing to failing health, he disposed of his interest in the sash and door factory, and shortly afterwards opened an architect's office, in which business he is still engaged. In 1880 he was engaged by the Board of Commissioners for the erection of a brick insane asylum building, to assume charge of several plans submitted by other architects and to prepare from them, introducing ideas of his own, a plan for the erection of a building calculated to accommodate 400 patients. How faithfully he executed that work the new and elegant building in the suburbs of Salem is evidence. It is said to be as perfect a building of its kind as can be found anywhere, and it has been erected at an expense, thus far, surprisingly small, aggregating only about $100,000. Mr. Boothby's services have been retained as supervising architect and superintendent of construction, and to his economical management and thorough knowledge of his profession is greatly due the success attending the labors of the board. He also prepared the plans for Warner Breyman's elegant new residence, now in course of construction in that city. Mr. Boothby is a pronounced Republican, but has never sought office. He was in 1870 a member of the Common Council of Salem. He is an exemplary citizen, to whose enterprise and energy Salem is greatly indebted for many of her most important and permanent improvements. His integrity and industry have made him very popular in Salem, where he is best known. He was married September 20, 1865, to Miss R. A. Dalgleish, of Salem, formerly of Lawrence, Mass.

REV. ROBERT W. HILL,

Superintendent of the Presbyterian Home Missions for Oregon, Washington, Idaho and Alaska Territories, was born in the city of New York November 13, 1845. He was educated in the public schools of that city until he entered the University of the City of New York. Early developing a taste for the ministry, he commenced a thorough course of study with the view of adopting that as a profession, and in 1878 graduated from the Union Theological Seminary. He was married May 29th of the same year to Miss Lois R. Hough, of Lewis county, New York, and, accompanied by his young wife, at once started for Oregon, having accepted a call from the Presbyterian church of Salem. Reaching here in June, he commenced his labors without delay and very soon made friends, not only with the members of his own congregation, but with our citizens generally. He is an earnest worker, and his field of labor afforded a rich harvest. His congregations increased and he proved one of the most popular ministers in that city. His sermons are practical and eloquent, and he succeeded in creating a warm interest in church work, and remained as its pastor until in 1882 he was called by the unanimous voice of the Synod of the Columbia to his present high and responsible position. Mr. Hill enlisted during the war as a private in Company L of the Second New York Cavalry, and to-day bears the scars of honorable service. He takes a warm interest in politics and is a strong Republican. He is a constant correspondent of several of the leading Eastern journals, and his letters have contributed in no small degree in informing our Eastern friends as to the resources of the great Northwest, in the development of which Mr. Hill is deeply interested.

HON. WILLIAM D. HARE.

There is scarcely a man, woman or child in the State of Oregon who has not heard of the subject of this sketch. Ever since the foundation of a government on this northwest coast Mr. Hare has taken an active part in the affairs of the community where he lived. He is an exemplification of the time-honored adage that "God helps those who help themselves," and his whole life has bristled with instances of this belief. He is a man of strong convictions and honest prejudices. His friends always know just where he may be found when he is wanted. His nature is positive in its character, and when once he has settled in his own mind that he is right, nothing short of utter annihilation can swerve him from his course. Such a character must succeed, and Mr. Hare has succeeded. Mr. Hare was born at Wheeling, Virginia, September 1, 1834, and with his parents removed to Ohio in 1835, where he continued to reside until 1853, when, in company with James Edwards, of Benton county, he came to Oregon. He settled in Portland, where he remained until 1857, when he moved to Washington county, where one year later he was elected County Clerk. He held that office until July, 1862. He had meanwhile devoted his spare moments to the study of law, and, having passed a successful examination, was admitted to the bar in 1863. He represented Washington county in the Legislative Assembly of 1870. He was the Republican candidate for Presidential Elector in 1872, and made an active canvass of the State. He was appointed Collector of Customs for the District of Oregon March 14, 1873, which important and responsible position he held until July 1, 1881, since which time he has been engaged in agricultural pursuits on his farm in Washington county. Socially, none are more genial, open hearted or courteous, and his native humor renders him popular in every circle and a welcome guest in every company. As a public speaker he combines the various elements of eloquence, logic, pathos, sarcasm and bitter invective. His energy is unremitting and his friendship sincere. He is a man of family and remarkably fond of his home circle. He is P. G. M. W. of the A. O. U. W., and is deservedly popular in that order. It were well if our young State had many such generous and enterprising men as Hon. W. D. Hare.

HON. ISAAC R. MOORES.

The sterling citizen whose every thought is for the good of the community in which he has reared his home and cemented his associations, must always command the respect and esteem of his fellow citizens. Of such metal and commanding such respect is he whose name is inscribed above. Like his father, whose name he bears, and of which family he is the only living representative, he is a man of sterling worth, whose word is as good as his bond. Isaac R. Moores, Sr., served in the Seminole Indian war, in two campaigns with General Jackson in Florida. He also held a commission as Colonel in the Blackhawk war of 1831, raising a regiment of four companies and being under marching orders within three days from the time the first alarm was given. He was also elected Captain of a company to serve in the Mexican war of 1846, the services of which, however, were not required, the quota of the State in which it was raised (Illinois) being filled, and he, with his family, came to Oregon in 1852 and settled in Lane county, which county he ably represented in the State Legislature of 1855 and in the first State Constitutional Convention held in Salem in 1857. He passed away in 1861, honored and respected by all who knew him. The subject of our sketch is, evidently, a chip off the old block, and a man whose friends are legion. He was born in Vermillion county, Illinois, on St. Valentine's day, in 1831. Enjoyed only the advantages of a common school education, the early portion of his life having been employed as a clerk in the mercantile business. He went to California with the argonauts of 1850 and spent two years in search of the golden fleece without success. Returned to Illinois and in 1852 accompanied his parents to Oregon and settled in Yamhill county, where it is claimed all great men originate, where he followed surveying until October, 1854, when he moved to Salem, where he has continuously resided ever since. Was married September 2, 1856, to Miss Ellen R. Lamon, who has proved an efficient helpmate in the struggles incident to life in a new country. He clerked for a year or more for J. N. McDonald, after which himself and brother (Hon. Jno. H. Moores, deceased) bought McDonald out and continued in the general merchandising business until 1866, when he accepted the position of clerk of the State Board of School Land Commissioners under Gov. Woods' administration, remaining there until 1870. Represented Marion county in the House of Representatives in 1862 and was re-elected in 1864, and was chosen Speaker, which position he filled during that session and the special session of 1865, and as such officer signed the amendment to the Constitution of the United States, abolishing slavery within its borders, a public act in which he takes no small degree of pride. In 1861 he was appointed Colonel of the Second Regiment Oregon Volunteer Militia, which was composed of fully 1100 men and two companies of artillery. Although equipped for active service their services were never required. He has been an active member of the Common Council of Salem for several terms, and in 1867 was one of the originators and incorporators of the Oregon Central Railroad Company, serving as its President and Vice President prior to its transfer to the Oregon and California Railroad Company. In 1870 he was appointed Land Commissioner by the O. and C. R. R. Company, which position he still holds. He has made himself popular in fraternal organizations, having joined the Odd Fellows in 1856 and held the office of Grand Treasurer for sixteen years. He joined the Masonic order in 1870 and has attained the honors of the thirty-second degree, and has acted as Grand Receiver of the A. O. U. W. since its organization in 1879. He has always been a Republican, resisting all inducements to swerve from his allegiance. His habits are such as to insure good health and the indications are that he is destined to many long years of usefulness. He is the very personification of sociability, and is a perfect storehouse of information and laughable incidents, and universally respected as a man among men.

HON. TILMON FORD,

One of the Representatives from Marion county, is an Oregon-raised boy; was born in 1845 and lived with his parents on a farm in old Marion until the year 1865, when he went to Idaho to try his luck in the mines, and being tolerably successful with the pick and shovel, accumulated sufficient means to enable him to return to Salem and enter the Willamette University as a student. He graduated from that institution in 1870 and immediately commenced the study of the law and was admitted to the bar by the Supreme Court of this State in the fall of 1872. He then opened a law office in Salem, where he has resided ever since, and has been favored with a lucrative practice in his profession. In 1880 he was nominated by the Republican County Convention and was elected to represent Marion county in the House of Representatives of the Oregon Legislature in that year. He was the author of the bill which passed at that session to erect the State Insane Asylum building at Salem. Mr. Ford was re-elected as one of the Representatives on the Republican ticket in 1882. At this session he was very active and energetic in procuring the passage of laws to complete and furnish the asylum and govern and control that institution under the charge of the State. He was a member of the Judiciary Committee of the House in 1880 and also in 1882. He became somewhat noted for being always on the side of economy upon all measures which required money to be paid out of the State treasury, and to his financial ability is due many of the economical features of measures requiring expenditures of money by the State. He was not given to "much speaking" as a member, but whenever he did speak upon any question before that body he was clear and forcible as to the position which he occupied on the subject under debate, and always received the close attention of the members while speaking upon any question before the House. It can be truthfully said of Mr. Ford that he was one of the real working members of that body.

PROFESSOR T. H. CRAWFORD.

Prominent among those who are in charge of the educational interests of our State stands the gentleman whose name heads this sketch. For years past he has been prominently connected with various institutions of learning, until the profession of a teacher, than which there is no higher or nobler, has become second nature to him, and none in the ranks of that profession stand higher or more universally command the respect and esteem of the general public than does Prof. Crawford. His record as a teacher and as a man and citizen is without blemish, and his friends and admirers are legion. He was born in Clarksburg, Indiana, June 24, 1840, and with his parents crossed the plains and reached Oregon in 1852, and settled on a farm near Brownsville, in Linn county. He attended the district schools until 1858, when he entered the Santiam Academy, where he remained several months. He commenced teaching in the fall of 1859, in the Cowan district, near Albany, and in November of that year he entered the Willamette University and graduated in the classical course in the class of '63. The succeeding three years were spent in teaching at Sublimity, and in September, 1866, he took charge of the public schools of Salem, where he remained until December, 1867, when he came to Portland and accepted a position in the Portland Female Academy, under Prof. T. M. Gatch. He remained here until July, 1870, when he was appointed Principal of the North Portland Public School, where he remained two years, when, in September, 1872, having been elected Professor of Natural Science in the Willamette University, he moved to Salem. This position he resigned in December, 1875, and for a few months devoted his attention to the real estate and insurance business. In September, 1876, he was elected to the Principalship of the

Central School in Portland, and remained there for one year, when he was elected City Superintendent of the Portland Public Schools, which high and responsible position he still occupies, this being the sixth year of his service in that capacity. He has been a prominent member of the I. O. O. F. since 1867, and in 1875 was one of the Grand Representatives to the Sovereign Grand Lodge, which met at Indianapolis, Indiana. During the years 1867-9 and 1876-7 he was Grand Secretary of the I. O. G. T. His parents, Dr. and Mrs. R. H. Crawford, are still living, in the enjoyment of a ripe old age, at Brownsville. Prof. Crawford's educational advantages were secured mainly by his own exertions; earning means to pay his expenses by engaging in various kinds of labor during vacations and on Saturdays. While attending the Willamette University, at Salem, he sawed wood, built fires, swept the university and acted as sexton of the old M. E. church to earn money to pay his school expenses, and during the greater part of the time "bached" in the old "third story." Among his classmates we note the honored names of Hon. J. B. Waldo, Rev. P. S. Knight, Hon. Syl. C. Simpson, P. L. Willis, Esq., and Hon. O. N. Denny. Prof. Crawford was married to Miss Emily B. Crandall, in Salem, July 24, 1864, four children being born to the family, the first three of whom fell victims to that dread disease, diphtheria, and died within one week in 1875, his wife passing away in August of the present year, leaving a daughter of about two years of age. Prof. Crawford is a fine-looking specimen of manhood, rather tall and well-proportioned, erect, with a good-shaped head, high forehead, heavy beard and hair of auburn, prominent features and attractive face and engaging manners. He makes friends rapidly and rarely loses one. He is a pleasant speaker, and in any legislative body is listened to with interest whenever opportunity occurs. His reputation is beyond reproach, and he is esteemed very highly by those who know him best.

HON. WILLIAM LAIR HILL.

No attorney in Eastern Oregon stands higher in the ranks of the profession than does he whose name heads this sketch. He was born on a plantation in McNairy county, Tennessee, August 20, 1838. His father, Dr. R. C. Hill, now of Albany, Oregon, moved to Missouri in 1848, and came to Oregon in 1853. W. Lair Hill was educated at McMinnville College, Oregon, and read law in the office of Hon. Geo. H. Williams and Hon. A. C. Gibbs, who, at that time, were partners in Portland; and was admitted to the bar in December, 1861. He was employed in the Paymaster's Department of the U. S. Army during the year 1862, and did duty at nearly all the military posts in Oregon, Washington and Idaho, the service in those days requiring constant travel. In January, 1863, he commenced the practice of law as the partner of Hon. A. C. Gibbs, who was then the Governor of Oregon. He was Judge of Grant county from 1864 to 1866. While a resident of Grant county he married the eldest daughter of the late Rev. Dr. Chandler, the marriage being the consummation of an attachment formed in school days, when Dr. Chandler was President of McMinnville College. He returned to Portland in 1866, and resumed practice here. His application, industry and strict attention to business, brought him clients who soon became his enthusiastic admirers, and his business increased rapidly, mainly as a real estate lawyer. In the fall of 1872 he assumed editorial management of the Daily and Weekly "Oregonian," agreeing to edit the paper a few weeks until satisfactory arrangements could be made with some other suitable person. The weeks ran into months and the months into years, until in March, 1877, his greatly impaired health necessitated the resignation of a position requiring such close attention and constant care. Under his management the "Oregonian" abandoned the position of a party organ and assumed the independent position it now occupies. In 1878, being still in feeble health, he sought benefit by change to a less humid climate, and with his family removed to The Dalles, where he now resides, in the enjoyment of greatly improved health and the leading law practice of Eastern Oregon. He lives on a farm about two and a half miles from town, driving in every morning. He has always taken an active interest in educational matters and is at the present time a member of the Board of Trustees of McMinnville College, and has been President of the Board of Directors of Wasco Independent Academy ever since its organization. Politically, he is a Republican with very decided views of party principles, and very little respect for the methods by which party organization is generally maintained. As an attorney, he has been the leading counsel in many of the most important cases in the Federal and State Courts, and has had a large number of the most important criminal cases in the last few years. As a journalist, he has few superiors, being a ready writer and dealing tersely with subjects of public interest and importance, and discussing all questions from the standpoint of fearless disregard of party consequences.

HON. THOMAS C. SHAW,

Who to-day occupies the important position of County Judge of Marion county, was born near Liberty, Missouri, on the 23d day of February, 1823. His early life was spent on the farm and his educational advantages were very limited, being confined wholly to the inferior common schools of that early day. In May, 1844, his parents started across the plains for Oregon, reaching The Dalles in November of that year. They remained there during the winter and in the spring of '45 started down the Columbia. In the fall of that year his father rented a farm near Wheatland. The subject of our sketch was one of Col. Gilliam's party, who in 1846 endeavored to find a pass through the Cascade mountains in Southern Oregon. On his return he lived for a short time with his uncle, Mitchell Gilliam, near Dallas, and then enlisted in Company C, First Regiment Oregon Volunteers, and was elected Second Lieutenant, serving with distinction during the memorable Cayuse war. Returning home in 1850 he remained on his father's farm for a short time, and eventually took up a farm of his own on Howells Prairie on which he still resides. A man of such sterling worth as Mr. Shaw, of course occupied a prominent place in the estimation of his neighbors, and in 1864 he was elected County Commissioner, which position he held for four years. He was County Assessor from 1870 to 1874, and at the general election in the latter year he was elected Sheriff and discharged the responsible duties of that office to the satisfaction of every one and credit to himself. At the last general election he was elected County Judge, and is discharging his duty without fear or favor, and promises to make as faithful an officer as he has in the past. He was married to Miss Josephine Headrick, November 28, 1850, and they have four children living. Judge Shaw is a man of unblemished reputation and stands high among those who know him for his integrity, industry and unwavering fidelity to the best interests of the public he has so frequently and honorably served.

HON. E. D. SHATTUCK

Was born in Bakersfield, Franklin county, Vermont, December 31, 1824. He was educated in academic and classical studies in the academies of Malone and at Bakersfield, and then spent four years in college at Burlington, graduating therefrom in 1848. During a great portion of the time in winter months he taught school to procure means to meet his college expenses. After he graduated he followed teaching in Bakersfield Academy, Vermont, for one year; then he received the appointment of Associate Principal of Newman Seminary, Georgia; six months after he gave up this position and went to Laurel Station, Maryland, and taught school until July, 1851. At this period he went to Malone, New York, and commenced reading law, afterwards going to New York City, where he was admitted to the bar in November, 1852. He came to Oregon in February, 1853, and was chosen Professor of Ancient Languages in the Pacific University. He next took charge of Tualitan Academy for two years. In 1855 he was elected Superintendent of Public Schools in Washington county, and in 1856 he was elected Probate Judge for the same county. In 1857 he was chosen delegate to the Constitutional Convention, and after the adjournment of that body he returned to Portland and entered into a law copartnership with David Logan. In 1858 he was elected to represent Multnomah and Washington counties in the last session of the Oregon Territorial Legislature. He was one of the original organizers of the Portland Library Association. At different periods he has served as a member of the Portland City Council and as a member of the Board of Directors of the Portland School District. In 1862 he was elected Judge of the Supreme Court for the Fourth District, which office he held for five years. In 1874 he was again elected Judge of the Supreme Court, and continued in office until the organization of the courts by the act of 1878. In 1858 Mr. Shattuck was a Whig. He afterwards joined the Republican party on its first organization in this State. In 1870 he joined the Independent movement, and worked earnestly and efficiently against the then existing abuses practiced by regular party nominees. In 1872 he was a candidate for Presidential Elector on the Greeley-Democratic ticket. Since that time, while still claiming to be an independent, he has acted and voted for the most part with the Democratic party. For the past year, on account of failing health, he has retired from the practice of law and from politics and engaged in agricultural pursuits on his farm, near Portland. In 1882 he was voted for for Judge of the Supreme Court, and at the last session of the Legislature received a flattering vote for U. S. Senator. His name was presented on both occasions without any solicitation or desire to be elected on his part, as he feels the necessity of devoting himself to the peaceful occupation of country life in order to regain his strength and vigor, which he has exhausted on the bench and in practice at the bar. In every position that Judge Shattuck has been chosen to fill during his busy life, he has always been guided by the purest motives, and firmly adhered to the cause of truth and justice. Both as judge and jurist he has few equals in the profession of law. He is a studious reader, a profound thinker and an earnest and logical talker. All of his actions through life have been marked by his judicious combination of wisdom, justice and mercy, and therefore he has always enjoyed the confidence and highest respect of his fellow men; and as his life has been an almost unceasingly busy and ennobling one in the past, it is safe to predict that, after he has sufficiently recuperated at his rural home, there will be places and positions of trust awaiting his guiding influence and executive ability.

HON. GEORGE H. BURNETT,

Who during the session of the Legislative Assembly just closed filled the important and laborious office of Assistant Clerk of the House of Representatives, is a full-fledged Oregonian, having been born and raised in Yamhill county, where, it is claimed by many, all smart men originate. It was near McMinnville, on the 9th day of May, 1853, that Mr. Burnett made his debut on the world's stage of action. He was reared on a farm until he was nine years of age, when his parents moved into town. In the fall of 1871 he entered the Christian College at Monmouth and graduated in June, 1873, delivering the Greek salutatory on that occasion. He taught school at Sheridan for about six months in 1874, and in the fall of that year went to Salem to pursue the study of law, entering the office of Mallory & Shaw for that purpose. He was admitted to the bar in December, 1875, and the following year was elected Prosecuting Attorney of the Third District, his opponent being Hon. W. M. Ramsey. During his two years' service in that office he displayed rare legal ability, and was considered a very efficient officer. In 1878 he formed a partnership with Hon. J. J. Shaw, of Salem, with whom he is still associated in the practice of his profession. He was elected a member of the City Council in 1880 and was one of the most active and influential members of that body. He was married December 31, 1879, to Miss Myra Belt, of Salem. Mr. Burnett is a Past Grand of Chemeketa Lodge No. 1, I. O. O. F., and one of the most active members of the Salem Fire Department, being at the present time foreman of Capital Engine Co. No. 1. He is a consistent Republican at all times and under all circumstances. As an attorney, he is careful and painstaking, guarding with zealous care the interests of his clients, and by the bench and bar is considered an able, influential and conscientious advocate of the law. He is still a hard student and ambitious to win honors by the pure force of meritorious intellect, and we bespeak for him unqualified success.

CAPTAIN FRELON JESSE BABCOCK

Was born in Burke, Caledonia county, Vermont, June 14, 1843, where he spent his youth and young manhood until May, 1861, when the tocsin of war sounded, and although scarce eighteen years of age, he enlisted as a private in the Third Vermont and went to the wars. Mr. Babcock's record as a soldier of the Union is way above the average, and one that he can be justly proud of. He was wounded three times during his service, once at Antietam and twice at the battle of the Wilderness. He rose from the ranks to First Lieutenant and was for some time Adjutant of his regiment. For meritorious services while A. A. G. on General L. F. Haskell's staff, he was promoted to the full rank of Captain. Captain Babcock participated in nearly all of the great battles fought by the Army of the Potomac from Yorktown to the surrender at Appomatox Court House of the Army of Virginia. After Lee's surrender he was sent with Sheridan's command to Texas, where he remained until he was mustered out in October, 1865. In 1868 Mr. Babcock came to Salem, Oregon, where he has since resided. In 1871 he was united in marriage to Miss Ida M. Pratt, a most estimable lady, daughter of Capt. L. E. Pratt. Capt. Babcock was one of the charter members of Pacific Lodge, No. 40, of A. F. and A. M. of Salem; is also a bright Chapter Mason, a Commandery Mason, and is at present Grand Secretary of the Grand Lodge of Oregon. His occupation is that of fine cabinet-making, and his artistic work may be found in the Senate Chamber, Supreme Court rooms and department offices at the capitol. Although in person he is small, he possesses a wonderful amount of vitality and is "sure fire" for any task he undertakes.

HON. J. W. WHALLEY.

The gentleman whose name is the title of this biographical sketch was born at Granville, near Annapolis, Nova Scotia, April 28, 1833. His father was rector of the parish, and both of his parents were well educated people of ancient and respectable families, his father being English and his mother Welsh. The family left Nova Scotia and went to England in 1835, and resided for a time at Garstang, in Lancashire, then removed to New Hutton, in Westmoreland, and thence Old Hutton, of which his father was afterwards perpetual incumbent. Here, amid the wild and grand scenery and beautiful lakes of the north he lived until thirteen years of age, pursuing his studies with his father. At the early age of nine years he was reading Cæsar, and Ovid at ten. Unable to educate all of his children in the learned professions, J. W. Whalley was apprenticed by his father to Captain Grundell, master of the good ship Speed in March, 1846, and sailed from Liverpool for New York the same month. Arriving in that city, where he had respectable and wealthy relations, he ran away and went to New Brunswick, New Jersey. Here he remained, at the home of Mr. Adrain, afterwards U. S. Senator from that State and a stepson of his grandmother, until the ship sailed, when he returned to New York and entered the office of his uncle, Mr. Thomas Jones, the author of an excellent treatise on bookkeeping, a teacher of that science, and often employed in settling matter of complicated accounts.

Remaining with his uncle about eighteen months, he obtained an excellent mercantile education. At this period of his history, Mr. Whalley's father insisted on his return to England, and, obedient to the paternal summons, he sailed for the Old World early in 1848, where he remained until 1849, when, finding the prospect for the future gloomy in consequence of the pecuniary embarrassment of his father he determined to go to sea and seek his fortune in the East Indies. Arriving in Liverpool, and hearing of the gold fields of California, he determined to become an argonaut. Concealing the matter from his father, he saw the old gentleman off on one Saturday morning, to attend to his every-day duties, and went immediately and bound himself to the owner of the ship Antelope, bound for California as apprentice boy. He arrived in San Francisco in July, 1849, and going to the mines he followed a miner's life with the varying fortune incident thereto until 1858. He began teaching school in Siskiyou county, California, reading law at the same time with Captain Fair and Hon. Joseph Roseborough, of Yreka, and was duly admitted to practice at the bar in 1861, after passing a good examination, but deferred entering into active practice until 1864. He was married in 1865. During the time he was teaching and studying he contributed to the columns of the "Hesperian" and of the local press, his productions being mostly poetical, exhibiting rare genius, and many of which were extensively copied. In 1864 he left California and came to Oregon. Settling first in Grant county, he began practice and soon, by honest dealing and strict attention to business, he built up a lucrative practice. In 1868 Mr. Whalley came to Portland and began the practice of his profession with Mr. Fechheimer (who was his student while in Grant county) as his partner. The firm has been very successful. They made the bankrupt law of 1867 a specialty, and most of the business in that department of the legal practice came into their hands. In 1870 Mr. Whalley was elected a member of the Lower House of the Oregon State Legislature by the Republicans, and served one term, when he retired altogether from political life, devoting his whole attention thereafter to his profession, of which he is master. In 1872 he was elected Grand Representative to the Grand Lodge of the United States I. O. O. F., which met at Baltimore, and embraced the opportunity to visit his old home in Europe, and he contemplates making another journey across the Atlantic during the coming year. Mr. Whalley is a ripe scholar, devoted to elegant literature and the classics, and possessed of rare fluency as a speaker, either conversational or oratorical. He is a true and devoted friend to those worthy of his esteem, and a dangerous antagonist to those who incur his righteous displeasure. Being still in the prime of manhood, and possessed of an easy fortune, his prospects for many years of active usefulness are far above those allotted to the average of mankind.

HON. O. S. SAVAGE.

This name is familiar to almost every resident of Eastern Oregon, and especially to those of Wasco county, where he has resided for years past, and where, by the votes of the people, he has been elected time and time again to positions of responsibility and trust. He was born in Lisbon, Grafton county, New Hampshire, in 1825. He moved to Boston in 1842, where he continued to reside until 1851. He came to this coast in 1852, and settled in California, where he remained until 1857, when he came to Oregon and took up his residence at The Dalles, where he has resided ever since. He represented Wasco county in the Legislature of 1870, and assisted in carrying out most of the important legislation of that session. He was elected County Judge of his county in 1876, and re-elected in 1880. In this position he has displayed marked executive and financial ability, and administered the affairs of that county honestly, economically, and without fear or favor. He has made a few enemies, it is true, but his disposition of aggressiveness would naturally create these, and being a man who always leads, and never follows, he rarely affords them an opportunity of doing him an injury. He is well thought of, however, by the better class of citizens, and none presume to question his honesty and integrity. He is an uncompromising Democrat, and a man of family.

WILLIAM A. HART.

The present Chief Engineer of the Portland Fire Department, was born in Albany, New York, October 12, 1852, and is the youngest man who has been elected to that position in this city. He was educated in the schools of New York until he was eighteen years old. He came to Portland in 1870, and since that time has taken a prominent interest in fire matters. In recognition of his labors in behalf of the department, he was honored with the position of Assistant Engineer in the years 1875-6-7, and in 1881 was elected Chief Engineer by the largest majority ever given to a candidate for that office. Since he has been Chief Engineer he has had several very difficult fires to contend with, and he handled the department so ably that he has invariably won the praise of property holders and insurance companies, and the press of the city has been unanimous in praise of his management of the department. He was presented with a handsome gold medal for the ability he displayed in extinguishing the fire on First street, between A and B, when the department was laboring under great disadvantage by reason of defective hose. Chief Hart was at one time connected with the State militia, having been captain of the City Rifles for many years. During the period that he had command of that company it enjoyed its greatest popularity, as it invariably won all the prizes for drilling, etc., for which it contested. He was married to Miss Maggie Lynch, of San Francisco, in December, 1880, and we may reasonably expect that he will retain his popularity in the additional responsible position of husband and father.

CHARLES P. BACON.

The subject of this sketch who to-day is considered one of the solid men of Portland, and possesses the well-merited confidence and esteem of its citizens, was born in Candor, Tioga county, New York, April 15, 1823. He moved with his parents to Coldwater, Michigan, in 1841 and to Illinois in 1847. In 1850 he crossed the plains and came to Oregon and settled in

Portland, where he has resided ever since. He went into the livery business in February, 1853, and for several years conducted a draying and delivery business in connection therewith. He was also interested in the saddlery and harness business with the late Samuel Sherlock, Esq., for some time. He is now farming and raising horses in connection with his business as proprietor of the elegant Black Hawk stables, on Second street between Stark and Oak. By judicious investments and a thorough knowledge of business principles, Mr. Bacon has succeeded in amassing sufficient of this world's goods to enable him now to enjoy life, and his love for his family and home enable him to do so without ostentation, but with none the less intensity. He is a Republican, but has never taken a very active interest in politics. He was elected City Assessor of Portland in 1855 and Collector in 1856, and at the last general election was elected County Commissioner by a very handsome majority. He was married in Portland January 17, 1855, to Clara A. Clark, formerly of Warren, Maine, and their family consists of two children, the eldest, a daughter, being the wife of George W. Weidler, Esq. Mr. Bacon comes of good Connecticut stock, his father and mother, Dr. and Mrs. William Bacon, now of Niles, Michigan, being both alive and enjoying good health at the advanced age of eighty-eight years, having been married sixty-eight years next February. Mr. Bacon is highly esteemed by those who know him best and honored and respected by all.

REV. L. J. POWELL, A. M.,

Late Superintendent of Public Instruction for the State of Oregon, and now President of the University of Washington Territory, has in his life that kind of a record which, to read and understand, explains the forces that have made the "Wilderness bud and blossom as the rose." He was born May 19, 1834, near Piketon, in Kentucky. His parents were David and Almedia Hurless Powell. In 1837 these parents removed to the then extreme Western frontier, and settled in Cass county, Missouri, where they remained until the spring of 1847. The training of these ten years was almost altogether in the line of farm work, amidst the inevitable deprivations of frontier life. One pair of shoes a year, made by his father out of leather tanned by himself, and a limited wardrobe made out of cloth for which his mother's hands had carded, spun and woven the wool, and then had cut and made the garments, a holy ministry of work and love to the boy. Few were the opportunities for learning, and consequently little the education of these ten years. In 1847 the star of Oregon was just arising in the west, and Mr. David Powell saw it, and started with his family to follow its guiding ray across the then trackless desert. The hardships and dangers of the journey of half a year were too many to attempt here to record. Late in the Autumn, weary and worn, the family arrived in the Willamette Valley, and settled about seven miles east of Portland, where the father, Hon. David Powell, still lives, respected by his fellow-citizens and beloved by his intimate friends. In the Spring of 1848, May 28, came the sad shadow of his mother's death over the life of young Leonard. To him she was not a mother only, but her motherhood was of that rare type that leaves a growing impress of good on the life of the son as long as he lives. On the 5th day of July, 1845, she had received the boy's promise never to taste intoxicating liquors. On her dying bed she gave him further charge to procure an education, and do all the good he could in the world. These promises have been the guide of all his after life; the pledge has been kept sacred, the charge he has sought and is seeking to meet. At the age of fifteen, he, hardly yet more than a child, went to California, where he spent a year working in the mines. When he returned he put into his father's hand $1,000, as the result of his year's toil. At the age of seventeen there was a new awakening within him. He found himself totally unable to write, and able to read only very poorly in the third reader. In his association with men in the mines of California, many of whom were highly educated and intelligent, he learned that education would be to him worth more than gold. He accordingly entered the Portland Academy, where, under the direction of C. S. Kingsley, one of the most competent instructors as also one of the most useful men of early Portland history, he prepared for college. During the Indian war of 1855 and 1856, he served five months as a private in Company C, First Regiment Oregon Mounted Volunteers; three months as First Lieutenant of Captain W. S. Buckley's Company of Multnomah county Rangers, and a short time as Captain of a company of volunteers, raised in the city of Portland to relieve the Cascades at the time of the great massacre there in 1856. Here he was associated with Lieutenant Phil. Sheridan, afterwards and now the famous general. Young Powell entered the Wesleyan University, Delaware, Ohio, from which institution he graduated with honor in 1861. Returning to Oregon in the Fall of that year, on the 22d day of December, he was married to Miss Martha Ransom, of Yamhill county, and went immediately to the Willamette University as a teacher in the Academic Department. The next year he was elected to the chair of mathematics in the University, and held that position with honor to himself and great benefit to the institution for fourteen years. For one year he was principal of the Tualatin Academy at Forest Grove, and for two years was President of the Albany Collegiate Institute. While serving in this capacity he was nominated by the Republican State Convention in 1878 for Superintendent of Public Instruction for the State, and at the election in June of that year was chosen to that highly honorable position. He served the cause of education in this office four years, giving the benefit of his large practical experience and wide observation to it without stint. During his term, and under his labors, the cause of popular education in Oregon received an impetus, and was placed on a basis it had never before attained. At the close of his term in this office he was called to the Presidency of the University of Washington Territory, one of the most honorable and useful educational positions on the coast, which position he now occupies. Mr. Powell is a man of medium height, but of large, compact and powerful frame, immense vital powers supply unlimited energy to his mind, and enable him to do most manly work in a most manly way. At middle life, much as he has been able to do in the past, more and grander is before him. Self-made, he is yet well made, and wearing without ostentation the honor of work well done, he is sure to reach the honor of better work more nobly done in the future. He has long been a member and minister of the Methodist Episcopal Church.

PROFESSOR I. W. PRATT

Was born in Waterloo, Seneca county, New York, March 17, 1838, and was the fourth son of a family of ten children. His father was a descendant of Matthew Pratt, one of the early Pilgrims to Massachusetts. The family removed to Ohio early in the '40s and located on the Western Reserve, where the then coming Professor spent most of his minority upon a farm, receiving only a common school education. He graduated at Norwalk Academy, at the age of twenty years, and followed railroading on Mad River and Lake Erie railroad for three years, advancing from brakeman to engineer. In 1860 he chose teaching as a profession and took a normal course in Michigan. In 1862 he came to California and taught successfully in El Dorado county until 1867, when he came to Oregon. Here he entered again upon the duties of his profession, soon after his arrival, in East Portland. In April, 1869, he took charge of Harrison-street school, in the city of Portland, where he still remains. He is the only teacher who has remained continuously in the public schools of the city since that date. Professor Pratt was married to Sophia C., eldest daughter of Peter Taylor, of Portland, July 14, 1874. He has served eight years on the State Board of Education, and has been appointed for another term of four years. He is a member of the Masonic fraternity, his relation with that organization beginning in 1865. In 1869 he helped organize and was first W. M. of Washington Lodge, No. 46, A. F. and A. M. in East Portland. He received Chapter and Templar degrees in Portland in 1875-7. In 1872 he took the degrees of the Ancient and Accepted Scottish Rite, and in 1878 was elected to and received the thirty-third and last degree of this Rite, with Hon. R. P. Earhart and Dr. E. I. Bailey, Medical Director of the Department of the Columbia, by the Supreme Council for the Southern jurisdiction of the United States, which met in that year in the city of Washington, D. C. He was elected Grand Secretary of the Grand Lodge of Oregon for 1879. At the present time he is Master of Portland Lodge, No. 55, High Priest of Portland Royal Arch Chapter, No. 3, Captain General of Oregon Commandery Knights Templar, No. 1, and the presiding officer in all the bodies of the Ancient and Accepted Scottish Rite.

JOSEPH BACHMAN,

Of the firm of J. Bachman & Bro., is one of the lively and energetic men whose interests are solely identified with the city of Portland. He has been a resident of this city for the past twenty years, and expects, if spared by Providence, to put in at least twenty years more in the same place. He has, however, little dread of the hereafter, as he is so well covered with insurance in this world that he has assurance enough that fire will not affect him in the next. At the present time he is agent for the Connecticut, North British and Mercantile, German-American, Scottish Union and National, Lion, of London, Hamburg and Magdenburg insurance companies. He is also marine agent, and represents the Fireman's Fund Insurance Company. The fact that so many responsible companies entrust their business in his hands is sufficient to show the standing in which he is held by business men abroad, and we take pleasure in testifying to his popularity at home. He is a pleasant gentleman, always willing to take a risk, and issue a policy to his neighbor, and no one is ever dissatisfied in doing business with him.

HON. B. F. BONHAM.

But few, if any, stand higher socially, morally, or in the estimation of his neighbors and friends in this commonwealth than the subject of this sketch. His name is a synonym for all that is true and honorable in a man and fellow citizen. Judge Bonham was born in East Tennessee October 8, 1828, and removed with his parents to Indiana in 1840. In 1853 he crossed the plains to Oregon and settled near Parkersville, on French Prairie, in Marion county, where he taught school for one year; removing from there in 1854 to Salem, where he has since resided, with the exception of two years spent at La Grande, in Union county. In January, 1856, he was elected Auditor of the Territory and Librarian, and held these positions until the admission of Oregon as a State in 1859. Judge Bonham was elected a member of the last Territorial and the first State Legislature of Oregon in 1858. The same year he was married to a daughter of Mr. John Baker, near Salem. In 1870 was elected from the Third Judicial District as one of the Justices of the Supreme Court of Oregon and ex-officio Circuit Judge of said district for six years, and was Chief Justice of the State from 1874 until the close of his term. He was admitted to the practice of law by the Territorial Supreme Court in 1856, and has followed his profession closely since that date, and is to-day considered one of the ablest lawyers and jurists on the coast. Judge Bonham has been a life-long, straightforward and consistent Democrat, and on the closing day of the memorable Senatorial contest in Oregon in 1882 received the vote of his party for the United States Senate.

HON. BEN SIMPSON.

In the armed band of State-builders, who, catching the earliest rays of that regal star which the prophetic spirit of poesy discovered long ago as the leader of advancing civilization, followed its course to the western verge of the continent and laid the foundations of the ultimate pillar of Union, few are deserving of more honorable mention than Hon. Ben Simpson, at present holding the important office of United States Postal Inspector for this district. He first saw the light in the grand old commonwealth of Tennessee in the year 1818. His parents immigrated to Missouri in 1820, and in that then bold border State he resided until 1846, the year of his departure for Oregon. In the interval, 1839, he was married to a young lady named Wisdom, whose death two years later left him a widower, with one child, John Thomas, as the fruit of their brief union. In 1843 he was married to Miss Nancy Cooper, a grand-daughter of Colonel Cooper, the companion and ally of Daniel Boone in the settlement of Kentucky, and who afterward settled in Missouri and built what was known as Cooper's Fort, in Howard county, a famous citadel of the pioneers in the early Indian wars. In 1846, as soon as the skies began to clear, accompanied by his wife and three children John T., Sylvester C. and Sam L. he set out on the memorable journey across the plains, borne, with all his household goods and gods, by slow but true and patient oxen. He acted as captain of his company, numbering about one hundred and fifty souls, on the long and weary route, and they crossed the Cascades in October, by the Barlow road, arriving at Foster's, on this side, the 15th of the month, nearly six months from the time they left Missouri. Inured to hard labor from his earliest boyhood, and bold, aggressive and persevering by nature, Mr. Simpson was little daunted by the frowning aspect of fortune on his arrival in Oregon: a wilderness to encounter, a young family to care for, no money in his pocket and little food in the larder; but, having found shelter for his household, shouldered his ax and sought and found a job of rail-making in order to secure the necessaries of life. The winters of '46 and '47 were spent at Oregon City. Early in the spring of the latter year he removed to French Prairie and engaged in husbandry. Thence, in 1848, he went to Clackamas City and gave his attention to lumbering and merchandising, succeeding well in both branches of business. Then came the Whitman massacre and the Cayuse war. Mr. Simpson promptly volunteered and served under Colonel Gilllam, and participated in the first general battle at Well Springs. While residing at Clackamas City he was elected to the Second Territorial Legislature as a member of the House. About this time the rush to California began, and Mr. Simpson made a sailing voyage to San Francisco, then a cluster of dirty tents and rude shanties, taking with him a cargo of lumber, which he sold at fabulous figures. On his return he sold out his business in Clackamas City and moved to Parkersville, where he also engaged in merchandising and the manufacture of lumber. During the time he built and launched at Fairfield a little town on the river, in Marion county—the second large steamer ever constructed above the Falls the Oregon. While at Parkersville he was elected to represent Marion county in the House, and afterwards in the Council of the Territorial Legislature. To follow up his legislation at this point, we note that he was a Representative from Polk at the outbreak of the war, and assisted in the election of B. F. Harding to the United States Senate. In the Legislature of 1872 he was a Representative from Benton county and strongly championed the cause of the successful Senatorial candidate, Hon. J. H. Mitchell. Beyond this his business and official experience has been varied and extensive. He served several years as post sutler and Indian trader at Fort Yamhill, during the time that the present General Phil. Sheridan was attached to the post as a Second Lieutenant and Post Quartermaster. He was afterward appointed Indian Agent for the Siletz Reservation, where he served for eight years acceptably, before the wild tribes had lost the verve of the war-trail. At the close of his official term he went to Yaquina Bay and erected the steam saw-mills at Oneatta and resumed the old line of goods and lumber, building two handsome schooners to ship the latter product to San Francisco. He, also, at one time owned a saw-mill at Santiam City, sold dry goods and groceries in Salem, and has, in fact, led an active and enterprising life. He was appointed Surveyor General of the State in 1872, and held the position four years. Mr. Simpson has nine children by his present wife, four daughters and five sons. Three daughters and two sons are graduates of the Willamette University. Sometimes the favorite and again the jest of fortune, he is still at the front in the strength of a storm-toughened age, a fast friend and a fearless foe, giving yet the promise of many years of usefulness.

JOSEPH BUCHTEL.

The genial, energetic Jo Buchtel is a good representative Oregonian. He was born in Stark county, Ohio, November 22, 1830, and moved to Urbana, Champaign county, Illinois, in 1839. He obtained such an education as was then afforded by the public schools of Ohio and Illinois. Quite early he was put at the tailor's trade, but not liking the sedentary life, engaged as clerk in a dry goods store, afterwards worked on a farm and then went into the daguerreotype business. Left Urbana for Oregon April 2, 1852, managing an ox team in the I. R. Moores emigrant train. He first stepped foot in the then little village of Portland September 18, 1852. Worked for Colonel Backenstos, helped load the Charles Devens with lumber, and then went to Oregon City, and soon after commenced his remarkable career at steamboating on the Upper Willamette river during the winter months. In the summer, when the water was too low for navigation, he ran a daguerreotype gallery in different places, including Oregon City, Astoria, Lafayette and Portland. It was while engaged as steward and in other capacities that he displayed many of those remarkable traits of bravery and courage so characteristic of the man. Joseph Buchtel's steamboating covered a period of four years, of the most perilous river navigation known in the history of the country. It was a period when the business was in its beginning in Oregon and all sorts of hazardous experiments were being tried. The stories of hair-breadth escapes and daring ventures to save his vessel, or the lives of men in peril, that is told of Joe Buchtel would make an interesting volume of itself, but we have not space to name them in this brief sketch. At length he got tired of this dangerous and toilsome life, and established a permanent photograph gallery in Portland, which he still owns, and which is now known as "The San Francisco Gallery." In this business, as in everything else he ever undertook, Mr. Buchtel took a leading position. The fame of Buchtel's pictures is world-wide, and his enormous list of negatives includes all the notable personages of Oregon and all distinguished visitors from abroad. In this business he always kept in the lead. Every new style of picture ever introduced into the United States was brought out at Buchtel's gallery. He would allow no one to excel him his line of business. Mr. Buchtel was married in 1853 in Oregon City, taking his wife from the old and highly respected Oregon family of Latourettes, his wife's first name closely resembling his own — Josephine. This union has been a prosperous and happy one, not a breath ever having been brought against Joe Buchtel's private and family relations, even in the most bitter political contests, when a man's character is sifted like fine flour. His family now consists of a wife and five children — two married daughters and three sons, whose ages range from twenty-one to eight years. He lost one bright and most hopeful son, Albert Z., at the age of twenty-three years. Politically, Buchtel is a Republican. Loyal to the core, decided and unyielding, during the Rebellion he could be nothing but a warm-hearted and true patriot. When the rebels laid down their arms he grounded the weapons of his warfare and has since been what may be termed a conservative Republican, too generous hearted to be a bitter partisan and too honest to vote for any one whom he deemed unfit for any office, even if forced upon his own party ticket. In 1880 he was elected Sheriff of Multnomah county, for two years filling the position with credit to himself and to the great satisfaction of all worthy citizens of the county. He introduced many reforms in the management of the jail and other departments of his office. He was firm but kind to a fault. Many hundreds of dollars were given from his private purse to the prisoners, when they were discharged, that they might have a start to get a living, and most of these were never returned to burden the county with expense. Mr. Buchtel has held other important positions in the associations to which he has belonged. He joined the Masonic order in 1853. Also the Odd Fellows and the Encampment. Was elected Grand Representative and attended the National Grand Lodge at Atlanta, Georgia. Has been an active fireman for twenty-six years, and a member of Number Two ever since its organization, and served as Foreman of that company and then served as Chief Engineer of the department for two years. He is an inventor, and will soon put in operation his electric signal fire hose, by which the fireman at the pipe can command the engine. He invented the silver-saving photo holder and the atmospheric background in photography. Mr. Buchtel, besides looking after his photograph gallery, is the lessee of City View Park, and proposes in time to make that a desirable public resort, in some respects equal to the famous Woodward's Gardens in San Francisco. He is turning his attention to the purchase and raising of blooded stock. This will yet become an important enterprise in his hands, and the time will come when the kindness of heart, integrity of purpose and native energy of the subject of this sketch will be fully appreciated in Oregon.

CAPTAIN GEORGE W. BELT,

Who is one of the best known among the young men of the State, was born near Salem, Oregon, on the 13th day of August, 1854, and nearly the whole of his life has been spent in the city of Salem. He was educated at the Willamette University, but did not graduate, leaving that institution at the beginning of his senior year. During the period of his attendance at the university, and for some time after leaving it, he was engaged in teaching. In June, 1876, he commenced the study of law under the tutorship of Judge B. F. Bonham. He finished his law course in the office of Bonham & Ramsey, and was admitted to the bar at the January term, 1879, of the Supreme Court. From this time until January, 1881, he remained in the office of Messrs. Bonham & Ramsey, acting during that time as Deputy Prosecuting Attorney for the Third Judicial District. In the year 1880 he was nominated by his fellow Democrats of Marion county for Representative in the State Legislature, but was defeated with the rest of his ticket. In January, 1881, he removed to Independence, where he formed a co-partnership with Hon. M. L. Pipes, and has since been engaged in the practice of the law. He was married on the 1st day of August, 1882, to Miss Olive L. Chamberlin, of Salem. No sketch of George would be satisfactory to the boys that did not refer to his service as a base-ball player, a fireman and a military man. As a base-ball player he was for years captain of the champion nines of Salem. As a fireman he was long the Foreman of Tiger Engine Company, No. 2, and afterwards Chief Engineer of the Salem Fire Department, and as an officer of the Capital Guards he made a practical study of military tactics, and in July, 1880, he was appointed Aid-de-Camp on the staff of Brigadier General M. V. Brown, with the rank of Captain. All of these matters, in which he was once regarded as an authority, have apparently lost their attractions for him, and he is now devoting himself to his profession with an assiduity that shows his love for it and that promises for him a most successful career as a lawyer.

DR. W H. SAYLOR.

As a rule, the ranks of the medical profession are made up of a class of gentlemen possessing great strength of mind, highly cultured intellects and a loftiness of character which is necessary to command for them the respect of the general public. They are therefore entitled to the great confidences which are necessarily reposed in them, and which they guard with all the great traditional honor of their noble calling. Amongst the physicians of the State of Oregon Dr. W. H. Saylor takes a foremost position. Well qualified by natural inclination, educational training and a vast experience, with a soul fully comprehending the greatness of his work and of his personal responsibility, he has built up for himself a very extensive practice and acquired an enviable standing. He was born August 17, 1843, in Wapelo county, Iowa, and at the tender age of nine years came with his parents across the plains to Oregon. The family lived one year in Portland, and then went to Olympia, W. T., where they lived three years. Returning to our State, the family permanently located in McMinnville, and young William was enabled to finish his education at the Willamette University, graduating from the medical department of that institution in the class of 1869. He then practiced for a term of five years in Forest Grove, and not being satisfied with his general and specific knowledge of the profession, went to New York and attended the celebrated Bellevue Hospital Medical College, from which he graduated in 1876. In that year he returned and commenced the practice of his profession in Portland, remaining here ever since. Although Dr. Saylor is a general practitioner, he has made a specialty of surgery, and has performed some of the most difficult operations on record. He was in 1872-3 Professor of Anatomy in Willamette University, and also Corresponding Secretary of the Oregon State Medical Society for two years. Dr. Saylor is at the present time, and has been for the past four years, attending physician at the Good Samaritan Hospital; he is also a member of the G. A. R., having when the Union was in danger joined B Company, Oregon Volunteers, with which command he served one year as Hospital Steward. Dr. Saylor was married in 1873 to Miss Phœbe A. Wing, who was at the time Preceptress of the University at Forest Grove; the Doctor lived happily with his young wife until the year 1874, when she departed this life.

HON. F. N. SHURTLIFF,

Present Collector of Customs at the city of Portland, was born in Blackland, Niagara county, New York, in 1836. He was reared to manhood at that place. Leaving his native State, he traveled throughout the Western States for a number of years and came to Portland in 1862, and located in Polk county. In 1864 he was appointed Commissary, in the service of the Government, at Grande Ronde Indian Reservation, in Yamhill county, in which position he served until 1869, when he made a brief visit East. Returning in 1870, he received the appointment of Deputy Collector of Customs, by H. W. Scott, then Collector at Portland. In this position he remained with Mr. Scott and Mr. John Kelly, who succeeded the former, until his appointment as superior officer in the same service, in 1880, by President Hayes. Mr. Shurtliff was married to Miss Viola B. Morton in 1858. He is a gentleman of retiring manners, an excellent accountant, and is highly esteemed, both in private and official circles, where he is known. During many years of Government service he has retained an unsullied reputation for business tact, energy and honest dealing.

A. J. MARSHALL

Was born in Baltimore, Maryland, February 11, 1832. He received a liberal education in his native State, and came to California in March, 1849. Here he engaged in mining, express riding and other active business until September, 1856, when he came to Oregon, where he has since resided. He was married to Miss Sarah R. Choat, in Clackamas county, Oregon. Mr. Marshall is a prominent Odd Fellow, having attained the high degrees of Past Grand Master of the Grand Lodge of the State and Past Grand Patriarch of the Grand Encampment. He was the first Grand Patriarch chosen to that position in Oregon. He is also a member of the Masonic fraternity, in good standing, holding, as he does at the present time, the important office of Secretary of Harmony Lodge, No. 12, of Portland, Oregon, of which lodge he is Past Master. He is also a member of several other societies, and is noted for his activity, sagacity and usefulness in all to which he belongs. Mr. Marshall has filled many places of honor and trust, and has always acquitted himself with credit and fidelity. He was Street Commissioner of the city of Portland from July, 1871, until July, 1873, during which time he made a good record. In July, 1874, he was appointed Deputy County Clerk for Multnomah county, which position he has held continuously ever since. In the discharge of his duties in this position he has won the confidence and esteem of all with whom he has been brought in contact. Possessed of quick perception, strong in his convictions of right, and honest in purpose, together with being a devoted and true friend, in sunshine and storm, he numbers, among a host of friends, many of the prominent men of the State. . He is a pronounced Republican, on principle, and takes a lively interest in politics, local, State and national. In fact Mr. Marshall, in all the avocations of life, is entitled to rank among the representative men of the State.

HON. RUFUS MALLORY,

Who, as an attorney at law, ranks among the foremost of his profession in this State, was born in Chenango county, New York, June 10, 1831, and during the same year moved with his parents to Alleghany county, in the same State. He was reared on a farm and enjoyed the advantages of a common school education only, with the exception of a few terms, attendance at the Alfred Academy, in Alleghany county. He commenced teaching school in 1847, relieving its monotony by laboring on the farm during the summer months and teaching during the winter. He moved to New London, Iowa, in 1855, where he remained until 1858, following his avocation as a teacher and devoting his spare time to the study of law. He came to Oregon in 1859 and settled in Douglas county, and taught in the public school at Roseburg until the following Spring. In March, 1860, he was admitted to the bar and at once opened an office at Roseburg. He was elected District Attorney of the First Judicial District in June of the same year, and his success as an attorney and counsellor was assured from that time on. He represented Douglas county in the Legislature of 1862, in the Fall of which year he removed to Salem, and was appointed Prosecuting Attorney for the Third Judicial District vice Hon. J. G. Wilson, appointed Circuit Judge of the Fifth Judicial District. He was elected as his own successor in 1864. At the general election in 1866 Mr. Mallory was elected Congressman from this State, where he served two years, and returning to Salem again resumed the practice of law. In 1872 he represented Marion county and was elected Speaker of the House of Representatives, in which trying and responsible position he displayed marked executive ability. In the Fall of 1874 Mr. Mallory received the appointment of United States District Attorney for Oregon, which office he continued to hold until the Spring of 1882. In the Summer of 1882 he, as a special agent of the United States Treasury Department, visited Singapore, India, to procure evidence in certain important questions then pending in the United States Circuit Court for Oregon. Mr. Mallory is a pronounced Republican and has always taken an active part in politics. He is an able and effective speaker and has canvassed the State several times in the interests of the Republican party. None excel him in industry, integrity and honor, and he has won a warm place in the hearts of the people of this State by his fearless and impartial discharge of every public trust confided to his keeping. As an attorney he has few superiors and as a pleader he leads the profession in this State. He was married to Miss Lucy A. Rose, daughter of Aaron Rose, Esq., of Roseburg, on the 24th day of June, 1860, and they have one son. Such citizens as Hon. Rufus Mallory well deserve mention as one of the "Representative Men of Oregon," his usefulness as which has, in reality, but just commenced, and we bespeak for him a prominent position in the future history of our State.

GEORGE L. STORY,

The gentleman whose name appears at the head of this biography, was born in Manchester, Massachusetts, in 1833; was educated at the private school of Fox Worcester, Esq., at Salem, same State. In 1847 he entered the employ of Brewer, Stevens & Cushing, wholesale druggists in Boston, and remained with them until 1850, when he came to California, where he remained until August, 1851, when he came to Portland, Oregon, and soon afterwards he, in connection with Devaux Babcock, Esq., bought out the drug store of Hooper, Snell & Co. In the following year he bought out Mr. Babcock and soon after formed a partnership with Story, Redington & Co., of San Francisco. After that he bought out the interest of his partners in the Portland branch, and in 1854 sold out to Smith & Davis, who had been employes of his in the store. In 1855 he went into the wholesale paint, oil and glass business in San Francisco, and in 1862 he returned to Portland, where he has since resided. For a number of years after his return to Oregon he was engaged in mining enterprises in Idaho, and in 1870 again embarked in the paint, oil and glass business in Portland, which business, however, he discontinued shortly after his election to the office of County Clerk in 1874. In 1872 he was elected by the Common Council of the city of Portland to fill the unexpired term of Cincinnati Bills, Esq. (who was a member of that body at the time of his death), and at the end of that term he was elected for the term of three years from the First ward. He is one of the newly-appointed Fire Commissioners to organize the Paid Department of the city of Portland, and he, having been for nearly five years past the manager of the Oregon branch of the Home Mutual Insurance Company of California, and more recently appointed agent and attorney for the State of Oregon for the Phœnix Insurance Company of London, his appointment as Fire Commissioner would seem to be well advised. Mr. Story has attained to high and honorable positions in the Masonic fraternity, and is universally respected by his fellow citizens. Mr. Story was married in 1854 to the eldest daughter of the late Anthony L. Davis, Esq.

HON. W. W. THAYER,

Who, by reason of his careful and economical administration of State affairs during his four years' occupancy of the gubernatorial chair, has become deservedly popular with the people and won their merited regard and esteem, was born at Lima, Livingston county, New York, July 15, 1827. His early life was spent on the farm at a period when school advantages were at best but crude and imperfect. He derived his education in the common schools of that State and labored industriously to secure a foundation for the profession he had resolved to enter as a means of livelihood. He read law and was admitted to the bar in the Supreme Court of the State of New York, at Rochester, during the March term of 1851. He practiced law at Tonawanda and Buffalo, New York, until the spring of 1862, when he immigrated to Oregon. He settled in Benton county, where he went into partnership in the practice of law with his brother, Hon. A. J. Thayer, afterwards Judge of the Second Judicial District, who died in 1873. Governor Thayer remained in Benton county until the summer of 1863, when he went to Lewiston, Idaho Territory, where he stayed until 1867. He was a member of the Territorial Legislature of Idaho in the winter of 1866-7. He was elected District Attorney of the Third Judicial District of that Territory in 1866, which position he resigned in 1867, when he removed to Portland, where he again entered upon the active practice of his profession, and where he has resided ever since, having built up a practice both lucrative and honorable. In 1878, when the Democratic party was casting about for a candidate to succeed Governor Chadwick as the Chief Executive of the State, the name of Hon. W. W. Thayer was proposed and it resulted in his nomination and election. He was inaugurated as Governor September 11, 1878, and at once set about correcting certain abuses of public trust and introducing in all departments under his immediate control much needed reforms. His appointments were made with a view to the fitness of the applicant, and his entire administration was characterized by an economical management of public affairs and an evident desire to make all things subservient to the best interests of the State at large. He was very popular as Governor, being one of those plain, every-day sort of men who are always the same wherever you meet them and having a kindly greeting for all. He took especial pride in the economical management of the Penitentiary, which institution was under his complete control, and in the judicious administration of other State matters he was ably assisted by his associates in office. Personally he is social, courteous and genial, and never fails to make friends with all with whom he comes in contact. The Governor was married November 11, 1852, to Miss Samantha C. Vincent, of Tonawanda, New York, their family consisting of one son, now a prominent attorney of Tillamook county. Since the Governor's retirement from office he has resumed the active practice of his profession at Portland.

WILLIAM REID, ESQ.,

The well-known banker and capitalist of Portland, although a naturalized citizen of the United States, was born in Glasgow, Scotland, in 1842, and is consequently forty years of age at the present time. He was trained for the legal profession and educated at the Scottish University of Glasgow, being admitted in 1867 as an attorney of the Scotch courts at Edinburgh, and afterwards practiced his profession at Dundee until 1874. In 1869, upon the recommendation of Mrs. Mary Lincoln, widow of President

Lincoln, he received the appointment of United States Consul at Dundee and held the office at that port until his removal to Oregon in 1874. While in Scotland he acted as counsel for the United States for several American claimants under the Alabama treaty. In 1873 he organized the Oregon and Washington Trust Investment Company at Dundee, and in 1876 he formed at Portland the Oregon and Washington Mortgage Savings Bank, which institutions have loaned the enormous sum of over $5,000,000 on mortgages under his control, without as yet making one single dollar of bad debts. Shortly after his arrival in Oregon he appeared before the Legislature of the State and urged the passage of the first Oregon Immigration Act, and was appointed thereunder, by Governor Grover, President of the State Board of Immigration for Oregon, in conjunction with Hon. W. S. Ladd, Hon. H. W. Corbett, B. Goldsmith and C. Leinenweber as Commissioners, which position he held for three years, and appointed Oregon immigration agents all over the United States and Europe, which was the direct means of securing a very large immigration to this State shortly afterwards. In 1874 he first organized, in conjunction with Captain A. P. Ankeny, the Board of Trade of Portland, and was its active secretary for a period of six years. In 1874, 1876 and 1878 he wrote various pamphlets, describing "Oregon and Washington as Fields for Labor and Capital," 40,000 copies of which were printed in the English, Flemish, German and French languages for the Paris Exposition. In 1879 he conceived the idea of constructing a system of narrow gauge railroads in Western Oregon, and, in conjunction with Mr. J. B. Montgomery, for that purpose was one of the organizers of "The Oregonian Railway Company, Limited," of Scotland, Mr. Montgomery having gone to Scotland to perfect the same The construction of this system met with great opposition from rival railroad enterprises and the city of Portland; its entering this city, in condemning and appropriating the public levee for a terminal depot and grounds; and the fight was taken into the halls of the Legislature in the session of 1880, where, after considerable opposition, a bill was passed by a two-thirds vote of the Senate and House, over the Governor's veto, entitling his railroad company, which, at that time was very popular with the farmers of the Willamette valley, as an opposition road, to occupy the public levee of Portland for its terminus and depot grounds. They constructed and completed 163 miles of this railway, and had his road bed graded to a point within eleven miles of Portland, when his efforts for its farther extension to that city were stopped by the Scotch owners of the enterprise, who, despite his opposition, leased the road against his wishes for ninety-six years to the Oregon Railway and Navigation Company in return for a guaranteed rent of seven and one-half per cent. per year upon the paid-up stock. Mr. Reid the same year reorganized the Salem Flouring Mill Company, and also formed a company with a capital of $200,000, called the "City of Salem Company," for the purpose of adopting and extending the gradual reduction system of milling into Oregon upon the Minneapolis process, which proved a success upon Oregon wheat. That company, of which he is President and the largest stockholder, owns the Capitol Mills, "A and B," of Salem, and the Turner "C" Mill, with a united capacity of producing eight hundred barrels of flour per day, the largest milling company in the State upon the new process. In the Fall of 1882 Mr. Reid formed the First National Bank of Salem, of which he is nominally the President, Mr. W. N. Ladue, from Detroit, the Vice-President, being the active manager at Salem. Mr. Reid is married and has a family of five children. Such, dear reader, is but a brief outline of the history of one of the most active, energetic and enterprising capitalists in our State. He is a man of indomitable pluck and perseverence, and as keen a financier as can be found anywhere. His enterprise is proverbial and his superior business sagacity unquestioned. His various business interests in Oregon are successful and his credit is almost unlimited. His management of foreign capital in our State has been the means of very greatly advancing its interest and prominence as a commonwealth, and we owe much to him for the rapid progress we have made during the past eight or ten years. Mr. Reid is a man who, while not of a tall, commanding form, would none the less attract attention in any assemblage. Of ordinary height, slight form, smooth face and the most piercing dark eyes. He is ever on the move, and many wonder when he secures the rest an active brain like his necessarily requires. He is an indefatigable worker, and despatches business with hasty precision. He has an eye to business at all times and is considered a very successful business man. He is genial and sociable with his friends and is esteemed by all who know him. Would we had more of just such men in Oregon. The latest acquisition he has brought to the State of Oregon is the American Mortgage Company of Scotland, having its head office in Edinburg, with a capital of two million dollars, the loaning of which, on mortgages, has been entrusted to his care and has caused a deal of rivalry and jealousy from the Dundee loaning companies for whom he formerly acted.

J. H. ROBBINS.

When we see a gentleman who is successful in his business, we know that his prosperity is not the result of chance; but rather that he has worked hard and long, and that he possesses a spirit which does not succumb to trifling discouragements. When one attains this proud distinction of being known as a solid man, his word is considered as good as his bond, and his reputation must necessarily be unblemished. Mr. Robbins is one of our citizens who, without aid or guidance, has followed the true instincts of his own progressive nature and to-day takes his place in the ranks of the very foremost. He was born in Decatur county, Indiana, in the year 1832. After receiving the educational advantages ordinarily accorded to youths of his station in life, he learned the trade of cabinet making, and meantime obtained an exceptionally good knowledge of music. At the early age of sixteen years young Robbins commenced his career as a teacher of vocal music, in the instruction of which he met with great success. He started for Oregon in the year 1862, and on the journey, in the Powder River Valley, his young wife, to whom he had been married in 1854, and who had borne him three children, died, leaving the weary traveler and devoted husband with his three infants to continue their weary way alone and motherless. Arriving in Oregon, Mr. Robbins at once commenced teaching music, as before, and very soon became known as one of our most proficient instructors. He was again married in 1861 to Miss Mary M. Harvey, daughter of the well-known Amos Harvey, and a few years afterward founded his present popular music house. Mr. Robbins' establishment to-day is a very extensive as well as attractive one, and his stock of organs, pianos, picture frames and artistic goods is one of the finest outside of San Francisco. He is the agent for the celebrated Whitney & Holmes organ, and although this instrument was comparatively unknown a few years ago, Mr. Robbins has introduced it to such an extent that now he can scarcely fill orders. Although not being a member of any society, our subject is temperate in all his habits, and his best friends know that he is an enthusiast against the use of tobacco and liquor. Mr. Robbins has a beautiful home, ornamented with all the beauties of art and blessed with happiness and contentment. He is, thanks to his own exertions, now in independent circumstances, and enjoys the friendship and esteem of our best citizens.

H. Y. THOMPSON.

One of the most prominent barristers, enjoying an extensive practice in Portland, is H. Y. Thompson. Mr. Thompson was born in Zanesville, Ohio, and there received his first knowledge of the world and its mysterious ways. He was favored with a liberal education, and well-fitted to struggle with life and win for himself positions of trust and prominence. He came to Oregon in 1865, and, settling in Portland, soon became an active member of the legal fraternity. He has also taken an active part in the politics of the State, and has been identified as a leader in the ranks of the Republican party. He served one term as City Attorney of Portland. He is a social, trustworthy gentleman, who always commands the respect of the community at large. He was married in 1871 to Miss Anna B. Smith, daughter of Hon. Joseph Smith, an estimable and accomplished young lady, and the happy couple count a host of friends amongst their acquaintances. Mr. Thompson is a member of the Knights of Pythias, and takes an active interest in that organization.

J. K. GILL,

The popular dealer in books and stationery in Portland, was born in Yorkshire, England, in the year 1841. In 1854 he crossed the Atlantic and settled in Worcester, Massachusetts, where he remained until he was twenty-one years of age. At that age he entered the Wesleyan Academy, at Wilbergham, in the same State, and graduated therefrom in the class of '66. In the same year he started for Oregon, and in the month of August arrived in Salem, where he immediately established himself in the book and stationery business, continuing there until August, 1871, when he removed to Portland, where he entered into a co-partnership with Mr. George Steel. The new firm purchased the stock and business of Messrs. Harris & Holman, who were at that time the leading book-sellers in the State. In 1872 Mr. Gill purchased Mr. Steel's interest, and has been in charge of the business ever since. As a specimen of Mr. Gill's business enterprise and capacity, we will state that at no time has he been dependent on the San Francisco market for his supplies. As he has always dealt directly with Eastern firms, he has been enabled to compete with the largest firms in San Francisco, and to offer to the people of this State and Washington Territory all the advantages that can be gained by his method of large purchases to supply the State as well as retail purchasers. Mr. Gill is a firm adherer to the doctrines of the Methodist Episcopal Church, and has always taken a prominent part in advancing the interests of that denomination. In musical circles he is both "useful and ornamental," being a first class violinist, and always contributing his valuable services to every entertainment that is worthy of encouragement. Whether in business or social circles, he is always the same—an obliging, liberal gentleman, who, whilst anxious to benefit himself, is never selfish or grasping. He was married August 17, 1866, to Miss Fanny A. Wilson, daughter of Mr. W. H. Wilson, one of the pioneers of this State. Mr. and Mrs. Gill are blessed with an interesting family, and thankfully enjoy all the blessings of a peaceful and happy home.

HON JOHN WHITEAKER.

"Honest John Whiteaker" is the familiar title by which the first Governor of the State of Oregon is known on both sides of this continent. He was born in Dearborn county, Indiana, May 4, 1820. His early life was passed with his parents on a farm in his native State. When twenty-five years of age he went to Illinois and the following year from there to Missouri, where he was married, in 1847, in Putnam county, to Miss N. J. Hargrave, daughter of Judge Hargrave, a prominent man in that part of the State. In the spring of 1849, attracted by the fame of the California gold mines, he left his wife at her father's and visited the new El Dorado of the far West. Arriving at Sacramento early in the fall, he turned his attention to mining, in which avocation he shared the fortune of a great majority of delvers for the precious metals. He next dealt in live stock, and for a short time managed a hotel in Sacramento City. In the spring of 1851 he returned East by way of the Isthmus, and crossed the plains the second time in 1852, to Oregon, bringing his wife with him. He arrived in Portland when the present city was a comparative wilderness, and remained but a short time when he proceeded up the valley to Polk county, where he passed the winter. The following spring he went to Lane county and settled on a tract of land under the donation law of 1850, and he has resided in that county up to the present time. The first office to which he was elected in the then Territory was that of Probate Judge for Lane county, to which position he was elected in 1856. In 1857 he was elected to the Territorial Legislature. In the meantime the convention to frame the State Constitution convened, and, upon its adoption, Hon. John Whiteaker was nominated by the Democrats and elected the first Governor of the new State. His term extended over the eventful years from 1858 to 1862, during which time Governor Whiteaker illustrated his patriotism and statesmanship by his wise and moderate course in all of his public and private acts. In 1862 he received the support of his party in the Legislature for United States Senator, which honor has since been frequently accorded him. He was elected to the Legislature in 1866, and was returned in 1868, at which term he was elected and served as Speaker. In 1870 he was once more honored by his constituents with a seat in the lower House, and was nominated again in 1872, but was defeated by a small majority. In 1876, his party having recovered the ascendancy in Lane county, he was elected to the State Senate, of which body he was elected President. So acceptably had he filled the important positions to which he had been called, that, in 1878, he was nominated by his party for a seat in the Forty-sixth Congress, to which exalted position he was elected by a large majority over his Republican competitor, Hon. H. K. Hines. At the called session of 1879 Congressman Whiteaker made the quickest trip ever accomplished from the Pacific to the Atlantic seaboard. By special train he was taken from San Francisco to Washington in four days, nineteen hours and fifty-three minutes. The great haste was necessary to secure the organization of the lower House of Congress to the Democrats at that session. During his term in Congress Mr. Whiteaker served as Chairman of the Committee on Pensions, an honor seldom conferred on a new member. He was also a member of the Committee on Indian Affairs. In 1880 he was renominated for Congress on his party ticket, but was defeated by the present incumbent of that office, Hon. M. C. George. He served on the committee appointed by Governor Grover to inspect the locks at Willamette Falls, and was also appointed on the State Board of Equalization and made Chairman of that body. In every position to which Governor Whiteaker has been called he has proved equal to all requirements imposed upon him. As a parliamentarian he has few equals and as a legislative and administrative officer his record stands above adverse criticism. Loved by his neighbors for his many noble and humane traits of character, possessing the confidence of his party because of his consistency, and trusted and respected by all who know him, Governor Whiteaker now resides on his farm in Lane county. He delights in his rural and domestic life, is in vigorous health, both mental and physical, and is still capable of performing any duty to which he may be called in the future by those who have so often delighted to honor him with their confidence.

HON. O. N. DENNY.

Office-holding is not always a recommendation to a man. There are those who seek office and those whom the office seeks. The subject of this biography is one of the latter class, and has, almost continuously, since attaining his majority, held official position. He was born in Washington county, Ohio, September 4, 1838. His father was of Scotch-Irish and his mother of English descent. He came to Oregon with his parents in 1852, crossing the plains with an ox team and settling in Linn county, near Lebanon, on a donation claim. Two weeks after their arrival the father died, leaving a widowed mother with six children, three girls and three boys, O. N. Denny being the oldest of the boys. The responsibility and chief labor of improving the farm and supporting the family devolved upon him and his mother, and, with the assistance of the younger children, they struggled on to the accomplishment of both. Meantime he attended the Lebanon Academy and obtained an education sufficient to qualify him for teaching a common country school. He taught six months and then attended Willamette University, at Salem, for two years. He then began reading law with Hon. A. Holbrook, at Oregon City. That gentleman being called East, on business connected with the National Sanitary Commission, of which he was chief agent for Oregon, he prescribed a course for his student, furnished him with text books and sent him to Salem, where he joined a class, consisting of the late C. G. Curl, Thomas Caton, H. A. Gehr and William Waldo. The class recited to Hon. L. F. Grover, at present United Senator, for one year, when they each entered law firms. Mr. Denny went in the firm of Hons. J. G. Wilson & B. F. Harding, and after being admitted to the bar in 1862 he went to The Dalles, in Wasco county, and began practice alone. In September of the same year he was appointed, by Governor A. C. Gibbs, County Judge of that county, which position he held one year. He then went to Idaho Territory to make collections for merchants at The Dalles, resigning his office to do so. The business detaining him, he opened an office at Centreville and practiced law for a short time, with marked success. He then returned to The Dalles, and at the following election was nominated for the office of County Judge on the Republican ticket, and elected by a large majority. At the expiration of his term he was renominated and, although the county went largely Democratic, he was only beaten eight votes. Mr. Denny gained great credit for his administration of county affairs while he held the office of Judge, the bonds of the county advancing from fifty cents on the dollar to par value during his term. He was married to Mrs. Gertrude J. White, an accomplished widow with one child, a daughter, in 1868. He then removed to California and located in San Jose, where he practiced law one year, when he returned to Oregon and, locating in Portland, he again began the practice of his profession. In 1871 he was elected Police Judge for the city of Portland, and was re-elected in 1873 on the Republican ticket. During his last term he was tendered the Consulship, at Amoy, China, by President Grant, which office he declined, not having been an applicant. In 1875 he was appointed Collector of Internal Revenue for Oregon and Alaska by President Grant, when he resigned the office of Police Judge and entered upon the duties of his new position. In May, 1877, he was appointed Consul at Tientsin, China, by President Hayes, and in 1879 he was promoted to Consul General, with residence at Shanghai. He entered upon the duties of that responsible position April 1st, 1880, and still continues in the office, although at this date he is visiting friends and attending to official duties in Oregon. Mr. Denny was appointed to the office which he now holds, at the request of Hon. William M. Evarts, then Secretary of State of the United States, without his having made application for the same and without his knowledge. He holds high relations with other foreign Ministers and Consuls to the Chinese Empire and is held in high esteem by them and also by the Chinese authorities. No higher mark of confidence could be given him than the fact that the whole Pacific delegation to Congress recently recommended him for promotion to Minister to Peking, a position still more distinguished than that which he is now holding. The writer of this brief sketch has known Judge Denny from his early boyhood, and is cognizant of the facts herein stated. His early struggles, his after triumphs, and his still promising future, are themes upon which much more could be written. But closing here, we leave him to still further

"Cast for himself the sounding line
In the deep ocean of futurity."

HON. JOHN M. GEARIN,

Who is prominently identified with the Portland legal fraternity, was born in Umatilla county, Oregon, on the 15th of August, 1851. His earlier years were spent in the schools of this State, and his education was completed at Santa Clara College, California. After graduating at that noted institution of learning he returned home, and immediately commenced the study of law. As he showed evidence of more than usual ability, his friends pressed him into the political field, and in 1874 he was elected a member of the Legislature on the Democratic ticket. In 1875 he was elected City Attorney of Portland, and in 1876 he was re-elected to the same position. In every position that he has been chosen to fill he has invariably acquitted himself in a highly acceptable manner, doing credit to himself as well as to those whom he was chosen to represent. As a lawyer he is quite successful, and his prominence commands for him a much larger practice than is usually accorded to so young a practitioner. He is at present associated with Hon. C. B. Bellinger, and no other law firm is more extensively and favorably known in this city than that of Bellinger & Gearin. Mr. Gearin was married in 1876 to Miss Tillie Raleigh, the esteemed daughter of the late P. Raleigh, one of the pioneers of this State.

Leading Journalists.

H. W. SCOTT.

One of the proprietors and Editor-in-Chief of the Daily and Weekly "Oregonian," the leading journal of the Northwest, was born in Tazewell county, Illinois, on the 1st day of February, 1838. At the age of fifteen years he removed to Oregon, coming across the plains with his parents. Washington Territory, then a part of Oregon, was selected as a place of settlement, but the family came to Oregon proper in 1854 and lived for two years in Clackamas county. Most of the time from his arrival on the coast till 1858 was spent by Mr. Scott in the hardest kind of farm work, of which he tired finally and undertook the task of securing an education. For this purpose he entered the Pacific University, and, after five years close study, came out of that institution with a mind well fitted for the prominent position he was afterwards called to take. About the close of the war of the Rebellion he assumed the editor's chair in the "Oregonian" office, which he has since continuously filled, with the exception of about two years, when the chief writer was Hon. W. Lair Hill. Mr. Scott's style as a journalist is peculiarly his own. While he is not dashing or florid, and by some is regarded as occasionally heavy, his writings are never pointless. He goes home to the root of his subject, and, with a logic that is strong if not always keen, he cuts to the quick. Trained as a boy by a Whig father, and receiving his first lessons in politics by reading Horace Greeley in the New York "Tribune," Mr. Scott has always been the staunch opponent of the Democratic party, though of late years he has shown a decided leaning to the Democratic idea of free trade. Under his editorial management the "Oregonian" has become the largest and most influential newspaper of the Northwest, and its utterances have been given more prominence in the country generally than those of any other journal on the Pacific Coast. Harvey W. Scott is conceded to be the ablest journalist in the Northwest.

A. NOLTNER.

Mr. A. Noltner, whose name occupies a foremost position amongst the politicians of this State, came to Oregon in the year 1857, and in the Fall of that year was initiated into the rudimentary elements of typography in the town of Corvallis. Two years later he became associated with Hon. James H. Slater in the publication of the Corvallis "Union." In 1862 they sold the "Union" to the late P. J. Malone. Mr. Noltner then removed to Eugene City, where he published the "Register" until 1865, when he removed it to Salem, In 1868 he sold the "Register," and for a time applied his attention to journey work. In 1870 he purchased the Oregon City "Enterprise" and conducted that paper until the Fall of 1875. In January, 1876, he commenced the publication of the Portland Daily and Weekly "Standard," and he is still at the head of that prosperous and able advocate of Democratic principles. Mr. Noltner is a member of the Independent Order of Odd Fellows, and has passed through the various official chairs. In 1873 he was a Grand Representative of the Order to the Supreme Grand Lodges, and he was also the instituting officer of the Grand Lodge of British Columbia, the Grand Encampment of Oregon and the first Subordinate Encampment of Washington Territory. He was married in 1861 to Miss Ellen Fox, of Albany, and two years later became a widower. He was married a second time, in 1865, to Miss Martha N., daughter of the late James E. Williams, one of the early pioneers of Oregon, having arrived here in 1845, Mrs. N. being born at their newly-settled home in Polk county in 1847. Mr. Noltner is what may be termed a thorough journalist, being a practical man in every branch of the business. Being endowed with good common sense, strengthened by a more than average education, and having a full knowledge of political matters generally, he has proven to be a valuable acquisition to the Democratic party in this State, to which he has been allied from "time immemorial." Personally, he is a quiet, genial, unassuming gentleman, and is well calculated to make friends at all times, both for himself and his enterprise.

T. B. MERRY.

The subject of this sketch was born in the city of New York in 1835, and came to California in '53. He commenced writing for the newspapers in 1855 as a free lance, and since that time has been employed almost continuously in journalistic work. In 1864 he edited the Sacramento "Star," and was connected with the "Bee" in the same city in 1865, in an editorial capacity. Some thirteen years ago Tom Merry journeyed to Oregon, where he has been engaged in several newspaper enterprises. He published the Coos Bay "News" from 1873 to 1875, and the "Inland Empire" at The Dalles from 1878 to 1880. About a year ago Mr. Merry, in recognition of his eminent fitness for the post, was selected as managing editor of the "Sunday Oregonian," which paper, since he assumed the tripod, has been conducted with marked ability. He wields a facile pen and is as brilliant in conversation as he is polished in diction. His English is pure, strong and sinewy, and he never impairs the force of it by a quotation from a foreign tongue. Out of his wonderful wealth of language, he can always hit the nail on the head in good, vigorous Saxon. Coming to California a boy, his mind was as wax to receive, and as marble to retain, the vivid impressions of the Argonautic era and pioneer days, which he has so faithfully and picturesquely portrayed in those reminiscences of which his readers never tire. Those who know genial Tom, and have listened to any of his good stories (and as a "raconteur" he is unrivaled), will always recall with a thrill of pleasure his many excellent qualities. Tom Merry stands in the foremost rank of Pacific Coast journalists.

ALFRED HOLMAN.

Among the young men of ability in this State who have come to the front is Alfred Holman, associate editor of the "Oregonian." He is twenty-five years old and a native Oregonian, having been born in Yamhill county, on the farm of his grandfather, the late Dr. James McBride. Until the age of fifteen he attended public schools and academies, and then began the foundation for a career in journalism— began it in the composing room and took "Excelsior" for his motto. His first reportorial work was in 1876, and he served at odd times on each one of the Portland dailies. In the position of reporter and of city editor he showed great energy as a newsgatherer and excellent judgment in handling the multifarious matters which every day come under the supervision of a local editor. He did not follow the beaten path of a plain record of passing events, but stamped his news items and comment with individuality of style that always made them readable. In the spring of 1878 he was engaged by the "Oregonian" as news editor, in which capacity he served three years, when he was promoted to the assistant editorship. During the past year he visited various sections of the new Northwest and contributed to his journal numerous descriptive articles. They were marked by evidence of keen observation, accuracy of statement and freedom from dry detail. They gave just what the public generally, and intending immigrants particularly, desired to learn, and no more, except occasionally descriptions of persons and places in a humorous vein. The letters attracted much attention and have been incorporated into pamphlets descriptive of Oregon and Washington for foreign distribution. He represented the "Oregonian" as editorial correspondent at the capital during the recent session of the Legislature, and while his daily contributions by no means pleased those who opposed the course laid out and followed by the journal in the Senatorial question, he showed vigor of thought and expression which opponents were compelled to admire. His writings, as a rule, evince terseness and strength. He has already attained a high place among Oregon journalists, and few young men of the State give promise of a brighter future.

S. A. MORELAND.

Editor-in-chief of the Portland "Evening Telegram," first saw the light of day in Jackson county, Tennessee, November 1, 1836. When he was twelve years old his parents removed to Illinois, where they resided for four years. Young Moreland, then a rugged lad of sixteen, started across the plains to Oregon with his parents, and like many another eminent pioneer, drove an ox team. In the fall of 1852 the family located at Hardscrabble, in Clackamas county, which was not a particularly inviting region at that period. The subject of this sketch was an ambitious youth, and soon tired of the plow on his father's farm. He came to Portland in 1857 and afterwards entered the law office of Hon. L. F. Grover, the present U. S. Senator from Oregon, where he prepared himself for the legal profession. While studying law he supported himself by his pen. Mr. Moreland has been honored by his fellow citizens in Portland in various ways, having been

Police Judge, Justice of the Peace, and City Assessor. In 1872 Judge Moreland was attached to the staff of the "Oregonian" as commercial editor. During the campaign of 1880 the leading paper was under the sole editorial management of Judge Moreland, whose articles were well-timed, vigorous and trenchant, and stamped their author as a man of much ability. Judge Moreland is at present Police Magistrate in the city of Portland. In private, as in public, life he is universally respected and esteemed for his many excellent qualities of head and heart.

W. H. ODELL.

Is the talented editor and proprietor of the Oregon Daily and Weekly "Statesman." His pen is an able and versatile one, and on many an occasion has proved itself "mightier than the trusted sword." He was born in Carroll county, Indiana, in the year 1830. Was raised on his father's farm, and prior to his majority received only the advantages of a common school education. In the year 1851 young William with his parents crossed the plains to the then far-off Oregon, driving an ox team all the way. When the family arrived here they located in Yamhill county, and the subject of this short sketch remained there with his parents till April, 1853, at which time he entered the Oregon Institute, now the Willamette University, where he spent two years drinking at the fonts of knowledge. After completing his education he was married to Mrs. E. F. Thurston, and for five years subsequently he lived on his farm in Yamhill county. In September, 1860, Mr. and Mrs. Odell took charge of the Santiam Academy, where he remained three years; from thence they removed to Albany and took charge of the public schools of that city. In 1864 Mr. Odell removed to Eugene City and accepted the appointment of United States Deputy Surveyor, which position he retained till January, 1871, when he was appointed United States Surveyor General of the State of Oregon. He remained in this important office till 1874. He was honored by the Republican party of the State of Oregon in 1876 and made an elector on the Hayes and Wheeler ticket. In May, 1877, he embarked in the newspaper business, and by his ability as a writer and his sagacity as a business man, has made the "Statesman" the influential journal that it is at the present time.

T. A. SUTHERLAND,

Editor of the Portland "Sunday Welcome," is well-known as one of the most promising journalists on the coast. He was born in San Diego, California, May 1, 1850, and was the first American child ushered into existence in that charming little town. He was educated at Santa Clara College, California, and finished at Harvard University, at Cambridge, Massachusetts. He subsequently studied law in Philadelphia, but never embarked in the practice of that profession. He regularly espoused the trying pursuit of journalism in 1875, having, however, previously contributed to Eastern reviews and newspapers. Since Mr. Sutherland's connection with the daily press, he has represented the New York "Herald" as war correspondent in the Nez Perce campaign, in which he served upon the staff of General O. O. Howard, with the rank of Lieutenant, and the San Francisco "Chronicle" during the Bannock war. Mr. Sutherland is a Democrat in politics, and was Editor-in-Chief of the Portland "Standard," the leading Democratic organ of Oregon, for nearly a year, from the Summer of 1881 to the same time in 1882. As a writer, he is clear, forcible and convincing. He never strikes a blow with a bludgeon, but pierces his adversary, as with the thrust of a rapier. He is well-informed, not upon State and national affairs only, but upon European matters as well, having passed nearly two years at one time abroad. About a year and a half ago he was united in marriage to a daughter of Rev. W. C. Chattin, of Portland. He has no children living.

W. S. CHAPMAN

Is a native Oregonian, having been born at Portland on July 3, 1850. In 1853 his parents moved to Southern Oregon, and returned to Portland in 1861, where they and he have resided ever since. At the time of his return to Portland he could not write his name, but he evinced due appreciation of the opportunities for schooling then at hand, and in July, 1867, he was employed by the City Surveyor of Portland, and, showing a knowledge of the business, was soon entrusted with the most important work. However, at the end of six months he quit the office, and went to school at the Portland Academy, pursuing several studies "on the side," caught up with his class and with them graduated in July, 1868. The next day he was employed as Assistant City Surveyor, which position he held almost continuously, under different City Surveyors, until the first election after he became "of age," when he was chosen City Surveyor of Portland. In the meantime he had been employed to make surveys and inaugurate systems of street grades for Vancouver, Astoria, East Portland and, eventually, the capital of the State, where he also set the stakes for the many corners and angles of the State Capitol building. He held the office two years, when a turn in the political wheel caused his removal, he having been a Republican, though he was at first elected by Democratic and Republican votes, and thereby beat the Republican caucus nominee. When his successor was elected, there were only two Republicans against seven Independents in the Common Council, and as he never took any stock in "half-breedism," he had to be punished. In 1878 he was again chosen City Surveyor, and held the office nearly four years. In the meantime he was engaged as editor of the Daily "Bee" in 1876, and became owner of it in 1877, and succeeded within one year in bringing the paper to a paying basis, though it was opposed by the O. S. N. Company, the "Oregonian" and "bank crowd," of Portland. On taking the Surveyor's office in August, 1878, the "Bee" fell into other hands and soon began to decline. The most deserving public work in which Mr. Chapman was engaged was the valuable assistance which he rendered his father, Colonel W. W. Chapman, in the latter's efforts in 1872-8 to establish a railroad from Portland up the Columbia river and to the Union Pacific, he having given his father for the cause over $6,000, a liberal sum from "the boy Surveyor," besides having graded several hundred feet of road and made a number of surveys along the Columbia river for the company. These efforts of Col. Chapman and his son finally attracted the attention of Eastern capitalists, and greatly conduced towards securing the present railroad development of the State. Another worthy public enterprise was the establishment of the Jefferson street ferry at Portland. The new ferry is a great public convenience, and is the only one of many which succeeded in overcoming the opposition of the parties who own the Stark street ferry. Mr. Chapman was also chiefly engaged in organizing and making successful the East Portland water company, which, after a long fight, gained a local franchise and promptly built water works. He still controls the ferry company and owns a considerable interest in the East Portland water company. Mr. Chapman has been quite successful as a journalist, having made the "Sunday Mercury," of which he owns a half interest, one of the most successful and best paying papers in Portland. He is temperate in all his habits, using neither liquor or tobacco, strange as it may appear in an active politician. He is still a young man, unmarried, and promises to be one of the "solid men" of the metropolis.

L. SAMUELS,

The enterprising and progressive editor and proprietor of the "West Shore," is a gentleman who has done as much as any other for the population and advancement of this State and the entire Northwest. He was born in Germany about thirty-four years ago, and came to America in childhood, drifting westward as far as Sacramento, California, where he was raised and received his education. Having a love for the newspaper business, he started out as a newsboy, and gradually worked his way up until in a few years later he became the proprietor of the "Traveler's Guide," a weekly publication, which he conducted successfully for three years. He then came to Oregon, and becoming impressed with the great natural advantages of the State, determined to do what he could to make them known to the outer world, and accordingly, in 1875, he commenced the publication of the "West Shore," as a monthly journal. Mr. Samuels' object in establishing the "West Shore" was for the purpose of setting forth the superior advantages which this country offers to the immigrant, and to give all the necessary information in a simple and comprehensive manner. From the very outset the "West Shore" has been a success; making its advent as a small and unpretentious newspaper, it has made for itself a world-wide reputation and stands to-day unrivaled in its particular field of journalism. And further than this, its object has been accomplished, and through its instrumentality thousands and thousands of immigrants have been encouraged to locate in our State. In order to bring about this grand result Mr. Samuels has spared neither time nor money; he has established agencies all over the United States and in Europe, and very frequently he has went so far even as to have editions printed in the German and Scandinavian languages and sent on to those countries, that their inhabitants might read in their native tongue. He has at the present time a corps of field artists and a number of lithographers constantly employed, and the leading journals of this State and country have justly commended the superiority of their work as beyond the reach of rivalry. At the present time the "West Shore" can be found in nearly every town and city in the United States and Europe, and it is gaining favor with each succeeding issue. This simply demonstrates that Mr. Samuels' efforts to make his paper first-class in every particular have been duly appreciated, and we might add here, that the Land officers also prefer it to any other publication. Anxious for the prosperity of the great State of Oregon, which is now in its infancy, and with a heartfelt desire to see her take her place in the constellation of States in the most exalted position, we hope that Mr. Samuels is but just entering upon the great work which is destined to accomplish it, and we know that his efforts will be successful.

JOHN J. BURNETT

Associate editor of the Portland "Sunday Welcome," first saw daylight on the 15th of September, 1845, in the city of Philadelphia. His parents were Virginians and while the subject of this sketch was very young they removed to Chicago, taking him with them. At an early age he entered the University of Chicago, and, while peacefully pursuing his studies, the threatening war clouds which long had foreboded disaster burst, and the nation was engulfed in strife. Though but a slender lad, young Burnett joined the Nineteenth Illinois Volunteers as a private in the early part of '61. Enough of his war record to say that he received his share of hard knocks and was gazetted an officer for brave and meritorious conduct. He served until August, 1864, when he returned to his home. After the close of the Rebellion he came west and settled in Idaho. In 1869 he found himself in Oregon, where he has remained almost without intermission ever since.. In 1872 he began his career as a journalist and has been actively engaged up to the present time in the arduous details incidental to the daily grind of the newspaper office. There is no occasion to dwell upon Mr. Burnett's standing as a writer. Contributing as he has been for years to one or the other of the Portland papers, he understands not only how to write but what to write about. His style is pure, clear and succinct, never aiming at brilliant figures of speech, nor straining after effect, but appealing directly and understandingly to the mind of every-day men and women with a terseness that is commendable. Politically, Mr. Burnett is a war Democrat; personally, he is one of the most affable and popular men in the State. He is married to an estimable lady, and one child, a girl, is the fruit of their union.

E. L. COLDWELL,

The well-known and popular city editor of the "Daily Standard," is one of those jovial, genial fellows that it does one good to meet. He is a Nova Scotian by birth and came to this State in 1869, since which time he has almost continuously been connected with some printing or newspaper office in the various capacities of pressman, compositor or reporter, in any of which positions he is equally at home. He is familiarly known by his printing office nickname "Jerry," to which he has become accustomed, and many who have known him for years suppose it to be his true name. He was employed in the job printing establishment of A. G. Walling for three years and afterward in the State printing office at Salem as pressman during three consecutive sessions of the Legislature. He was city editor of the Portland "Daily Standard" for over a year, and has been connected with the "Bulletin," "Herald," Salem "Mercury" and "Statesman," and a number of other papers, until nearly every one knows him. He tried farming on a ranch near Salem for a time, but not liking the life of a granger, "hung up the shovel and the hoe" and struck out for Portland, where he "kicked for a job" at the first printing office he came to, securing a situation on the "Bee" on the day of his arrival. It is evident that "Jerry" has now adopted a business for which he is by nature particularly adapted. He is a "hail fellow well met" with all classes of people, an industrious, indefatigable worker, with quick eyes and ears, a pleasant writer, possessing rare descriptive faculties, and enjoying the reputation in Portland of being the peer of the very best in his profession. "Jerry" is destined to meet with well merited success in the profession he has chosen, and the writer, who has known him for years, wishes him prosperity meted out full measure and overflowing. He has resigned his position, to accept one on the "Oregonian."

A. M. CLINTON,

The city editor of the Daily Evening "Telegram," is a native of New York City, where he was born May 1, 1836. He was educated for that most trying of all pursuits, teaching, which vocation he followed faithfully for seven years, and during this time he became an occasional contributor to the press, his articles invariably denoting no little thought and vigor. He entered regularly into newspaper life years ago, and has been everything from reporter and correspondent to editor and business manager. He afterwards embarked in mercantile pursuits, but the old fascination of journalism coming upon him, in 1874 he returned to newspaper work. Since that time he has been editor of the "Pacific Monthly," on the staff of the Portland "Bee," and for a brief while has been city editor of the Daily "Standard." For the past eighteen months Mr. Clinton has ably filled the position of city editor of the Evening "Telegram." Since he assumed the tripod, that paper has been noted for the clean and wholesome tenor of its articles and is eagerly sought for by many citizens on that account. Those who have been associated with Mr. Clinton in newspaper work regard him as a man of sterling traits of character, who is always striving with pen and tongue to lift up his fellow men.

M. F. BLAKE,

Reporter of the "Daily Evening Telegram," is a native of New York City, twenty-five years of age. He received a sound education in the public schools at the great metropolis, and afterwards studied medicine for some years. Before graduating he gave up the study, and after contributing for some time to several weekly papers of his native city, he followed Horace

Greeley's advice to "Go West and grow up with the country." He landed in San Jose, California, about three years ago, and during his stay there was connected with the "Times" and other daily papers. Allured by the accounts he heard of the Northwest, he drifted to Oregon. Within a few days after his arrival in Portland he was attached to the morning "Standard" in the capacity of reporter. After a very brief stay in the Webfoot metropolis he journeyed to Oregon City, where he accepted the position of traveling correspondent for the "Enterprise," one of the best interior journals in the State. His articles, written over the nom de plume of "Wilkins Micawber," were widely read at the time. After performing some very creditable work on the last-named paper, Mr. H. L. Pittock, of the "Oregonian," having conceived a favorable impression of young Blake sent for him and offered him a position on the city staff of the "Oregonian." After remaining for some months on Oregon's leading paper, Mr. Blake was transferred to the "Evening Telegram," where he had an opportunity of showing his mettle as a journalist. He has won an enviable reputation as a writer and as one of the most energetic and indefatigable news-gatherers in Portland, no trouble, labor, or danger being considered too great if thereby he can secure for the "Telegram" the first publication of a piece of news. He is an enthusiast in his profession, and by his energy and enterprise has contributed largely to the reputation of that paper. He is a genial, whole-souled young man, and a close student, not only of books but of human nature, and as his soul is in his work it is certain that he will achieve distinction in the field of labor he has chosen. Mr. Blake has resigned his post on the "Telegram," and his connection with that paper will cease about December 1, 1882. He has been offered an advanced position on the "Morning News," a new journalistic enterprise, the publication of which is to be commenced in Portland during the month of December. He has decided to link his fortunes with the new venture, and his many friends wish him success.

HON. THOMAS J. STITES.

The subject of this sketch was born in Putnam county, Indiana, October 25, 1839, and with his parents moved to Illinois (Edgar county) in 1841, where he resided until 1854, when they moved to Missouri, where they remained until 1862, when with an older brother Mr. Stites came to Oregon, having crossed the plains with an ox team. His early life was spent on a farm and his educational advantages were very limited, being embraced chiefly in twelve months' attendance at a private country school. He has been a deep reader, however, and by this means has acquired an extensive knowledge on general subjects and succeeded in making himself a very successful teacher, which profession he followed for a number of years both in Missouri and since his arrival in Oregon, having taught in Clackamas, Benton, Lane, Linn and Yamhill counties. He has always been a Democrat, and for a number of years past has taken an active interest in politics. He was elected a member of the House of Representatives from Linn county in 1868, and took a prominent part in the railroad fight over land grants during that session. He was elected County School Superintendent of

Linn county in 1870, and re-elected in 1872, in which year he took charge of the Albany public schools. In 1876 he was elected County Clerk of Linn county, running over one hundred ahead of his ticket, and in 1880 was the Democratic candidate for State Superintendent of Public Instruction, and was defeated by but seventy votes. He served four years as Private Secretary to Gov. Thayer, during which time he read law and was admitted to the bar in July, 1880. He has recently purchased a half interest in the Albany "Democrat," and will hereafter devote his attention to journalism. He was married in 1868 to Miss M. J. Martin, of Harrisburg, and they have two children living. Mr. Stites is a member of the I. O. O. F. and of the A. O. U. W., having occupied positions of trust in each. Mr. Stites is of rather more than medium height, slim and sharp featured, with heavy hair and beard, in which we find a silver thread quite frequently. He is not handsome, but passes well in a crowd. He has a host of warm personal friends, and feels more at home in old Linn than elsewhere. We may expect a lively paper in the "Democrat" during ensuing political campaigns.

JOHN ROCK,

Editor and proprietor of the Oregon City "Enterprise," is one of the rising men of Oregon. He was born at Barnstaple, England, in December, 1848. He received his education in the schools and academy of his native city, and afterwards at the Wesleyan College, Taunton. He then went to Les Andelys, France, where he studied for some time longer. He returned to England and entered a merchant's office in Swansea, South Wales. He next embarked in business at home, and shortly after we find him a clerk in a London railroad office. Mr. Rock's father had lived in America for some years, and his glowing accounts of the country, together with the reading of American newspapers, fired the young man's mind with the idea of coming to the United States. He landed in New York City, in 1870. After a very brief stay in western New York he drifted to Illinois and thence to Iowa. He reached Oregon in 1872, and the conviction resolutely settled itself upon his mind that he struck the desired spot. After teaching school for six years in various parts of this State, he settled at Oregon City and for a brief while was engaged in buying wheat. All his life, since early manhood he had been a scribbler for one paper or another. In 1878 he visited Europe, and upon his return he assumed the editor's chair of the "Enterprise," which he has ably filled. Mr. Rock is a Republican in politics, and his editorial utterances are carefully read by most of the leading men in the State.

MAJOR ENOCH G. ADAMS,

Nothing can be found in the pages of this book that will prove more interesting than the genealogy of the historic family from which Major Enoch G. Adams has descended. As we trace his lineage back to Revolutionary times, we find that each son has proven to be a worthy successor to a valiant sire, and that the noble blood which flowed through the veins of Major Adams' ancestors has not lost any of its patriotic purity or been degenerated in being transmitted from one generation to the other. Major Adams was born in Bow, Merrimac county, New Hampshire, about fifty years ago. His father was Rev. John Adams, a Methodist preacher, and a descendant of Rev. Joseph Adams, uncle of John Adams, second President of the United States. His mother's name was Sarah Sanderson, of Waterford county, Maine. Her father, Stephen Sanderson, was a soldier of the Revolutionary war. On his mother's side Major Adams is descended from the Dudleys, also Bradstreets and Aldens, Governors of Massachusetts colony. On his father's side he is descended from the Gilmans, who were noted in the early history of Massachusetts. His father, being a man of wealth, spared no expense to educate his two sons properly, and the result was that Major Adams and his brother John were, in their younger days, provided with tutors at home, and afterwards completed their studies at Yale College, Major Adams graduating therefrom in 1849, the youngest of his class, and his brother in 1850. After graduating, the Major taught school in the States of New Hampshire, Massachusetts, Maryland and Missouri, and through his occupation as teacher he has become widely known to the rising generation throughout the length and breadth of the land. He was married to Miss Sarah C. Plumer, of Newburyport, Massachusetts, in 1850, and three years after his wife died, and in addition to this bereavement he also lost the two children she bore him. The Major was a regular contributor for the "Olive Branch," in Boston, and the "Ladies' Repository," in Cincinnati, Ohio, his contributions being chiefly of a poetic nature. In April, 1861, he enlisted in Company D, Second N. H. Regiment, and was afterwards wounded at the battle of Williamsburg, the bullet yet remaining in his body. He fought in the peach orchard, at the battle of Gettysburg, and is the only officer living of the Second New Hampshire that escaped being wounded. Twenty-four out of twenty-six officers were either killed or wounded, and the other officer was afterwards killed at the battle of the Wilderness. At Point Lookout, Maryland, his time having expired, he was discharged from the Second New Hampshire, and was commissioned Captain of Company D, First United States Volunteer Infantry, (enlisted prisoners of war,) under General Butler, by order of President Lincoln. In 1864 his regiment was transferred to Fort Rice, Dakota Territory, and from May 10 till September 1, 1865, he commanded that fort, and during that period met and vanquished the famous Sitting Bull and three thousand warriors, killing with his own hands two of the most noted chiefs of the Minnesota massacre —Red Dog and Big Thunder. He was brevetted Major on the 13th of March, 1864, by the President and the United States Senate, and was mustered out of service in Leavenworth, Kansas, November 27, 1865, with the most distinguished and well-merited honors. He was married to his present wife in 1863, whilst at home on a leave of absence. She is the daughter of James Libby, of Berwick, York county, Maine. They have two children living. Major Adams came to Portland early in 1866, and for a time taught high school in the vestry of the Baptist church, afterwards removing to Astoria, where he continued teaching until 1867. In that year he was appointed Grand Lecturer of the Good Templars, and whilst filling that position he organized about forty lodges in Oregon and Washington Territory. In 1867 he pre-empted the claim on which he lives at St. Helens. He then went to Vancouver and bought the "Register," which paper he ran for the next three years, in the meantime being appointed Register of the Land Office at that place. In 1871 he sold his paper and moved to St. Helens, where he has since resided, and during most of the time has been Justice of the Peace of the district in which he lives. Two years ago he started the "Columbian," and it is now regarded as the liveliest country paper in the State, and is certainly the most original in its character of any paper we have ever seen. The Major has a happy and pointed way of expressing all the passing thoughts that crowd on his busy brain, and whilst these expressions are amusing to some, they cause others to become quite antagonistic; but woe betide the man who takes up the cudgel against the Major, for he is noted for being not only mighty with the pen and the sword, but also dexterous in flourishing his trusty cane. For special valor displayed on one occasion, in Oregon City, Major Adams was presented, by the citizens of that place, with a silver mounted cane, with the suggestive words, "For use," engraven on it. On July 4, 1881, he delivered an original poem at the grand celebration in Vancouver, before ten thousand people, and received the highest encomiums from all for his spirited and appropriate production. In a volume entitled "New Hampshire Poets," nine selections have been chosen from the pen of Major Adams, as well as selections by his sister, Mrs. Mary A. Senter, and also his brother, both now deceased. The whole family were infused with a poetic nature. It will be seen from the foregoing brief synopsis that Major Adam's career has been an eventful one. He is a man of more than average height, splendid build, a quick eye, sturdy and impetuous in temperament, an entertaining conversationalist, ready wit, and a man whose imposing address and general bearing will always command attention in a multitude. Considering the prominence of his origin, coupled with the praiseworthy record he has earned for himself, he possesses little of that unenviable quality of vanity and conceit that is found so distasteful in the majority of men who possess such a historic pedigree in addition to their natural talents, and he is therefore entitled to greater praise for his becoming modesty. Whilst he takes a deep interest in the welfare of the community in which he lives, he is also closely devoted to his interesting family.

SAMUEL FINLY BLYTHE

Was born in Fairfield, Adams county, Pennsylvania, February 14, 1842. At the age of fourteen he commenced learning the printer's trade in the office of the "Repository and Whig," at Chambersburg, Pa., and after serving two years as apprentice, removed to Eaton, Ohio, and finished learning his trade in the office of the "Eaton Democrat." After a year's tramp as a "jour." through the States of Ohio, Kentucky and Indiana, the breaking out of the Rebellion found him at Eaton, where he enlisted and served three years and three months in the Twenty-second Ohio Infantry, participating with that regiment in the battles of Fort Donelson, Shiloh, Corinth, Siego of Corinth, battle of Corinth, Siege of Vicksburg, capture of Little Rock, and other engagements of lesser note. Mustered out in 1864, he re-enlisted in the Second United States Veteran Volunteer Infantry, under General Hancock, and served a year in the Army of the Potomac. In 1866 he crossed the plains from St. Joseph, Misiouri, to Montana, with an ox team, coming by way of the Black Hills, through the Sioux country. The train with which he traveled was harassed and detained several times by hostile Indians, and from Fort Reno it was piloted to Gallatin valley by Jim Bridger, the celebrated scout and Indian fighter. Mr. Blythe settled on a quarter section of land in Gallatin valley in the fall of 1866, but abandoned it the next Spring for a "sit" on the "Montana Post," in Virginia City. After setting type for a year at one dollar per thousand, during which time he had a "fat take" for forty days on bill work during the legislative session, he thought he had all the money he wanted and went to the States in the Spring of 1868, making the trip down the Missouri by steamboat from Fort Benton to Sioux City. He returned to Montana in the fall of 1868, by way of the Union Pacific railroad as far as Green river, the end of the road at that time, and passed over ground along the Platte river in a few hours where he had toiled for days and weeks with an ox train but two years before. He went to California in 1869 and came to Portland July 5, 1870, along with the material for the old "Bulletin." Of the large force of employes that came with the "Bulletin" material, Mr. Blythe is the only one left in Oregon. He was a compositor on that paper up to the time of its suspension in 1875, with the exception of one year, when he was employed on the "Evening News." He was married July 30, 1873, to Miss Emma J. Nation, of Portland, and they have two children. He was one of the incorporators of the "Portland Bee," in 1875, but disposed of his interest when a majority of the stockholders voted to change its independent character. His health becoming impaired, in 1877 he removed to Hood River, where he engaged in farming for three years. In 1881 he came back to Portland and has since been associated with Edward Casey in the publication of the "Farmer and Dairyman."

CAPTAIN J. R. WILEY,

Whose name is familiar to all those who have resided in Portland for any number of years, is a gentleman whose natural aspirations are such that it is with a positive degree of pride we place his name on record as one whose example is worthy of emulation by the ambitious students who are destined to occupy prominent positions in life for years to come. Captain Wiley, as he is familiarly called, is the step-son of the late William P. Burke, who was foremost amongst Oregon's best citizens. Captain Wiley was born near Mineral Point, Iowa county, Wisconsin, December 30, 1847, and with his parents removed to Portland in December, 1852. His school-boy days were spent principally in the Portland Academy, from 1861 till 1664. In the latter year his parents sent him to the Jesuit College, Santa Clara, California, and he graduated therefrom in 1867. The devoted fathers of that institution still refer with pride to young Wiley's adaptation to his studies whilst under their charge. Returning home after graduating, he started a parochial school in connection with the cathedral of this city, and remained there for one year, when he was elected County School Superintendent, in 1868, which position he resigned one year later to accept the deputy County Clerkship under Mr. B. L. Norden, and retained that position until the close of the term in July, 1870. During a portion of the time that he was School Superintendent he was also Deputy Marshal under Mr. A. L. Zieber. In July, 1870, he took charge of the commercial and advertising departments of the "Daily Herald," and resigned that position several months after to accept the captaincy of the Portland police force, being the first man chosen for that office, and he held it until March, 1875. Two months after he was elected to the Common Council, and in that capacity served the city's best interests for a term of three years. During his spare moments he applied himself to the study of law. In the Spring of 1879 he was appointed Justice of the Peace, and served for one and a half years, at the end of which time he started a real estate agency. In February, 1882, he purchased the "Catholic Sentinel," and since that time has ably conducted it, and his literary efforts entitle him to rank amongst the foremost literary men of our State. He has at all times taken an active part in military and civic matters, and has been for many years an active member of the Board of Fire Delegates from Multnomah Engine Company No. 2. He served for four years, from 1871 till 1875, as Captain of the Emmet Guard. He was also appointed on Major General Effinger's staff, with the rank of Major, in 1878, holding that position until the present time. He was Sergeant-at-Arms of the House, in 1876, when ex-Governor Grover was elected to the Senate. In the societies connected with the Catholic Church, of which he has always been a faithful and consistent member, he has held many positions of trust, having been President of the St. Vincent de Paul Society for eight years. He is also State Treasurer of the A. O. H., and for four years has been successively elected President of the Father Mathew Temperance Society. The above is a short summary of his career, and it certainly is a commendable one. Without any desire to flatter, we can say that no man ever looked more earnestly after the welfare of the suffering and needy, or is more ready to aid them in accordance with his means, than is this gentleman; and he is amongst those whose unostentatious acts of friendship and charity resound the praise more eloquently than all the laudations that language can devise. Captain Wiley was married February 9, 1874, to Miss Maggie Hickey, a highly-esteemed young lady. A trio of fine, healthy children now occupy their parental solicitation and add to the ornamentation and comfort of their household.

J. F. ATKINSON.

Amongst the several Portland printers who are well known, there are few who have had a more varied experience than the one whose name appears above. His early life was spent in roving, and we are satisfied he is correct in the statement that a recital of his perigrinations when between the ages of fifteen and twenty-five would alone almost fill this book. He came to

Portland in 1867, where he was engaged as a compositor on the "Oregonian." In November, 1868, he made his first venture in the field of journalism, and started the "Daily Evening Bulletin"—the first evening paper published in Portland. He labored late and early, filling the positions of editor, business manager, foreman and compositor, for seven months, but finding more labor than pay in it, he became discouraged and buried it amongst the things of the past, although there was a brilliant outlook ahead. In February, 1870, in partnership with Mr. H. L. Herman, he started the "Catholic Sentinel." For two years he was connected with that paper, and then disposed of his interest to his partner. For the next few years we find him "working at the case" on Ben Holladay's "Bulletin," and also for his late partner, Mr. Herman. In 1874 he started a small job office, and in July of that year purchased the "Commercial Reporter," and continued the publication of that paper for the next seven years, and to his efforts are the business men indebted for a vast amount of valuable statistics of this State. In March, 1875, he started the "Sunday Welcome," the first Sunday paper in Oregon, and under his guidance it gained the largest circulation and influence of any family publication in the State. On January 1, 1880, he took in a partner, one who had been employed by him on the "Reporter" for four years previous. On the 26th of June the new firm purchased the Daily and Weekly "Bee" and the "Northwestern Newspaper Union," and ran them in connection with their other publications. On the 23d of August they changed the name of the "Bee" to the ill-fated one of "Bulletin." In September of the same year Mr. A. started a livery and hack stable on Front and Taylor streets, and had good promise of success. About two months later he became afflicted with his eyes, finally resulting in the loss of sight of one optic. During the period of his prostration his business ran on the down grade and the result was a dissolution of co-partnership, followed by a disposition of the enterprises and the discontinuance of the "Evening Bulletin." After a brief rest, he started the "Sunday Chronicle," February 13, 1881, and continued the publication of it until December 10th of the same year, when he sold out in order to embark in another enterprise with R. C. White, who was formerly employed by him. The disastrous result of this last enterprise is familiar to all Portlanders, and as Mr. Atkinson at the time published, over his own signature, a statement in the public press which has never been controverted, it is generally believed that he was the sufferer. With all Mr. Atkinson's misfortunes, he is sanguine that the future has something brighter in store for him, and his numerous friends certainly desire that his expectations may be fulfilled. He was united in matrimony to Miss Mary I. Stephens, a highly-respected young lady, on the 9th of January, 1871. The ceremony was performed in the Catholic Cathedral of this city, solemn High Mass being sung on the occasion, this being the first time that that honor was extended to a newly-married couple in this diocese. Mrs. Atkinson came to this coast quite young, on the steamship Continental, in company with her brother-in-law, Hon. A. S. Mercer, whose fame, achieved in his early efforts to people Washington Territory and Oregon, is world-wide. An interesting and happy little family add comfort and hope to Johnny's ambition, and we know of no one whose future success will give such general satisfaction to the people of Portland than the subject of this sketch.

WALLACE R. STRUBLE,

Another editor of the "Sunday Welcome," was born in Chesterville, Ohio, on June 4, 1856. He entered the Central Ohio College at an early age and remained there for some years. Before graduating he severed his connection with the above-named institution, where his time had been chiefly devoted to literary pursuits. He continued his studies after leaving college, and soon found himself writing for the press. In 1873 he came to Oregon and has been so favorably impressed with the climate and people that he wisely concluded to remain. Since his advent in this State he has been connected in various capacities with different journals and has always shown himself competent and efficient. As a writer, Mr. Struble is light and vivacious, rather than deep and penetrating. As a delineator of humorous sketches, he stands prominent, and has the faculty of seizing upon the most prosaic facts and by a mere touch of the pen transform them into laughable episodes. He belongs to the noble army of benedicts, having married some years ago.

J. B. FITHIAN

Was born Virginia, June 30, 1850, and commenced schooling in Philadelphia, Pennsylvania. Before the breaking out of the war in 1861, he went to Western Missouri and there remained until after the struggle. He then went to Wisconsin and finished schooling in the Seminary at Hudson, studied law at that city with Glover & Clinton, and was admitted to the bar at Eau Claire, in 1871. Proceeding to Omaha he was there connected with the law firm of Redick & Briggs for a time, and then went to Kansas where, after about two years' practice, he embarked in the publication of the Topeka Daily and Weekly "Blade," and, after the assassination of his partner, became editor. In 1876 he was commissioned Captain of Company F, Second Kansas Regiment, called out by Governor Osborn to aid the Federal troops in the Indian war. In 1877 he was a delegate to the Kansas Democratic-Greenback-Labor Convention, which met in Wyandotte, and was elected Chairman of the State Central Committee of that party. The Convention represented 80,000 votes, but at the subsequent election polled about 30,000, the Democratic strength. As Chairman of the Committee, he published a letter dissolving the combination and advising the Democrats to maintain their organization distinct. He was afterwards editor of the Sedalia, Missouri, "Bazoo" (daily, weekly and Sunday morning editions). Coming to Portland, Oregon, he was for a time editor of the "Evening Telegram," and a reporter of the "Evening Bee." Then went to Oregon City and published the "Democrat" two years. During his stay there he was Chairman of the Democratic Central Committee of Clackamas county, and a member of the State Convention, which elected delegates to the Democratic National Convention, which placed General W. S. Hancock in nomination for the Presidency. Shortly after the defeat of Hancock the "Democrat" was suspended. He was a member of Governor W. W. Thayer's staff with the rank of Lieutenant-Colonel of the militia. He is now city editor of the "Standard."

EDWARD CASEY,

The editor of the "Northwestern Farmer and Dairyman," of Portland, was born in Queenstown, Ireland, on the 29th of February, 1852, was brought to America when an infant, his parents locating at the Flower City, Rochester, New York, where his early life was spent in school and on the farm. At the early age of twelve years he was imbued with the patriotic spirit of the times, and ran away from home to join the United States Navy. He was soon taken out by his parents, but left home again, after one night, and joined the Sixth Tennessee Regiment, in transit from the Potomac to the Cumberland Army, and commanded by Jim Brownlow, son of the famous Parson Brownlow. Young Casey became known as "the child of the regiment," and was a pet with the officers and the men on account of his endurance, fearlessness and general usefulness. He was mustered out of service in 1865 and for the next few years worked at farming at Knoxville, Tennessee, in Greene county, Indiana, and in Illinois, in the meantime taking every opportunity to improve his mind at school during winther months. In Illinois, he learned the rudiments of the harness and saddlery trade, following that business for the next few years in Greenfield, Ohio, and then at home in Rochester, New York. In 1870 he bid farewell to his friends and started for Helena, Montana, where for two years he followed the various avocations of mining, harness-making, stage-driving and gardening. He next joined the Eastwick surveying party of the N. P. R. R. Company, which made the first survey from the mouth of Snake river to Pend d'Oreille lake. Leaving the party in Walla Walla, W. T., he entered a printing office and in the next two years acquired an excellent knowledge of that business in every branch—as devil, compositor, pressman, city editor and chief scribe. He was also employed, for a short time, as publisher of the "Pendletonian," the first paper issued in Umatilla county, Oregon. Branching out again, we next catch him punching tickets on Dr. Baker's wooden railroad. In a few months more we find him employed on the "Statesman," in Salem, until the spirit of restlessness again seized and prompted him to start the "Itemizer" at Dallas, Polk county, a journal that he conducted ably for the next four years, until 1878, when he disposed of it and settled on a farm near Dallas, where he is considered a model farmer by his neighbors, and where for the next three years his labors as a practical agriculturist were crowned with success. Whilst a resident of Dallas he was elected a member of the City Council and by that body was unanimously chosen President—quite an honor for so young a man. Conceiving that there was an opening for the establishment of a business that embraced the principal study of his life with the acquiring and disseminating of knowledge congenial with that study, he rented his farm and came to Portland in June,

1881, and secured the "Northwestern Farmer and Dairyman," and has made it a valuable monthly visitor to the agriculturist. In December, 1881, he secured Mr. Samuel F. Blythe as partner in the publication of the journal. Mr. Casey is the editor and business man of the enterprise, and to no more worthy and intelligent gentleman could such an important position be entrusted. He has received flattering recognition from some of the most eminent and practical writers on agriculture, and the "Farmer and Dairyman" is often quoted by the leading agricultural journals of the East. He has traveled through about twenty-five States and Territories, and at all times has taken a deep interest in agricultural pursuits. He is well qualified to give the result of his observations to the patrons of the "Farmer and Dairyman," as he is thoroughly practical in all his ideas. Mr. Casey is an honored member of the order of Odd Fellows. He was married to Miss Ellen Robbins, a highly accomplished young lady of Dallas, on the 3d of July, 1875, but on the 17th of January, 1879, his beloved wife passed from this life to "that bourne from whence no traveler returns," leaving two children, a boy and a girl, to occupy the care and attention of her sorrowing husband. He is yet unmarried, and now devotes his time to improving and perfecting the "Northwestern Farmer and Dairyman."

www.ingramcontent.com/pod-product-compliance
Lightning Source LLC
Chambersburg PA
CBHW021813230426
43669CB00008B/735